THE ORIENT ON THE VICTORIAN STAGE

The Orient on the Victorian Stage examines the representation of the Middle East in a variety of nineteenth-century entertainment forms, such as panoramas, melodrama, pantomime, ballet, and opera. Ziter argues that changes in stage craft reflected the emerging idea that the significance of objects was evident in contextual relations, and he relates the development of this stage craft to orientalist exhibitons and museum displays. Unlike other theatre histories and studies of orientalism, this book examines broader strategies of spatial represention and focuses on performance and popular culture. Ziter explores the plays, productions, and displays at a number of venues, including Drury Lane, Covent Garden, the Great Exhibition of 1851, the Crystal Palace at Sydenham, and the British Museum, among others. The book also includes an analysis of Byron's image in the theatre and an analysis of his play *Sardanapalus*.

EDWARD ZITER is Assistant Professor in the Department of Drama at New York University. He has published articles in *Theatre Survey*, *Theatre Journal*, and *The Wordsworth Circle*, and in the anthology, *Land/Scape/Theatre*. He has coedited the reviews section of *Theatre Journal*.

THE ORIENT ON THE
VICTORIAN STAGE

EDWARD ZITER

New York University

CAMBRIDGE
UNIVERSITY PRESS

PUBLISHED BY THE PRESS SYNDICATE OF THE UNIVERSITY OF CAMBRIDGE
The Pitt Building, Trumpington Street, Cambridge CB2 1RP, United Kingdom

CAMBRIDGE UNIVERSITY PRESS
The Edinburgh Building, Cambridge, CB2 2RU, UK
40 West 20th Street, New York, NY 10011–4211, USA
477 Williamstown Road, Port Melbourne, VIC 3207, Australia
Ruiz de Alarcón 13, 28014 Madrid, Spain
Dock House, The Waterfront, Cape Town 8001, South Africa

http://www.cambridge.org

First published 2003

Printed in the United Kingdom at the University Press, Cambridge

Typeface Adobe Garamond 11/12.5 pt.   *System* LATEX 2ε [TB]

A catalogue record for this book is available from the British Library

ISBN 0 521 81829 x hardback

Contents

Illustrations

Illustrations 3.1, 3.3, 3.4, and 3.6 are reproduced by kind permission of the Ohio State University Libraries. Illustrations 2.1, 4.1, 4.2 and 4.3 are reproduced by kind permission of the Board of Trustees of the Victoria and Albert Museum. Illustrations 2.2 and 2.5 are reproduced by kind permission of the Billy Rose Theatre Collection, the New York Public Library for the Performing Arts, Astor, Lenox, and Tilden Foundations. Illustration 2.7 is reproduced by kind permission of the Stuart Collection, Rare Books Division, the New York Public Library, Astor, Lenox, and Tilden Foundations. Illustrations 2.9 and 4.4 are reproduced by kind permission of the Asian and Middle Eastern Division, the New York Public Library, Astor, Lenox, and Tilden Foundations. Illustrations 2.3, 2.4, 3.2, and 3.5 are reproduced by kind permission of the Fales Library, New York University. Illustrations 2.6, 2.8, and 2.10 are reproduced by kind permission of the University of London Special Collections.

Acknowledgments

Many people have contributed to the writing of this book. W. D. King gave invaluable advice in the early stages of this project when he directed my doctoral dissertation on orientalist scene painting, as did the other committee members, Simon Williams and Bert States. Simon again provided important guidance in the final stages of this manuscript. I am especially indebted to my colleagues at the Drama Department of New York University, particularly Una Chaudhuri and Robert Vorlicky who have not only encouraged my writing but have modeled exemplary lives in the academy. Parts of this book were completed while I served as a visiting professor at the Ohio State University, and there I benefited from Tom Postlewait's expert advice on writing and publishing as well as the intellectual camaraderie of Lesley Ferris and Brian Rotman. Richard Schoch helped me develop the argument well beyond its initial formulation and Pieter van der Merwe made his excellent dissertation on Clarkson Stanfield available to me. At Cambridge University Press, Vicki Cooper has gently shepherded this work to publication. The anonymous readers at Cambridge were very useful in streamlining my argument. I consider myself part of a generation of theatre scholars who have not only been inspired by Joseph Roach's writing but have directly benefited from his efforts to expand the parameters of performance historiography in scholarly societies and journals. I greatly value his encouragement. There is probably not an idea in this book that has not been sharpened in conversations with Jill Lane, whose intellectual generosity and contributions to the field of performance studies have long inspired my esteem and gratitude.

Portions of chapter one appeared in *Wordsworth Circle*. Portions of chapter three will appear in the anthology, *Living Displays*. Portions of chapter two appeared in *Theatre Journal* and my argument was sharpened with Harry Elam's editing advice. Portions of chapter four appeared in *Theatre Survey* and developed considerably due to the intelligent comments of the editor, Gary Williams, and the anonymous peer reviewers. Portions of chapter five appeared in the anthology, *Land/Scape/Theatre*, edited by Una Chaudhuri and Elinor Fuchs; Elinor's suggestions greatly added to the piece's clarity and focus.

The initial research for this book was funded in part by a dissertation research grant from the American Society of Theatre Research. A Godard fellowship from New York University provided me with the time to prepare the manuscript for publication.

Introduction: "real sets," geography, and race

Geography, we have learned, is no less constructed than history. In 1885 Sanger's Amphitheatre depicted the British army's successful relief of Khartoum, which had been under siege by Sudanese rebels throughout the previous year. In fact, Sanger's revision of the Sudanese War, *Khartoum! or, The Star of the Desert*, came one month after papers reported the fall of Khartoum and the death of its British commander. In order to convincingly stage this fantasy, Sanger's – which specialized in military spectacle and equestrian drama – populated its recreation of Khartoum with "a large herd of Camels and Dromedaries" and actual "Soudanese Natives."[1] Britain's entertainment industry had long enlisted fragments of the "real" to support what were actually fanciful depictions of the East; however, in few cases were the contradictions of this project so glaringly evident. If we take the playbill at face value, *Khartoum* had recourse to the very people who had won independence from British Egypt in order to provide a compelling and realistic depiction of Britain's unshakable dominion.

Not to be outdone by a minor theatre, that same year Drury Lane's *Human Nature* similarly transformed the failed Sudanese Relief Expedition into a British victory. Despite its disregard for the historical record, *Human Nature* was widely praised for its realism; in its review, the *Truth* asserted that "the accuracy displayed in the scenes illustrative of Egyptian warfare are beyond praise."[2] Drury Lane did not try to pass off the supernumeraries in *Human Nature* as Sudanese natives (though the production did feature "real police officers" in its most stirring scene, the return of the troops to cheering crowds in Trafalgar Square). Instead, Drury Lane augmented its production's aura of authenticity with a Sudanese exhibition in the theatre's Grand Saloon. The exhibition featured maps and sketches of the region, "interesting articles illustrative of African life and warfare," as described by the *Era*, and a recreation of Ahmad Urabi's Cairo cell, designed from on-the-spot sketches and featuring the actual carpet and furniture used by the Egyptian nationalist leader during his confinement.[3] The depiction of widely reported events followed by fictional victories in *Khartoum* and *Human Nature* would seem to be entirely in keeping with the elaborate mix of the "real" and the "represented" featured on stage and in exhibitions. In such a context, it is not entirely surprising to see that one review for *Human Nature* marveled at the "skill that gives us real sets of rural villages."[4]

How are we to read the oxymoron, "real sets"? It could be seen as a mere slip, though the fact that the quote was later reproduced in playbills for *Human Nature* would suggest that the phrase did not strike nineteenth-century readers as strange. Instead I would suggest that the phrase be read as evidence of the nineteenth-century need to find new terms to describe staging innovations and the confusion generated by the increasingly common juxtaposition of the "real" and the "represented." Audiences that had been accustomed to settings composed of painted sliding flats with limited numbers of three-dimensional properties now witnessed fully built-out and molded settings that featured objects taken from everyday life and people who could claim to be the things they represented. Sanger's "natives" and Drury Lane's "real police officers" are examples of a theatre that increasingly had recourse to the "real" at the same time that this theatre attempted to recreate known settings, not simply by copying details onto flat surfaces, but by reproducing the shape and arrangement of objects.

In this book, I read these staging innovations and use of the "real" as the culmination of a slow transformation in how Europeans understood and interpreted space, a transformation that is also evident in the emergence of new academic disciplines such as geography and anthropology. In productions such as *Human Nature*, the theatre replaced wings on a raked stage with three-dimensional environments that purportedly reproduced Eastern architecture and geography. At roughly the same time, the emerging science of geography was arguing that geographic conditions determined the physical and mental characteristics of its native races, and anthropology's focus on material culture and the anatomical characteristics of different races eclipsed ethnology's interest in philology. In *Human Nature* and *Khartoum*, the behavior and temperament of Arab characters was described as the product of desert conditions, in language that was more literal than metaphorical. Careful attention was given to the weapons and procedures of desert warfare. On stage and in the academy, topography and material culture became keys to non-visible drives and processes that defined racial difference. In this sense, race was not simply depicted in face-paint, but in built-out sand dunes, huts, and "articles illustrative of African life and warfare."

This new understanding of context enabled nineteenth-century Europeans to interpret the surface of objects and people as manifestations of internal laws and organic processes. It is for this reason that exhibitions and museums began to create elaborate sets in which to stage fragments of the "real." When a theatre in the late-nineteenth century recreated objects displayed in museums and exhibitions (or displayed in its own Grand Saloon) and when various entertainment forms placed supposed native people in exotic reconstructions, the entertainment industry was similarly attempting to draw the "real" and the "set" into the closest proximity possible.

This book argues that nineteenth-century British theatre and entertainment, like the new disciplines they emulated – such as ethnology, anthropology, biblical archeology, and, most significantly, geography – both reflected and helped constitute the modern British colonial imaginary. Throughout the nineteenth century, British audiences marveled at depictions of desert storms and harem dances as well as Nile steamers and colonial armies at theatres, panoramas, and exhibition rooms. The features of this theatrical East attained a remarkable currency throughout British culture as a wide population became versed in an emerging pictorial vocabulary that organized and interpreted the regions east of Europe. I argue that the entertainment industry, as a primary site for the dissemination of visual information, was central in the creation of Europe's image of the East as well as in popularizing and shaping the new vocabularies employed in defining and managing Eastern bodies.

In the process, both popular and elite forms of orientalism engaged a new spatial logic. Attention was no longer focused solely on the object in itself – be it an actor on an apron or an artifact in a case – but instead on the relation between that object and the surrounding space. Theatres, museums, and monographs discovered meaning in the interaction of objects and people with a larger environment, whether scenery or text represented that environment. I hope in this book to illuminate how *Khartoum* and *Human Nature* function within a tradition of orientalist entertainment, and to examine how this tradition developed in conjunction with those disciplines that emerged in colonialism's shadow throughout the nineteenth century. I turn to the entertainment industry, not simply because it is a rich archive of orientalist imagery, but because in the space of orientalist performance one can trace the changing parameters of what could be known and said about the East.

MAKING SPACE EXOTIC

This project began as a desire to understand the phenomenology of the stage space in orientalist plays. It was prompted by the impression that changes in the use of the stage space paralleled changes in the use of the museum space. I was struck by the fact that period rooms, in situ displays, and native villages at exhibitions were first employed at about the same time that theatre practitioners were flattening the stage floor and relying more heavily on built-out scenery. It seemed that there had been a fundamental shift in how space functioned in both the theatre and the museum: meaning did not naturally emerge from the presented object but was instead generated in the relation of the object to its display or acting environment.

The point has already been made that realism elevated the stage space to the status of dramatic character. As Bert States has written, when Hedda Gabler complains in the opening scene of the play, "Good heavens – what a nuisance! That maid's opened the window and let in a whole flood of sunshine," it suggests "a speaker who is in her world in a certain way; she is, in fact, imbedded in it, surrounded by actuality. One might say that the speech is centripetal, the product of a world in which speech is conditioned by the persistence of environment and the passage of clock time."[5] I would suggest that the shift evident in the emergence of theatrical realism was in no way confined to the stage. A year before Hedda's entrance, George Brown Goode, director of the Smithsonian Institution (then the US National Museum), announced that the cathedrals of Europe should be considered "national or civic museums." According to this logic, spaces are meaningful in that they tell us about the people who reside within, whether that meaning is the result of centripetal force (environment shapes behavior) or centrifugal force (behavior shapes environment). Goode's transformation of sacred space into museum space might not strike the modern reader as innovative, any more so than the choice to have a dramatic character comment on her surroundings. However, Goode's importance in museology lies in part in his ability to explain how the manipulation and delineation of space – through the arrangement of objects and construction of descriptive labels – could generate information. Goode, no less than Ibsen, is evidence of a new modern sense of how space makes meaning.

It is important to note that individual societies determine in advance what kinds of meanings potentially reside in specific spaces and that these meanings are delineated by such conceptions as race and national identity. For most audience members, Hedda's response to her surroundings is evidence of a distinct and idiosyncratic personality, not a racial essence. By contrast, nineteenth-century visitors to a "national museum" like Westminister Abbey might read their surroundings as a manifestation of the "Anglo-Saxon" and visitors to the Alhambra Court at Sydenham's Crystal Palace were specifically instructed to read their surroundings as evidence of the "Oriental spirit." One cannot bracket off this spatial discourse from racial and colonial discourses, nor can one address these other discourses without first making sense of the changes in the ways space produced meaning. As Foucault has noted, "the tactics and strategies of power" are invariably deployed through spatial formations, through "implantations, distributions, demarcations, control of territories and organizations of domains which could well make up a sort of geopolitics."[6] Not only is power articulated through spatial formations, spatial formations are themselves the product of power structures and their supporting ideologies. Richard Peet has argued that geography only became a respected discipline once it became a means of explaining how and why the separate races developed; as he states, "environmental determinism was geography's entry into modern science."[7]

My interest in how performance space changed during the nineteenth century took me into the vast area of "imaginative geography," a phrase coined by Edward Said to describe how regions become poetically endowed in such a way that the Orient could come to mean "more than what was empirically known about it."[8] Said introduces the term while discussing Gaston Bachelard's *The Poetics of Space*. The reference is significant, for as much as Said presents orientalism as a discourse that is instantiated in individual texts but in no way original to an individual consciousness, he also shares Bachelard's desire to trace the variations of an image as it emerges in each individual consciousness. As Johannes Fabian has written in reference to Said and himself, "I believe we both struggle to restore past experiences, which were buried under layers of 'enculturation' in other societies and languages, to a kind of presence that makes them critically fruitful."[9] One almost discerns a phenomenologist's stance in Said's assertion that "imaginative geography and history help the mind to intensify its own sense of itself by *dramatizing* the distance and difference between what is close to it and what is far away" (my italics). Said's debt to Bachelard – and the implication that exoticism is inherently a process by which space itself is dramatized – is an important, if sometimes overlooked, feature of Said's work and one that is central to my own analysis. Basically, I am arguing that the idea that space could function as a dramatic character emerged both on and off the stage at about the same time and that new orientalist disciplines show as great a debt to the theatre as the theatre shows to these disciplines. In the process of making this argument, I too demonstrate the influence of phenomenology, for like Said I am attempting to recapture orientalism as a recreation of self and other in the consciousness of a reader or spectator.

Said has primarily examined this process of dramatization and the marking of difference within the human sciences (most notably in *Orientalism*) and literature (most notably in *Culture and Imperialism*), and most scholars of orientalism have followed Said's lead and focused on elite texts.[10] Nonetheless, popular entertainment is possibly the most important area in which to examine transformations within orientalism. This is not simply because, as John MacKenzie has stated, "a full understanding of Orientalism requires some comprehension of the extensive range of artistic vehicles through which representations of the Orient were projected,"[11] but because the history of the theatre in the century of orientalism's accelerated development is a history of radical transformation in the strategies by which distant spaces were dramatized within the familiar space of the stage, the panorama, and the exhibition. Theatre and related venues allow us to examine both the dissemination of specific images of the East and how an evolving poetics of Eastern spaces was generated within evolving strategies of spatial representation.

In examining this popular orientalism, it is important to remember that these venues were frequented by both men and women. To argue, as I do later, that in many entertainments the East was imagined as a space of female indolence and sensuality is not to assume a uniformly male audience. Rather, it is more accurate to assert that orientalism was partially structured by and helped structure emerging definitions of the female, and that these definitions were consumed by both men and women. Presumably male audience members would experience a staged-harem dance differently from female audience members. However, for both men and women such a harem dance articulated power relations between East and West and between women and men, helping to define these terms.

RACIAL INTERIORS

In this book I hope to show that changes in nineteenth-century stage aesthetics were closely related to wider conceptual shifts that underlay the emergence of orientalist study. In doing so, I read strategies of spatial representation in orientalist entertainments as evidence of the epistemological shift described in Foucault's *The Order of Things: An Archeology of the Human Sciences*. Foucault argues that a modern *episteme* arose in the nineteenth century, which organized existence according to "transcendentals" (such as the force of labor, the power of speech, and the energy of life) outside the realm of the visible. In doing so, this modern *episteme* replaced the classical order in which existence was organized in a table governed by resemblance. According to Foucault, at the end of the eighteenth century this table essentially broke under the weight of the increasing documentation of dissimilarity, throwing the authority of the visual and the place of humanity into question. The rise of this modern *episteme* marked a movement from knowledge as the nomination of the visible to knowledge as the apprehension of the independent historicity of form. It was no longer sufficient to record and compare external form. Instead meaning was generated in the organic nature of forms, in the patterns and transformations that give rise to forms and can only be glimpsed in activities and relations that exist in time. Whereas classical science focused on the similarity of form, the human sciences employ concepts such as succession and analogy. The classical botanist measured pistils; the modern biologist, however, examines the function of the organs, the movement of the blood, the invisible force known as life.

As suggested in the subtitle, *An Archeology of the Human Sciences*, Foucault presents this vocabulary of invisibility so as to describe the human sciences within the parameters of a historically constituted discourse. His argument has an obvious relevance to the series of "sciences" prompted by the greater accessibility of once remote regions and people in the nineteenth century. Like the sciences discussed by Foucault, ethnology, anthropology, biblical archeology, and geography similarly made succession and analogy markers of knowledge. Within these sciences, exotic topography and culture were shown to reveal a litany of historical, social, and economic forces evident in the concentration of resources, the lie of trade routes, the traces of historical change, even the conditions of human evolution. Moreover, these sciences also "discovered" a single animating force within existence – race. Throughout this book, I rely on the work of writers such as George W. Stocking, Jr., Johannes Fabian, and Felix Driver who examine ethnology, anthropology, and geography within the context of an emerging racial ideology.[12]

Taken together, the history of these disciplines can help us to trace out the epistemic principles that gave racism its modern form. As Ann Laura Stoler has explained, the resonance between Foucault's "great hidden forces" and nineteenth-century theories of race are striking. Stoler writes:

Racism is not only a "visual ideology" where the visible and somatic confirms the "truth" of the self. Euro-American racial thinking related the visual markers of race to the protean hidden properties of different human kinds. Nineteenth-century bourgeois orders were predicated on these forms of knowledge that linked the visible, physiological attributes of national, class, and sexual Others to what was secreted in their depths – and none of these could be known without also designating the psychological dispositions and sensibilities that defined who and what was *echte* European.[13]

The authentic European was not only defined by external difference from a racial other, but by internal differences – drives, proclivities, temperaments, evolutionary history – that accounted for the perceived low level of culture and technology outside of Europe as well as an emerging colonial power structure. As Stoler points out, this hierarchy of the human species informed the entirety of the bourgeois order and similarly allowed for the creation of internal others. It is no wonder that the idea of homosexuality emerged at this same time, according to Foucault, as "a kind of interior androgyny, a hermaphrodism of the soul."[14] Modern racism was generated from within the same epistemological field as the human sciences and the one cannot be understood without analysis of the other.

The ways of knowing that circumscribed the object of study in the above-mentioned disciplines can be related to the ways of knowing offered to audiences of new popular entertainment forms in the nineteenth century, as particularly evidenced in a new spatial aesthetics. Implicit in Foucault's argument is the idea that space took on a new role in the generation of meaning, and it is here that the study of the entertainment industry can lend important insight into these new structures of meaning. Even Focuault's image of disciplinary society as a vast panopticon suggests radically new technologies of space. As Timothy Mitchell has shown us, these new technologies of space were central to Europe's construction of a totalizing view of the East in the nineteenth century. In examining the spatial aesthetics of nineteenth-century entertainment in relation to structures of knowledge and processes of social control, I ally my work with that of theorists such as Timothy Mitchell, Edward Soja, and Tony Bennett, who have reexamined the idea of space in Foucault's writing.[15]

A GENEALOGY OF THE PERFORMANCE SPACE

In focusing on an emerging spatial logic uniting popular entertainment with new orientalist disciplines, I hope to produce a genealogy of performance that acknowledges the competing interests and structures of power that shape this epistemological field. This is not to deny causal relations or the contributions of specific practitioners. In the nineteenth century, playbills noted specific Eastern authorities; scene painters copied images from scholarly folios; and story lines sometimes made reference to theories emerging from the human sciences. This has been documented elsewhere and will be further documented here. Nor do I overlook those changes in the conditions of production that made it possible to dramatize space in new ways, such as improvements in lighting and scenic technology, the enlargement of auditoriums and stages, and the lengthening of production runs. However, I would argue that to simply cite these developments as evidence of the "natural progress" of the theatre without examining their place within discursive formations is to side-step the more important question of what made these developments possible. We should not tell the story backwards, to decide in advance that realism is the inevitable summit in the evolution of the arts and then discover the harbingers of realist stage practice in every document we uncover.

There are obvious reasons for asserting that the story of nineteenth-century theatre represents a march towards realism. Traditional histories of nineteenth-century theatre depict a huge accumulation of specific and finely crafted detail. Settings were transformed from simple "backings to a stage, apt for almost any occasion" to an ultimately "excessive realism and display."[16] Attention in acting switched from the "dignified stance and graceful pose" of eighteenth-century actors like Barton Booth to the "kaleidoscope of business" and minutely organized gestures of a Henry Irving.[17] From romantic theatre's early interest in character and picturesque settings to naturalism's laboratory of human behavior and carefully reproduced settings, the stage has displayed a voracious appetite for ever more gesture, business, set pieces, properties, supernumeraries, and above all else, significance. Every space is filled and every detail made meaningful. In the midst of this accumulation, the director is said to have emerged. Macready's insistence that his actors act when they rehearsed is seen as harbinger of Beerbohm Tree's ensemble acting and well-drilled crowds all tastefully incorporated into a massive stage architecture. The evolution is sufficiently clear, the contributions of specific theatre practitioners so obviously important, that few theatre historians have felt compelled to ask, "Why?" Why all this stuff? I believe that until theatre historians ask such questions, theatre history will remain a marginal discipline rather than becoming a central tool for articulating genealogies of the human consciousness.

My answer to the question of proliferating "stuff" is simply stated if not simply explained: the accumulation on stage was a response to the tremendous dispossession that accompanied the loss of the classical order. The realization that forms have their own historicity that is neither subordinate to nor homogeneous with humanity ultimately became the means, according to Foucault, of reconstituting the human subject from the fractured space of the classical order. At this point, the human being "now realizes that he not only 'has history' all around him but is himself, in his own historicity, that by means of which a history of human life, a history of economics, and a history of languages are given their form."[18] The search for internal processes and transcendental laws through scrupulous examination and surveillance was the means by which a history and meaning of the human being could be written as the foundation for all other histories and meanings. According to this line of argument, the human sciences (as well as such modern institutions as the clinic and the prison) were driven by the need to create the human subject, and it is this same need, I argue, that organized the nineteenth-century stage.

It is in this context that one begins to understand the tremendous outpouring of orientalist entertainments in the nineteenth century. Panoramas, dioramas, and other optical entertainments depicted the regions east of the Mediterranean in such tremendous detail that reviews compared them to actual journeys east. When images alone lost their power to transport an audience, live performance and native peoples were incorporated into shows. An equally extensive range of exhibitions presented a wealth of Eastern objects, architectural recreations, and oriental peoples. The theatre was no less prolific in its orientalism: melodrama, pantomime, ballet, and opera all depicted Oriental people and places with increasingly spectacular detail. In doing so, the entertainment industry followed the lead of the human sciences, disseminating popularized versions of the theories emerging in disciplines such as geography, ethnology, and archeology, shaping public perception of these disciplines, and ultimately influencing their methods. While I note several instances in which later scholars first found employment or inspiration in the entertainment industry, I do not wish to limit the influence of the entertainment industry to such moments of direct contact. As Richard Peet has pointed out: "Society structures the direction theory takes by posing great issues in a certain way... The need to be socially and politically functional directs inquiry in directions productive of ideology but not necessarily productive of scientific principles."[19] I have taken the entertainment industry both as an arena in which society poses questions, ultimately "structuring the direction theory takes," and as a vehicle for popularizing those lines of inquiry "productive of ideology."

BRITAIN'S ORIENT, ROMANTIC AND TIMELY

The proliferation of orientalist sciences and entertainments was not confined to one country; however, there are compelling reasons to focus on the British experience. Britain's changing and often contradictory concerns in the East helped produce a particularly varied and complex history of performance. From the time of Napoleon's invasion of Egypt, the Eastern Mediterranean has been considered a primary British strategic interest – particularly once the overland route from Cairo to Suez became central to trade with India. The perceived need to maintain the integrity of the Ottoman Empire often ran into conflict with a growing philhellenism and concern for the Holy Land. British military involvement in the region, from the Battle of Aboukir Bay in 1798 to the occupation of Egypt in 1882, inspired a great number of performances. Advances in British scholarship similarly precipitated and informed orientalist entertainments, particularly given the popular interest in biblical geography and archeology.

While India was obviously of much greater economic value to Great Britain, it arguably did not exercise the same hold on the British imagination as the Middle East. From the Ayyubid reconquest of Jerusalem to the Ottoman sieges of Vienna, the neighboring dynasties of the Eastern Mediterranean had long commanded Europe's attention and fear. Islam, which incorporated many stories from Judeo-Christian tradition while denying Christ's divinity, struck many Europeans as a dangerous and unholy inversion of Christianity. Not only were the religious roots of Europe and the Eastern Mediterranean entwined but their cultural and intellectual roots were as well. It is worth remembering that many of the foundational texts of Western humanism were not translated from the original Greek but from Arabian copies. Europeans openly emulated the learning and cultural achievement of the Eastern Mediterranean. From a university system modeled on the Umayyad jami'a to the use of arabesque in Renaissance tapestry and painting, pre-Enlightenment Europe frequently turned to its eastern neighbors for intellectual and cultural inspiration. It is no wonder that Europe defined itself against the Eastern Mediterranean rather than such distant and little known regions as China or India. The world was divided between the Occident and the Orient, with the Christian West on one side and the Islamic East on the other.

This formulation underwent considerable revision in the nineteenth century so as to include a greatly expanded and detailed Orient. The area east of Greece and west of India was now read in the light of imperial interests that extended well beyond the Levant. This area became one of crossing – the middle terrain that lay between England and India, the home of a dying dynasty, and a contest of the Great Powers. Though the term "Middle East" was not coined until 1903, during the nineteenth century the far-flung regions of the Ottoman Empire and Persia were already coalescing in the British imagination as a single entity. Today, this area roughly corresponds to Turkey, Syria, Lebanon, Jordan, Israel, the Arabian Peninsula, Iraq, Iran, Egypt, Libya, Tunisia, Algeria, and Morocco; it is the depiction of this considerable area that concerns this study. (The term "Middle East" has gained such international prominence that the Arab nations themselves employ it, as if, imaginatively they too sat with their backs to the Atlantic staring at India across the Isthmus of Suez.) However, at the same time that the Islamic East shrunk to a mere portion of the Orient, it retained the connotations ingrained over centuries. The Islamic East had become a middle, but a middle that stood in for the whole. Consequently, when Britons discussed the Orient they were most often referring to the Islamic East as imagined over centuries.

The Orient, then, was both timeless and timely. As home to the Holy Land, the Orient did not simply house its own past but the past of all nations. However, the British also depicted this area as an arena in which the future of empire would be decided. The Orient was a space in which distinctly modern crises arose and were resolved (often with gunboats) and it was a sacred and unchanging space, unaffected by such colonial realities. This duality in British representations of the Orient was also the legacy of its depiction in romantic texts as a refuge from modernity. At the same time as the Eastern Mediterranean was seen as central in the economic and political developments transforming Europe, poets, painters, and playwrights created an Orient that was free from these and other features of modernity – an exotic world of Bedouins, corsairs, houris, and jinn.

At first sight it would appear that this romantic orientalism shared little with the disciplines that followed; the Orient was precisely that last space in which the visionary might experience the essence of a place unmediated by contextual frameworks and material relations, according to one strain of British romanticism. One went East because there vision induced, rather than obscured, pure apprehension. However, it was precisely this fact, that one *went* east, that insured the inscription of contextual frameworks into the retrieved sights. The Orient, after all, could only be imagined as the space outside modernity because of its spatial and cultural distance from London. The Orient's status as a preferred romantic other was the product of an incipient interest in ethnology and geography even as the source of this preference was the belief that in the Orient one could be free of such intellectual frameworks.

In the course of this book I investigate precisely how scientific and aesthetic attitudes are complicit by examining specific borrowings between their respective discourses. The question of modernity – its constitution and its impact – is a central concern. Here I am prompted by Saree Makdisi's suggestion that romanticism be understood as "a diverse and heterogeneous series of engagements with modernization," as well as by his argument that romanticism was not simply a response to modernization but a "key constitutive element."[20] Drawing on this line of analysis, I explore the possibility that orientalist discourses in the entertainment industry and the human sciences – discourses that developed out of a romantic engagement with the exotic – both were shaped by and shaped modern colonial practice. My analysis draws a circle of reciprocal influences with modernization and romanticism forming the vertical axis and colonialization and orientalism the horizontal axis. Conceptions of race that were disseminated in and shaped by artistic venues affected British activities abroad. To return to the example with which I opened, *Human Nature* and *Khartoum* rewrote the failed Relief Expedition into a story of British reconquest and white supremacy over a decade before the second Sudan campaign retook the territories despite little strategic or economic motivation. While it would be untenable to argue that Sanger's Amphitheatre and Drury Lane caused the British victory at Omdurman, the campaign and its reporting would suggest that melodramatic conventions impacted upon policy decisions.

HISTORICAL AND ETHNOGRAPHIC OTHERS

In both the scientific and aesthetic orientalisms of nineteenth-century Britian, exteriors are meaningful to the extent that they can afford some knowledge of an interior process. In this respect, Foucault's analysis of early-nineteenth-century thought uncovers a stance that is consistent with the skepticism towards the visual and investment in the internal world of imagination attributed to romantic writers. This stance is often cited in explanations as to why no lasting dramas emerged from the romantic period. It might appear, then, that the theatre would be an inappropriate location for exploring the repercussions of vision's increasingly suspect authority, whether one arrived at this conclusion through Foucault's analysis or through that of romantic studies. To the contrary, I contend that it is precisely this skepticism towards the visual that accounts for the specific nature of the entertainment industry during Britain's romantic period and after. Particularly in orientalist productions, one encounters an insistence that the image was simply a means to accessing a non-visual order. The theatrical tableau, the panorama, and the exhibition room all promised to reveal Eastern manners, the oriental essence, or the balance of power. Increasingly, these productions cited some originating poet–painter–scholar whose unmediated experience of the Orient was now transmitted via the production like a vital spirit.

I am asserting, then, that romanticism and the human sciences sit within the same discursive field, and that the theatre not only disseminated their respective stances but helped shape them. Here, I follow Stephen Bann's work on nineteenth-century historical consciousness, particularly his efforts to open up historical painting, fiction, and panoramas, as well as architectural reconstructions, as sites for historiographical analysis. In Bann's analysis, nineteenth-century venues of popular culture emerge as arenas in which modern European identities were generated out of examinations of the historically distant, and I would extend such analysis to include the geographically distant as well. For Bann, the profound desire for an engagement with history evident in such diverse sites as the Musée de Cluny and Sir Walter Scott's neo-gothic mansion is the product of the shattering of the human subject, an event that he sees outlined in Foucault's description of the collapse of the classical order and the overwhelming experience of dissimilarity.

Edward Said also identifies a search for self within the development of orientalist study. For Said, the Orient is a Western idea employed for "identifying 'us' Europeans against all 'those' non-European peoples and cultures," and the major component of this Orient is "the idea of European identity as a superior one in comparison with all the non-European peoples and cultures." It is this component which gives orientalism such durability and, according to Said, possibly what has made European culture "hegemonic both in and outside Europe."[21]

My juxtaposition of Bann and Said underscores an important commonality between historical and ethnographic writing. To quote Michel de Certeau, both the past and the exotic are a means of "representing a difference." The idea that at distinct periods societies have constructed racial others in projects of self-definition is now a familiar idea, but de Certeau suggests that a similar operation informs the writing of history. He explains, "the historical operation consists in classifying the given according to a present law that is distinguished from its 'other' (the past), in assuming a distance in respect of an acquired situation, and thus in marking through a discourse the effective change that precipitated this distancing."[22] The process "stages the present time of a situation" just as the ethnographers Said examines drew attention to their status as Europeans through their complete mastery of, and simultaneous disengagement from, patterns of Oriental life. One can even remark that the shift from an antiquarian veneration of the past to nineteenth-century historicism's critical manipulation of historical fragments parallels the shift evident in the decline of the myth of the noble savage and the rise of anthropology.

Even if similar operations have informed the creation of the past and the creation of the exotic, these operations have had different consequences. The people of past eras were obviously unaffected by their representation in the nineteenth century and the same cannot be said of the people described by orientalism. The British in the nineteenth century wrote extensively on medieval England, but they did not rely on the past for raw materials, open markets, and strategic position. Only in a metaphorical sense can the British be said to have colonized the past, even as historical writing both presupposes and informs systems of power affecting entire populations. Ethnographic writing by contrast defines a community of readers unfolding in time in opposition to an unchanging object of study. As Johannes Fabian explains, the use of the present tense in ethnographic statements like " 'the X are matrilineal' is taken [by some critics] to imply a static view of society, one that is unattentive to the fact that all cultures are constantly changing... At the very least, say these critics, the present tense 'freezes' a society at the time of observation; at worst, it contains assumptions about the repetitiveness, predictability, and conservatism of primitives." According to Fabian, this literary practice is one of many "distancing devices" that produce a "denial of coevalness... a persistent and systematic tendency to place the referent(s) of anthropology in a Time other than the present of the producer of anthropological discourse."[23]

The Orient was an object of both ethnographic and historical analysis. Many nineteenth-century entertainments created a uniform and unchanging Orient; scholarship on contemporary Egypt was adapted to theatrical productions depicting ancient Nineveh while native Syrians in London exhibition halls performed ceremonies that reportedly dated back eighteen hundred years. However, as this last example makes clear, the Orient was also seen as a space of considerable antiquity and past cultural achievement. Unlike tribal peoples who were granted no past, nineteenth-century "Orientals" marked the distance from both a "culturally superior" modern Europe and the distance from the Oriental's own "culturally superior" past. As we shall see, this question of how to account for the apparent decline of Eastern cultures became a central concern for both orientalist writing and orientalist entertainments. This marking off of the Orient from both Europe and itself was circumscribed within material relations; this marking was accompanied by an adverse balance of trade, growing debt, and direct intervention. Whether or not an ethnographer like Edward Lane directly contributed to British colonialism, it is incontestable that he benefited from the fact that "the colonial power structure made the object of anthropological study accessible and safe," as Talal Asad has written in reference to a later period.[24]

OVERVIEW

What follows is not only a history of the vocabulary, images, and ideas about the exotic as developed in both the entertainment industry and the human sciences, but also a history of how space and bodies came to have different meanings. My trajectory begins with early-nineteenth-century optical entertainments that used flat surfaces to give the illusion of depth and movement to their depictions of exotic topography. In these entertainments, as in the romantic theatre I next examine, authenticity resided in the careful copying of architectural details on canvas or in the inclusion of a native term in descriptive guidebooks. Both theatre and optical entertainments of the romantic period invited an imaginative engagement with the exotic through fanciful combinations of authentically reproduced fragments. It was a process, I argue (following Bann and others), that typified the antiquarian's creation of – and reverence for – the historically or geographically distant. I then examine the emergence of the idea that human behavior itself carries the marks of authenticity. The new vocabulary of ethnography changed the meaning and significance of longstanding entertainments such as human displays and native performance, and created different expectations for acting. Moreover, the idea that authenticity was evident in how a person interacted with those objects that we now refer to as "material culture" placed a new emphasis on mise-en-scène, a term that had only recently entered into English usage. This process ultimately gave rise to the widespread use of three-dimensional reconstructions in museums, exhibitions, and theatres.

I develop this spatial history while examining popular entertainment forms of the nineteenth century and their relation to specific orientalist images and ideas that anticipated or emerged from within the human sciences. In the first chapter, "Spectacle and Surveillance in Orientalist Panoramas," I argue that exotic optical shows at panoramas, theatres, and exhibition halls in the first half of the century reveal a tension between an inherited landscape sensibility (in which a spectator subjectively engaged and shaped an engrossing topography) and an emerging geographic imagination (in which topography was placed before the spectator and its internal meaning interpreted). These entertainments often created absorbing images, in which audiences reportedly felt sucked into the exotic lands depicted. At the same time, keys, written descriptions, and lectures distanced the audience from the image, creating a sense of orientalist mastery. In the course of tracing the changing stance of optical entertainments over a fifty-year period, I introduce many of the issues that inform my analysis of other entertainment forms. I argue that this tension between engagement and identification with the exotic and its masterful control is a central characteristic of the antiquarian stance. I explore the relation of this stance to the stance evident in codified disciplines that emerged later in the century, and examine the changing meaning of orientalist depictions in relation to ideas of spatial control central to the development of disciplinary society.

In the second chapter, "Fantasies of Miscegenation on the Romantic Stage," I examine the often cited romantic preference for the visionary over the visible in relation to the nineteenth-century fascination with and anxiety at racial spectacle. I argue that exotic plays presented detailed depiction of race as a means to abstraction – a way to reveal the drives, desires, and environmental effects that were thought to constitute race. Looking at Edmund Kean's exotic performances, the theatrical adaptations of Byron's oriental romances, and the theatre's use of the Byron myth, I argue that romantic theatre imagined genius–travelers who not only mastered the exotic but embodied its internal essence. These acts of penetration were frequently staged within harem plays and dances in which the East itself become coded as a closed female space of indolence and lascivious pleasure awaiting the Western male's discovery.

The authenticity of such performance was demonstrated by varied face-paint, detailed scene painting, and transliterated terms; however, there was as yet no concept that authenticity resided in an individual's interaction with a surrounding environment. Chapter 3, "The Built-out East of Popular Ethnography," examines the use of three-dimensional environments in the human displays, exhibitions, and pleasure gardens that grew in popularity after the Great Exhibition of 1851. Orientalist display in these venues reflected a new ethnographic world-view that transformed exotic bodies into documents of cultural practice. The exotic body became meaningful through its placement in a highly detailed display environment. These displays reflected a new imperial world-view that defined regions by their raw materials, whether products or peoples, at the same time that they perpetuated older tropes of exotic display that defined the East as an over-sensual odalisque.

The fourth chapter, "The Biblical East in Theatres and Exhibitions," examines the relation of biblical exploration and archeology to a surge of mid-century exhibitions, spectacles, and plays depicting the Holy Land. These productions created three-dimensional display environments that employed archeological and ethnographic research to reproduce and inter-pret the shape of distant spaces, whether that distance was geographic or historical. Authenticity resided in both the artifact's form and its use and placement in space. The role of the theatre, like that of the museum, was to trace out this use and placement – to *perform* authenticity rather than simply provide authentic renderings. This chapter gives extended analysis to two productions, *Azaël the Prodigal* (Drury Lane 1851) and *Sardanapalus* (Princess's 1853), and considers a range of exhibition spaces such as the Egyptian Hall, the British Museum, and the Sydenham Crystal Palace.

In the final chapter, "The Geography of Imperial Theatre," I argue that late-Victorian theatre created a new geographic mode of representation by combining exotic and colonial imagery with new scenic methods for rep-resenting space, which I describe as "environmental mise-en-scène." This geographic mode was evident in the theatre's near obsession with the colo-nial infrastructure and the technologies that supported it. In imperial melo-drama, Gatling guns and transcontinental cables linked colonial armies to England and protected colonials from "savage hordes." Even ballets fea-tured "Suez canal" scenes, and pantomimes Cairo steamers. The theatre was a principal space for the creation and dissemination of the modern geographic imagination, not only rallying support for Britain's imperial wars and familiarizing audiences with distant regions, but also adopting an emerging conception of geography that was informed by the growth and popularization of the discipline at a time when new racial theories were coming to the fore. Both theatre and geography examined how physical environment affected culture, civilization, and – in the words of one early geographer – "the mental processes of its inhabitants."[25] Such study, in both academic societies and theatres, accounted for the low levels of civ-ilization and the mental inferiority thought to exist outside Europe and justified British domination of indigenous peoples. This chapter examines the melodramas, pantomimes, ballets, and spectacles that made reference to the British occupation of Egypt in 1882 and the fall of Khartoum to Sudanese rebels in 1884.

In the course of this book, I describe many changes in scenic technology and theatre licensing; however, it might be useful to outline some of these developments for readers who are unfamiliar with the theatre of the eighteenth and nineteenth centuries. Throughout the eighteenth century, settings were painted on wings, borders, and a backshutter at the rear of the stage. Settings tended to be anonymous so that the same scenery could be used in different plays, a practice necessitated by frequent changes of bill and facilitated by the neo-classical view that identifiable locales undermined universality. Greater specificity in stage settings was introduced in the second half of the eighteenth century, notably with David Garrick's management of Drury Lane. Garrick commissioned new scenery for new productions, as when he produced Samuel Johnson's *Mahomet and Irene* in 1749 with "scenes splendid and gay, such as were well adapted to the inside of a Turkish seraglio."[26] Garrick also fitted new scenery to old plays, as in his 1759 production of *Antony and Cleopatra*. In 1771, Garrick hired Paris Opera scene painter, Philippe Jacques de Loutherbourg to oversee all elements of spectacle.

De Loutherbourg brought a new level of realism to the theatre's depiction of local and exotic locales, reportedly researching the regions he painted. He improved stage lighting, installing overhead battens and using silk and gauze to subtly color light. It was at this time that oil lamps began to replace candles in stage lighting, making the quality of the scene painting more visible to audience members. De Loutherbourg broke up the stage image with the use of low extensions of scenery known as ground rows. He was also a pioneer in optical entertainments; his 1781 optical entertainment, the Eidophusikon, produced settings throughout the Mediterranean unencumbered by actors, with lighting effects ranging from a sunrise to moonlight as well as fire and storm effects. The use of rear-lit transparencies, colored plates and gauze, and panoramic pictures in this show all precipitated later practice but, more importantly, the Eidophusikon defined the presentation of exotic locales as a theatrical event in itself.

De Loutherbourg even influenced oriental romances, arguably inspiring William Beckford to write *Vathek*. Months before creating the Eidophusikon, Beckford hired de Loutherbourg to transform his estate into a labyrinthine and necromantic environment for a three-day Christmas performance–masquerade. According to one de Loutherbourg biographer "the realization of this exotic world bore many allusions to oriental and Egyptian imagery" and Beckford himself described the event as "the realization of romance in all its fervours, in all its extravagance...I wrote

V[*athek*] immediately upon my return to London at the close of this romantic villegiatura."[27]

In the nineteenth century, changes in lighting and design accompanied more detailed and varied representations of place. In 1817 Drury Lane and the Lyceum installed gas lighting. With the development of "gas tables," theatre practitioners could control the intensity of light at separate parts of the stage. In 1837 Covent Garden first used limelight, in which a block of quicklime was heated by an oxygen flame so as to cast an intense spotlight. In 1881, electric lights were introduced at the Savoy Theatre. With greater intensity and control over lights, practitioners extended de Loutherbourg's early experiments with coloring light. More attention was placed on design during this period as well. Even before the installation of gas lighting, theatre managers, notably John Philip Kemble at Drury Lane at the turn of the century, began to commission historically accurate scene painting. Later, scene painting became a central attraction of the theatre, and painters such as John Henderson Grieve, David Roberts, and Clarkson Stanfield became famous for their lavish settings in the 1820s and 30s.

New techniques for depicting locations also emerged in the nineteenth century and some practitioners abandoned wings when reproducing interiors. Madame Vestris is credited with introducing the box set on the London stage in 1832, though she may have continued to use borders rather than a ceiling cloth. However, she undoubtedly furnished these interiors with real objects, from quality furniture and rugs in domestic scenes to actual goods in shop scenes. Painted flats continued to be used, even as they were complemented by built-out properties. Henry Irving is notable for relying more heavily on free-plantation at the Lyceum in the 1870s, even removing the stage floor grooves that guided flats on and off stage. Throughout this period, the apron was repeatedly shortened at several theatres, so that actors increasingly performed *in* settings rather than *in front of* settings separated from the actor by a proscenium arch.

The nineteenth century also saw a growing number of entertainment forms. This was largely the result of new interpretations of the Licensing Act of 1737. This act had originally given a theatrical monopoly to two royal theatres in London, Drury Lane and Covent Garden (the Haymarket was later permitted to stage plays during the summer months). In the early-nineteenth century, theatrical legislation was reinterpreted to allow for additional theatres as long as they did not perform regular drama. This resulted in the development of various minor forms such as equestrian and nautical spectacle, pantomime, melodrama, and burletta. The popularity of these forms prompted similar offerings at the patent houses, so that when theatrical monopolies were revoked in 1843 there was already considerable overlap in the fare offered at the patent and minor theatres. In 1843 there was no shortage of entertainment venues in London, with twenty-one theatres as well as numerous optical entertainments, and lecture and exhibition halls. London's entertainment industry was well equipped to absorb the volume of detail generated by orientalist travelers and scholars. In the process, the entertainment industry became – and remains – a primary site for the formulation of modern conceptions of race, gender, and nation.

CHAPTER I

Spectacle and surveillance in orientalist panoramas

In the first half of the nineteenth century, scores of panoramas, dioramas, cosmoramas, and other optical entertainments presented Eastern terrains and architecture to London audiences. These entertainments reportedly recreated a painter–traveler's encounter with the East, celebrating his mastery of a foreign topography at the same time that they delighted in that topography's power to induce vertigo. Audiences, like the painter–traveler that preceded them, took possession of the discovered landscape while also being possessed by its expansiveness. Individual entertainments carefully delineated a wide range of terrains and architecture and then asserted that this variety overwhelmed the senses. These images seemed both to narrate centuries of immigration and dynastic change and to reveal an underlying timelessness. They provided access to the complexities of history, geography, and race – all of which were summarized in cycles of "sack and slaughter." These contradictions are much more than conceits or an emerging stylistic convention; I will argue that they speak of a new mode of being in the world and in time that was generated out of modernization and new colonial realities.

The sheer number of vistas housed in London contributed to both their authority and their disorienting effect. Most venues changed their views regularly, some venues housed multiple views, and a stunning number of venues were springing up all over London. From the privileged vantage point of the panorama platform, audiences looked upon a dizzying succession of locales. In 1851, the apogee of panorama production, there were nearly thirty views on display at various panoramas and optical shows. Nine of these featured Middle Eastern locales.[1] While the actual displays were dispersed throughout London, the places they represented were carefully organized in the popular consciousness along commercial and military routes. The year 1851 also witnessed the Great Exhibition of the Works of Industry of All Nations, a mammoth undertaking amassing goods and raw materials from around the world. Such ambitious collecting relied heavily on the movement of soldiers and seamen, as was demonstrated in numerous panoramas depicting military routes to the East.

FROM LANDSCAPE TO GEOGRAPHY

The panorama maintained a tension between visual surrender into disorienting landscapes and a sense of mastery produced by commanding views. Art historians such as John Barrell and Jonathan Crary have argued that in the eighteenth century vision was increasingly seen as a subjective faculty.[2] Panoramas reflect a continuing ambivalence towards vision's authority and the value of spectacle. Panoramas were, of course, visual entertainments par excellence in which pleasure was produced by the medium's ability to fool the eye. However, over the fifty years of the panorama's popularity, panorama spectacle was increasingly inscribed in abstract relations. Souvenir pamphlets provided panorama patrons with information on the region's topography and ethnic breakdown, as well as other natural and cultural features. Entertainment innovations such as the moving panorama and accompanying performances, travel narratives, and lectures also attempted to infuse a geographic sensibility into panorama landscapes. More importantly, panoramas drew upon the growing geographic knowledge of their patrons. If the visual offered a dubious authority, geography – manifest in a growing number of exchanges between London and peripheral regions but never directly perceptible – discovered a new and distinctly colonial authority in the contextual. Meaning did not exist in objects, but in the relation between objects (whether this relation was defined by geography, ethnography, or history).

The history of London's panoramas and optical entertainments in the first half of the nineteenth century reveals the increasing dominance of a geographic sensibility (focusing on abstract contextual relations) over a landscape sensibility (in which artistry and subjectivity informed the apprehension of the visible). In a corresponding development, new entertainments developed that more effectively conveyed a sense of authority while minimizing disorienting effects. The tendency of reviews for optical entertainments to provide lengthy discussions of the depicted region's history, ethnic breakdown, or role in the current power balance, indicates that these entertainments were taken as informative, rather than disorienting, spectacle. Paradoxically, presenters assuaged concerns for topographical accuracy by directing attention away from the visual. Increasingly, these entertainments became lessons in geography, ethnology, and history, realms that avoided the anxieties of vision in their abstract nature. Invariably, this non-visual information was directed back to specific features of the image – transforming these features into markers of abstract relations. The obsessive amassing of informative detail became a means of obscuring the visual nature of these obviously visual entertainments. They became opportunities to see past the visual into the incontestable authority of scholarship. The rise of geography was indicative of this process; however, this is not to imply that geography eventually vanquished landscape or that a landscape sensibility ever existed independent of a geographic framework. Rather, the two sensibilities were dialectically linked.

The tension between landscape and geography was especially pronounced in the depiction of Eastern terrain. Britain's long-standing fascination with an Orient imagined to be lawless and lascivious contributed to a tendency to imaginatively engage the depicted terrain. At the same time, Britain's burgeoning sense of cultural superiority, intensified by military interventions and a trend towards economic domination, found its corollary in commanding views. As the Eastern Question prompted Britain to more direct involvement in the region, the region became Britain's to delineate, arrange, and analyze. However, this was far from the case at the start of the century when the panorama craze first erupted in London.

In 1794, Robert Barker opened a large circular building in Leicester Square for the exhibition of giant topographical canvases depicting 360-degree views. Barker had been exhibiting giant canvases since 1788, which he began calling "panoramas" on the advice of one of his "classical friends" in 1791. However, it was not until the Leicester Square Panorama was in operation that the full illusionary capacity of his display was realized. Though not the first view to completely surround the spectator, the scope and illusionistic lighting of the Leicester Square Panorama provided an unprecedented experience. Spectators entered through a dimly lit narrow passage and then mounted to a 30-foot (9-metre)-wide viewing platform in the center of a 90-foot (27-metre) rotunda (known as the Large Circle). From this platform, spectators looked upon a brightly illuminated cylindrical canvas. The image was hung at the uniform distance of 30 feet (9 metres) from the edge of the platform. A second smaller panorama rotunda (the Upper Circle) was built directly above the viewing platform. Central skylights cast sunlight onto both canvases, but the floor of the Upper Circle prevented spectators on the viewing platform in the Large Circle from discerning the source of the light. A canopy in the Upper Circle produced the same effect. In the Large Circle, false terrain was built into the floor to prevent the appearance that the landscape terminated in a bottom frame. Moreover, the spectators in the Large Circle were unable to see the top edge of the canvas because the floor of the Upper Circle blocked their view of where the image met the roof.[3] The Leicester Square Panorama retained this configuration (with the exception of a short-lived third circle) even after it passed to Robert Burford, who operated the business from 1826 to 1861.

The panorama did not strive at realism, but produced an illusion of the real. The panorama erased any reminders that the spectator examined a work of art separate and apart from their position. The image had no frame (thanks to the false terrain and the floor of the Upper Circle). Instead, the image appeared to extend endlessly, enveloping the spectator. At no point could the spectator break from the image and examine the surrounding reality; the panorama completely filled the field of vision, blotting out anything that might reveal its artificiality. The indirect light ensured that the spectator's shadow would not be cast on the image, destroying the illusion. Moreover, the diffuse light recreated the experience of outdoor lighting. The darkness of the corridor leading to the viewing platform further undermined the spectator's awareness that they were still indoors; once emerging and stepping onto the platform, the depicted terrain "appeared as bright as the remembered daylight outside," in the words of one historian.[4] Spectators attested to the disorienting effects. Queen Charlotte reportedly grew seasick when attending Barker's first panorama in the Leicester Square building, *The Grand Fleet at Spithead in 1791*.[5] Spectators at other early Leicester Square panoramas complained of "dizziness and nausea" caused by the "impossibility of withdrawing from the delusion," and attributed the effects of the panorama to its lack of a frame or "any object that could serve as a comparison."[6]

The panorama's pronounced effects on spectators diminished with its novelty, and it is in this context that Robert Barker quickly turned to foreign subjects. As early as 1799 Robert Barker's son, Henry Aston Barker, traveled to Turkey to make sketches of Constantinople. It was his first sketching trip and the success of the resulting two panoramas secured a life of travel. *View of Constantinople from the Town of Galatea* was exhibited in the Large Circle from 27 April 1801 until 15 May 1802, and *View of Constantinople from the Tower of Leander* was shown in the Upper Circle from 23 November 1801 to 14 May 1803. Notices for the larger panorama drew attention to the fact that it was only through the intervention of Lord Elgin, British envoy to the Ottoman Sultan, that Barker obtained an "Order from the Porte" to execute his sketches. Moreover, these notices explained that an Ottoman Janissary attended Barker while he made the sketches.[7] The image of Barker under the surveillance of a member of the elite war corps, combined with the fact of Lord Elgin's intervention with the Porte, underscored the danger and exoticism of his sketching expedition. Constantinople would become one of the most frequently reproduced cities at the Leicester Square Panorama; new Constantinople panoramas were exhibited in 1804, 1846, and 1853–1854, the last two panoramas being based on new sketches by William J. Smith. In addition, the Strand panorama, which, like the Leicester Square Panorama, was owned by Robert Burford after 1826, exhibited a Constantinople panorama in 1829 based on Henry Aston Barker's original sketches.

While none of these canvases are extant (Barker began painting over old works soon into his career) their souvenir pamphlets, which contained an illustrated key and descriptions, suggest that a sense of geographic mastery came to overshadow the panorama's disorienting effects. The key for the 1801 Larger Circle view of Constantinople is anamorphic, whereas the keys for the 1829, 1846, and 1853 panoramas convert the panorama into two rectangles. The switch from anamorphic to rectilinear keys underscored the legibility of the panorama. Rectilinear keys are designed to be read from left to right; important features are numbered beginning at the left as are their corresponding names. Anamorphic keys are harder to read; the circular view produces distortions, there is no clear order to the depicted features, and there is not an obvious place to list the names of the numbered features. Anamorphic keys emphasized the sensationalism of a 360-degree view. There is no clear route into the image. Instead it is all available at once and yet inaccessible precisely for its overwhelming simultaneity. The spectator's position is marked at the center of the image, emphasizing the spectator's inability to separate from the terrain and make a picture of it. By contrast, in the rectilinear keys the spectator is outside the frame and the terrain is neatly organized. The fact that, according to Stephan Oettermann, most European panoramas switched to rectangular keys after 1815[8] under-scores how quickly the sensationalism of a 360-degree view waned.

As the effects of the panorama grew less sensational, the subject matter grew more so. The pamphlet for Burford's Constantinople panorama of 1846 provided a description of the baths, which seems largely drawn from orientalist painting. One portion of the description reads:

It may seem that the process of bathing occupies at least one or two hours, but females frequently remain talking, laughing and singing, five or six, yet the price of the bath, exclusive of refreshments, seldom exceeds six or seven-pence, and the attendants are all well skilled in shaving, hairdressing and other necessary arts. A female bath attended by thirty or forty bathers, with their beautiful children and numerous slaves, all sumptuously attired and blazing with jewels, is described as a splendid scene.[9]

By mid-century, Eastern baths summoned images of female dalliance, with refreshments and music. Eastern females were quickly translated into spectacle; together with their children and slaves, they automatically compose a "splendid scene."

This sensational pictorialism is similarly evident in the pamphlet's description of the "small chambers" of the slave market, which "are most appropriate to the use of female slaves, and present to the eyes of those privileged to see them, an extraordinary assemblage of frame and beauty of every age and colour."[10] No longer was the spectacle of the panorama its disorienting 360-degree view, but those small female chambers, normally closed but now opened to viewer's knowledge through the descriptive materials of the panorama. By contrast, the only mention of female space in the pamphlet for Barker's first Constantinople panorama was the explanation that that part of the Seraglio "which is called the harem, strictly signifies the apartments of the women, and the enclosures appropriated to their use."[11] The description makes no attempt to open up the harem. Instead it remains one of the countless features that surround but elude the spectator.

The ability to open closed female chambers was only one aspect of comprehensiveness of the view offered at the 1846 panorama. Its pamphlet asserted that from the spectator's position atop Seraskier's Tower, "the whole of [Constantinople's] curious internal economy is at once visible in its fullest extent and magnificence."[12] The pamphlet then delineated this economy in a somewhat haphazard fashion, discussing the present state of coffee-houses, the prevalence of public and private fountains, as well as providing extended discussions of the surrounding topography and the ethnic breakdown of the city. The spectator's view was as pervasive as the Western influence, which was evident in the fact that "the Turks possess all the elements of civilization, and time, example and a perfect confidence in their European allies, is working a great revolution." This new-found confidence in the Ottomans followed Palmerston's insistence that British interests in the region demanded the protection of the integrity of the Ottoman Empire against incursions by Russia and the growing independence of Egypt. However, the belief in an all-pervasive Western influence is striking even given the political context. Consider, for example, the pamphlet's assertion that "the habits of industry have made their way into many harems, and have totally changed the habits and feelings of the women." The same women, presumably, who formed the "splendid scene" at the baths were in fact open to a Victorian ideology of progress and usefulness.

Constantinople's "curious internal economy" apparently combined Western habits of industry with odalisques. The East would eventually develop into a somewhat inferior version of Europe, only with a lot more sex. This development would appear to have more to do with Constantinople's receptiveness to British commerce than any moral reform. It was Western *products* of industry (rather than habits) that had actually infiltrated Eastern homes. According to the pamphlet for the 1846 panorama of Constantinople, the real proof of the city's civilization was that the Turks were adopting Western clothing. The pamphlet cites as an example the fact that the turban was being replaced by the red fez, which – the pamphlet need not remind – was manufactured in England. The comprehensiveness of the panorama view was a corollary to the pervasiveness of British industry.

The pamphlet for Barker's first Constantinople panorama describes a strikingly different relation between British spectator and Eastern city. Rather than manufacturing Turkish costumes and shipping them east, the British in 1801 relied on chance events to make indigenous costumes visible. The pamphlet for the first Constantinople panorama explained that if the costumes were accurately rendered, it was only because of a fortunate "display which took place at the time of the drawing; the Grand Signior having passed close by the Tower, with the officers of his household, and a numerous train of barges, &c. as he sailed from Constantinople to one of his palaces on the Bosphorus."[13] Beyond the curious choice to describe the Sultan as "the Grand Signior" (a tendency to conflate the Eastern Mediterranean with the Western Mediterranean which was also evident in exotic scene painting at this time) the quote is interesting for its acknowledgment of happenstance in the preparation of the image. Sights rise up for the artist without his control, just as they do for the spectator at the panorama.

The 1801 pamphlet describes an active landscape, whereas the 1846 pamphlet describes a landscape that has been, by and large, subjugated. There is a sense of movement in the earlier pamphlet's description of barges making their way to a palace on the Bosphorus, filled with exotically clad officers of the Sultan's household. Unexpected images greet the spectator from a landscape performing its otherness. By contrast, the later pamphlet from 1846 asserts that from the viewing platform "mosques, minarets, palaces, and kiosks, in countless variety...spread out like a map." Even here, though, the exotic undermines attempts at its containment. After rather dry descriptions of the above-mentioned mosques, the 1846 pamphlet concludes:

...these [mosques] with the towers, ports, palaces, and the vast masses of heavy-looking, party coloured houses, together with the myriads of small domes, intermixed with vast woods of cypress, and groves of stately pines, which meet the eye in strange but pleasing confusion, press an appearance so Oriental, and so different in character from anything European, as to defy description.[14]

The pamphlet provides a long and clear list of structures, and then announces that these objects defy ordering and "meet the eye in strange but pleasing confusion." This active landscape, with its combination of brightly colored and vastly different structures, epitomizes the "Oriental." This is not the Orient as object of imperial objectivity, but an Orient that confronts the spectator with a character so different as to "defy description." Mastery folds before an absorbing confusion.

ANTIQUARIAN VISION

Just as the panorama maintained a tension between landscape and geography in its depiction of space, it also maintained a tension between antiquarianism and historicism in its depiction of time. The Orient was conceived of as an antiquary's haven, not because its past was visible in physical remains, but because past and present were thought to coexist in a kind of always-antiquity. In many examples of romantic orientalism, the region seems to possess its own proper time independent of Europe's forward historical development. The resulting image is "not a *pre-modern*, but an *anti-modern* Orient," as Saree Makdisi has written in reference to the East of "Childe Harold's Pilgrimage."[15] This was especially pronounced in representations of Jerusalem, whose importance in scriptures contributed to its remove from a Western secular timeline. This "anti-modern" Orient came into increasing conflict with the developing imperial world-view, especially once the British began to prop up the Ottoman Empire against the threat of Russian aggression. As we have already seen in the 1846 panorama of Constantinople, once the city was repositioned within Britain's sphere of influence, it was discovered to possess all the vestments of civilization including proper haberdashery.

Just as the exotic panorama prompted both disorientation and mastery, similarly contrasting attitudes are evident in the panorama's representation of the exotic past. Stephen Bann describes such contrasting attitudes when he compares the antiquarianism of the romantic period with the historicism that emerged later in the nineteenth century. According to Bann, the development of a historicist outlook entailed the ability to see beyond isolated facts and old objects so as to grasp their relation. Historicism is the attempt to separate oneself from the object of study so as to gain a proper perspective for the writing of history. Bann explains, "writing imposes a regime which is comparable to that of the perspectival painting, in that no detail, or object, is accessible in itself, but is simply an element integrated within the stimulating space of the perspective."[16] By contrast, antiquarian fascination attached itself to the ancient object proper. The antiquary sought to surround him or herself with the material of antiquity, regardless of its "real" position in a historical narrative. Antiquarian collections amassed artifacts and fragments from daily life, such that – as a contemporary journalist said of the Musée de Cluny – "you are as if enveloped by the good old chivalric times."[17] For Bann, this antiquarian envelopment is distinct from historicist perspective, and marks distinctly different attitudes to the past. He explains, "Envelopment is, of course, a concept particularly appropriate to an experience of the senses which is not directional – not subject to the ordering of a visually coherent space."[18]

Bann's choice to translate nineteenth-century historical consciousness into spatial metaphors (envelopment versus perspective) underscores the degree to which tensions between attitudes to the past and the tensions between attitudes to landscape trace a single dialectic in the epistemological field. Geography, in this sense, can be read as one of the several abstract frameworks (such as historicism) that emerged in the nineteenth century, replacing a classical order organized by resemblance. Geography attempts to include ideas of development and change in its representations of place, examining the distribution and interaction of physical, biological, and cultural features that change across regions and over time. In short, geography attempts to communicate the "whole of an internal economy" (to quote the Constantinople pamphlet of 1846). It examines processes beneath the surface rather than simply enumerating what is already visible.

In this respect, the relation between landscape and geography can be said to parallel the relation between antiquarianism and historicism. While antiquarianism limits itself to the material objects of the past (from chipped artifacts to musty documents), historicism uses such objects to arrive at ideas of succession and analogy. Similarly, only by seeing through depicted features to abstract relations could the panorama spectator remove herself from an enveloping landscape, even though these abstract frameworks were generated out of a physical topography. This was especially pronounced in orientalist depictions, in which "strange but pleasing confusion," often replete with sexual connotations, drew spectators into a densely material landscape, at the same time that clearly demarcated differences marked the spectator's mastery over the depicted terrain.

Britain's antiquarian interest in the East was stimulated at the start of the century by the wealth of iconographic material produced during the French invasion of Egypt. Prior to the nineteenth century, British interest in Eastern antiquities focused on those Egyptian remains scattered in Rome (the principal destination of the eighteenth-century Grand Tour) or those documented by a handful of Eastern travelers such as Richard Pococke, Frederick L. Norden, and James Bruce. However, this all changed in the aftermath of Napoleon's invasion of Egypt in 1798. The full effects of the short-lived occupation became evident in the years after the French evacuation of 1801, when reams of documentation and artifacts arrived in Europe. Though Napoleon's ultimate goal of reinforcing French domination of the Mediterranean and obstructing Britain's route to India was foiled when Nelson destroyed the French fleet at Aboukir Bay in August of 1798, the impact of the French occupation on European culture was lasting.

Napoleon's expedition was accompanied by one hundred and sixty-seven scholars from fields ranging from literature to engineering and charged with documenting all facets of Egyptian life. Napoleon returned to France soon after the defeat at Aboukir Bay; however, the French army and his troop of scholars remained in Cairo. Despite their tenuous situation, these scholars relentlessly went about their work recording and cataloguing nearly everything they encountered, from ancient and Islamic monuments, to arts and crafts, to flora and fauna. After the French capitulation, these scholars were allowed to leave with their manuscripts, drawings, and casts (after the French threatened to destroy their work rather than relinquish it to the British). In the years following the invasion, a series of lavishly illustrated French folios documenting Egypt appeared.

While the most famous and exhaustive of these publications was the twenty-three-volume *Description de l'Egypte*, Vivant Denon's *Voyages dans la Basse et la Haute Egypte* published in 1802 was by far the most important for the British entertainment industry. *Voyages*, with 141 plates and accompanying lengthy descriptions, roamed widely over all things Egyptian, inviting readers to an antiquarian immersion into the world of the exotic. In addition to extensive documentation of pharaonic ruins, the book includes images of Arab physical types, Egyptian costumes, interior views of the harem, even scenes from French battles in the region. Several editions of *Voyages* rapidly appeared in England, including a very popular pocket-sized edition with reduced prints. The *Edinburgh Review* asserted that "Few publications, we believe, have ever obtained so extensive a circulation in the same space of time as these travels."[19] *Voyages* was adapted by the theatre almost immediately following its publication and would become, in the words of one historian, "the theatre's major source of Egyptian subjects."[20]

In the same year as the publication of *Voyages*, Mark Lonsdale – theatre manager, dramatist, and stage mechanic – produced *Ægyptiana* in the upper room of the Lyceum, beginning the entertainment with eighteen large paintings based on prints by Denon and accompanied by explanatory readings, according to handbills. Charles Dibdin, Jr., the nineteenth-century playwright, was presumably referring to this production when he wrote of Lonsdale's "Egyptiana" in his *History and Illustrations of the London Theatres* (1826). According to Dibdin, the production "consisted of panoramic paintings, mechanical transformations, and recitation; and was illustrative of everything connected with the history of Egypt, natural and philosophical; its inhabitants, animals, customs, and localities."²¹ *Ægyptiana* apparently surrounded the spectator with images, stage effects, and narration. Its scope was as expansive as its source text. In this light, Dibdin's unlikely assertion that *Ægyptiana* illustrated "every thing connected with the history of Egypt" becomes an indication of the production's enveloping exoticism, rather than its thoroughness of subject.

The antiquarian response to the ancient East is clarified by John Britton's description of *Ægyptiana*. Britton, who would later publish extensively on antiquarian and topographical subjects, wrote and delivered accompanying descriptions for *Ægyptiana*. In his 1850 autobiography, Britton explains that "on the publication of Denon's splendid work on Antiquites &c. of Egypt," Lonsdale arranged to have these images "adapted and applied as to produce a moving panorama for the stage."²² It is unclear whether Britton used the term "moving panorama" to mean a series of images painted on a long cloth that was unfurled across the stage on rollers (which is what the term usually meant at the time he wrote) or if he simply intended to suggest a progression of images pulling the spectator into an enveloping (i.e. panoramic) stage world. The latter is most likely the case, as there is no evidence of such mechanical moving panoramas at the time of *Ægyptiana*'s production. Regardless, Britton remembers *Ægyptiana* as a theatrical event, rather than the mere exhibition of Denon's images. The exotic image, in its adaptation to the stage, is either literally or figuratively animated. This is not a static view, not simply a "splendid work on Antiquities," but a moving panorama.

The eclectic resources of this early theatrical orientalism are evident in the full bill for *Ægyptiana*. The images of Egyptian antiquities were followed by an "intermezzo" of readings from Gothic romances "Illustrated by Machinery and Painting in Six Picturesque Changes" which was then followed by "an Embellished Recitation of Milton's L'Allegro" with "Ten Successive Pictures" taken from the work.²³ In juxtaposing images from Denon with scenes from gothic romances and scenes from Milton of pastoral and ancient locales (such as consecutive views of "A Splendid Tournement" and "Ancient Hall, with a Banquet"), Lonsdale simply complemented the anti-modern with the pre-modern. There was no disjuncture in the move from pharaonic ruins to medieval recreations, both acted as markers of distance, both fulfilled a desire for a space outside modernity.

This antiquarian fetish for the non-modern is even more evident in Britton's account of *Ægyptiana*'s strange theatrical combinations. Britton explains that for his benefit night (a performance in which a specified performer or performers received the house proceeds after expenses), he and three friends "made up an evening's programme of the Egyptiaca, recitations, songs, &c." The use of the term "Egyptiaca," which was already obsolete, suggests the same love of the remote that animated *Ægyptiana*. It was not that the performance fully delineated the Egyptian past or created – to paraphrase Bann – a visually coherent space in which no detail was accessible in itself but only as part of a larger whole. Instead, *Ægyptiana* provided delightfully musty fragments, specimens of "Egyptiaca," arranged in the theatre so as to create the effect of antiquity. Songs, recitations, and Egyptology all pleased in themselves producing an atmosphere thick with the old and unusual.

Britton's early theatre career might seem inconsistent with his later renown as a writer on antiquarian and topographical subjects and his position as vice-president of the Sussex Archaeological Society and of the Archaeological Institute at Salisbury; however, he was not alone among antiquarians in his dabbling in the popular entertainment industry. The new theatricality of the early-nineteenth century was entirely consonant with the antiquarian impulse and a surprising number of scholar–travelers doubled as showmen, such as Giovanni Belzoni, Henry Salt, Joseph Bonomi, and Robert Ker Porter. The panorama is the most obvious manifestation of antiquarianism's figurative envelopment in an actually enveloping performance form (though theatre, as we shall see, similarly adapted new scenic strategies to this end). One of the most prolific of these antiquary showmen, both in terms of scholarly and entertainment output, was Frederick Catherwood. Catherwood is probably best remembered as the illustrator for John Lloyd Stephen's Central American travel accounts; however, at the time of their first trip to the region Catherwood was known as the proprietor of Catherwood's Panorama in New York City. Catherwood entered the panorama business in 1835 after three years of travel in Egypt and the Holy Land. According to his biographer, Catherwood was unable to find a publisher for his drawings of Jerusalem, and so allowed Robert Burford to use them at the Leicester Square Panorama. Catherwood assisted in the archaeological details of the buildings. This collaboration was followed by

Catherwood's contribution to three other Middle Eastern panoramas at the Leicester Square Panorama: "Thebes" of ancient Egypt, "Karnak," and the "Ruins of Baalbec."[24]

Antiquarian writing, like other writing of the romantic period, often sought to induce an empathic relation to the actors and events of the past. Such imaginative projection is suggested by Catherwood's inclusion of himself and fellow traveler Joseph Bonomi wearing Arab clothes in the Jerusalem panorama.[25] From the height of the Ottoman governor's house, from which the view was taken, Catherwood places himself and his friend in the ancient city, passing as Arabs. In doing so, he invites spectators to imagine leaving the panorama viewing-platform and entering Jerusalem as well. Such recourse to the imagination is also evident in the souvenir pamphlet's extended selections of poetry by Tasso and Henry Hart Milman. Such poetic invocations of place were repeated in the souvenir pamphlets for other Eastern panoramas at Leicester Square: Byron was quoted in the *Damascus* pamphlet (1841) and Pope was quoted in the *Bombardment of St. Jean D'Acre* pamphlet (1841). Such inclusions implied that poetry is as necessary to make place present and legible for the spectator as ethnic and topographical statistics.

Jerusalem was thought to exercise a considerable power over the emotions, as is evident in the unusually evocative language of the souvenir pamphlet of 1835. It is worth quoting at length:

... the general aspect of the city and its vicinity, is blighted and barren, the sycamore and cedar are no more, bare rocks present their rugged points through the languishing verdure, the vineyards are gone, and the vine cut off; the Holy Temple is destroyed, and the Sons of Jacob, favoured as no other people were, are driven out, and scattered over the face of the globe; all is loneliness and wildness, where once was every luxury; the glory is departed from the city, and ruin and desolation alone remain, to mark the tremendous power and righteous judgement that smote and so fearfully laid waste; yet there is nothing in antiquity more impressive or wonderful – the most powerful emotions are excited, and the most enthusiastic interest felt; each mouldering ruin recalls a history; and every part, both within and without the walls, has been the scene of some miraculous event.

Looking beyond the glaring anti-Semitism, one is struck by the passage's incessant delineation of loss. While the language cues topographical description, promising "the general aspect of the city and its vicinity," it rapidly becomes a list of what is *not*. Sycamore and cedar are no more, the Temple has been destroyed, even the population has been driven out and scattered. All that remains are moldering ruins, each of which "recalls a history." What appears to be a space of absence is suddenly filled. The barrenness is replete with the spectator's own sacred history. The love of antiquity is here conflated with the veneration of relics, for just as the relic is already imbued with holiness, the ruin is already dense with the past.

It is this very sense of veneration that Nietzsche found so contemptible in the antiquarian for whom "the possession of his ancestor's furniture changes its meaning in his soul, for his soul is rather possessed by it." There is no sense of a perspective or narrative that gives meaning to the remnant; instead each object "gains a worth and inviolability of its own from the conservative and reverent soul of the antiquarian migrating into it and building a secret nest there."[26] Just as Nietzsche's antiquary projects his own personal history into the old furniture and doorknobs with which he surrounds himself, the panorama antiquary finds a home for the soul in the Eastern canvas, placing himself and his spectators in Jerusalem, dressed in Arab costume. This is an East divested of inhabitants in order to make room for its rightful residents, London spectators. The panorama pamphlet's requisite ethnic breakdown simply describes the squatters. These transients find no home in moldering ruins and are – like the Arabs in Denon's images – oblivious to the past that towers over them. It is not surprising, for it is not their past but the specta-tors' past (and future) that was depicted in the topography and antiquities at the panorama. As the *Athenaeum* explained when a Jerusalem panorama was mounted in a newly created third circle at the Leicester Square Panorama in 1841, "On the interest of the subject it is needless to dwell, at a time when so many eyes are turned upon the Holy Land, and the Holy City, in veneration of their past, or curiosity as [to] their future destinies."[27] While Nietzsche's antiquary found his past in an old armoire, panorama antiquaries found both their past and their future in the ruins of the East.

WARTIME CANVASES

Projecting one's past and future onto fragments lodged thousands of miles away is a much more complicated process than waxing eloquent on one's ancestor's furniture. The former required a host of organizational and tech-nological innovations. New systems of transportation opened the East to greater numbers of travelers, new methods of reproduction facilitated the circulation of orientalist images, and – perhaps most importantly – new military technologies ensured a lasting European presence in the region. Increasingly, orientalist panoramas became imbued with Britain's growing sense of imperial importance. To summon up the East with an illusionistic surfeit of detail seemed indication of Britain's technological advances and ascendancy on the world stage. By contrast, barrow-digging in Wiltshire hardly inspired the larger public. One need only to recall Gaev's speech on the bookcase in *The Cherry Orchard* or Scott's Dr. Dryasdust to recognize how vulnerable to scorn were the parochial obsessions of antiquarianism. The *Athenaeum* was right, it was a time in which all eyes turned to the East "in veneration of their past, or curiosity as [to] their future destinies," a reference to both biblical narrative and Britain's recent capture of Acre from Egyptian forces.

Napoleon's invasion of Egypt prompted depictions of battles at a variety of entertainment venues. Astley's Amphitheatre and the Royal Circus both recreated British victories in Egypt with scores of actors on horseback, while Sadler's Wells reproduced the Battle of the Nile with model ships in a 90- by 20-foot (27- by 6-metre) tank installed in the stage floor. Optical entertainments similarly capitalized on the increased British interest in the East generated by the Napoleonic Wars. In 1799, the Leicester Square Panorama produced a spectacular recreation of the Battle of the Nile prompting Admiral Nelson to thank Barker for "keeping up the fame of his victory in the battle of the Nile for a year longer than it would have lasted in the public estimation."[28] In addition, of the six military panoramas that Robert Ker Porter displayed in the Great Room of the Lyceum, two depicted British victories against French forces in the Middle East, the Siege of Acre and the Battle of the Nile.

Porter's panoramas made much of exotic settings and properties. One spectator remarked that in Porter's *The Storming of Seringapatam* (1800), "The oriental dress, the jeweled turban, the curved and ponderous scymitar [sic] – these were among the prime objects with Sir Robert's pencil."[29] The descriptive pamphlet for Porter's *The Siege of Acre* (1801) drew attention to sites in Syria, such as "the splendid Mosque of the Pacha, with its Towers and Minarets rising amidst the ruins of a Christian Convent," Mount Tabor, which was "the scene of various events recorded in Holy Writ," and Mount Carmel, which – the pamphlet explained – was named by the Prophet Elijah.[30] Moreover, the pamphlet also included extensive historical and topographical information on Acre. The exotic wartime panorama privileged exotic details, placing British victories within the context of biblical history and imperial geography.

Entertainment venues continued to reproduce British military intervention in the East following the Napoleonic Wars. The British fleet's bombardment of the Algerian coast in 1816 prompted a spectacle at the Royal Circus, a panoramic depiction of the battle inserted into a pantomime at the Adelphi Theatre, and two other privately displayed panoramas – in at least one of which individual scenes painted sequentially on a long canvas were slowly advanced on rollers.[31] These "moving panoramas" were frequently inserted into pantomimes from the 1820s onward and were also displayed independently. When a European fleet defeated Ottoman forces at Navarino, ultimately forcing Ottoman withdrawal from the Greek city, moving panoramas depicting the victory were quickly inserted into at least three Christmas pantomimes.[32] Venues such as Astley's and the Royal Coburg followed with dramatizations of the battle.

Moving panoramas often foregrounded the military's use of geographic knowledge, transforming terrains into transport routes. However, this is not to say that these panoramas undermined the imaginative appeal of the exotic. For example, when the Russian government took advantage of Ottoman weakness to secure a route to the Dardanelles in 1828, Covent Garden inserted a moving panorama into that year's Christmas pantomime that transformed the Russian march on Constantinople into a showcase of exotic iconography. Charles Farley's libretto for *Harlequin and Little Red Riding Hood* describes the fancifully titled panorama:

'Poreibasilartikasparbosporas' Or the Northern Ruler's Route to the Dardanelles: Comprehending the following scenery: St. Petersburg at the time of a grand festival. Mountains and Fortresses. The Night-Watch – Soldiers Bivouacking, &c. Ambuscade and Battle. The Halt of the caravan in the Desert, at sunset; the approach through the Dardanelles to the Castle of the Seven Towers; and the General View of Constantinople.[33]

A desert caravan would be an unusual sight on the western coast of the Black Sea; however, the desert vista had proved a popular attraction at such early shows as the Leicester Square Panorama's Cairo of 1809 and so found its way into a surprising number of productions. The panorama for *Harlequin and Little Red Riding Hood* was roundly criticized in the press for its alleged plagiarism of artists such as John Martin, Francis Danby (himself an imitator of Martin), and Horace Vernet.[34] The fact that so much of the panorama felt familiar to its critics is testimony to how quickly exotic topography had been disseminated. If the panorama artist plagiarized, it is just as likely that he adopted the now increasingly familiar imagery of theatrical orientalism as that he borrowed from any one gallery artist.

Under Robert Burford's management, the Leicester Square Panorama gave increased attention to the sites of British military intervention. At the same time as theatres were displaying their panoramas of Navarino, the Leicester Square Panorama was hurriedly mounting its own depiction of the battle from drawings made at the scene and plans lent by the Admiralty.[35] Following the Russian invasion of Turkey, Burford mounted a view of

Constantinople at the Strand for audiences wishing to revisit the area that
was arousing the interest of the world's most powerful nations. When
England next interceded in the region, Burford responded with two new
panoramas. The continuing weakness of the Ottoman Empire enabled
the Governor of Egypt, Muhammad Ali, to extend his power over Syria,
Crete, and Adana, and to declare independence from the Porte. Fearing that
the further weakening of the Ottoman Empire would increase French or
Russian influence in the region, a combined British–Austrian fleet landed
troops at Beirut and captured Acre in November of 1840. The English then
forced Muhammad Ali to accept a compromise that granted him hereditary
governorship over a smaller region. Burford quickly mounted panoramas
of both Damascus and the Bombardment of Acre at the Leicester Square
Panorama.

Burford's *Bombardment of St. Jean D'Acre* provides a vivid example of
how he allied his Panorama with the military, stressing the patriotism of
his presentation of imperial and religious subjects. The speed with which
Burford mounted the panorama was itself a source of some amazement.
The *Mirror of Literature* marveled, "little more than three months have
elapsed since the brilliant deed and scarcely have Parliament voted thanks
to the conquerors, when here we have a perfect pictorial representation of
the brilliant deed."[36] Burford's souvenir pamphlet expressed "sincere thanks
to Capt. [sic] Stopford for the very important and useful information, and
various details he kindly furnished, also for his polite attention during
the progress of the painting, to which he is indebted for its accuracy."[37]
In addition, the pamphlet included the text of the letter from Admiral
Stopford announcing the victory to the Lords, as well as the Admiral's
own description of the thick of battle. Certainly warfare was good business
for Burford. As the *Athenaeum* explained, "The military contests in which
England is engaged have fallen in good time for Mr. Burford,"[38] referring
to the fact that the Acre panorama replaced a view of Macao, an important
base in the ongoing Opium War.

The pamphlet for *Bombardment of St. Jean D'Acre* moves with striking
ease from citing the city's biblical significance and elaborating its beauty to
glorying in its destruction. The panorama depicted the moment at which
the city's principal powder magazine and arsenal ignited, "spreading dismay
and desolation in every direction," presenting it as a marvelous spectacle (2).
Shortly after quoting the Admiral that "the state of devastation was beyond
description" (4), the pamphlet explains that "there appears little doubt that
[Acre] was the Accho of Scriptures, Judges i. 31"(5). The pamphlet even
quotes Pope to properly convey the beauty of Mount Carmel, though a

very different sense of beauty emerges from the pamphlet's explanation that "at the back of the spectator is seen a great portion of the city; the citadel, mosque, and minaret, the most prominent objects, just emerging from the sublimity, a perfect volcano" (3). The pamphlet explained that such beautiful cataclysm had long been a feature of this landscape:

It is most probable that it was on the eastern side [of Mount Carmel] near the river, that the people were assembled when Ahab "Gathered all Israel into Mount Carmel," 1 Kings xviii. 19, and where the fire of the Lord fell and consumed the burnt sacrifices which Elijah had prepared; a situation admirably chosen for the display of the wondrous miracle, for to the people assembled on the plain of Esdraeldon, and even on the hills of Samaria, and Gilboa, the whole must have been distinctly visible. (10)

It is as if destruction were inherent in the beauty of the region, and Britain's bombardment simply a repetition of a wondrous and picturesque miracle. God, no less than the British, dropped fire from the sky with an eye to the most compelling landscape.

Not all spectators thrilled at the depiction of "dismay and desolation." Two Bombay naval architects residing in London attended the panorama and recorded impressions that show little of the pride in the military's destructive capacity that marks Burford's souvenir pamphlet:

We observed some of the Egyptian troops lying here and there killed, and wounded, while others were busy firing at the ships. The blowing up of the powder magazine, which was supposed to have taken place by one of the shells from the steamers finding its way into it, and which killed nearly three thousand Egyptians, it was a terrible sight as we saw hands, legs &c., of these unfortunate beings flung into the air. The town of Acre also presented a galling and heart-rending spectacle, it was a mass of ruin and every house was shattered to pieces.[39]

The Bombay naval architects were in a decided minority.

The following year the bombardment of Acre was a prominent feature in Charles Marshall's Kineorama. This moving panorama cut a broad swath, illustrating "the leading characteristics of history, manners, customs, and coercive powers, combined with events of the late war, with delineations of the most interesting portions of landscape and architecture of the associated districts of Turkey, Syria, and Egypt, constituting the Ottoman Empire."[40] The Kineorama took audiences on a full tour of Ottoman provinces – maintained by the grace of the English military. The Kineorama included such standard sights as the Sublime Porte, the Sultan's Barge, pyramids, and Arab encampments. However, unlike many previous moving panoramas, the Kineorama was not framed by aerial views of cities but by aerial views of military reviews. At the opening, the audience saw the Sultan surrounded by Ambassadors of the Allied European Powers as the "newly-organized Troops of Turkey pass[ed] under Review." At the close, the audience saw "Aspects of the Modern Egyptian Army." The defining features of this new East were not monuments and landscape features, but native modern armies under European tutelage. It was further evidence that the empires of Europe had spread their influence to distant regions.

GEOGRAPHIC MASTERY

The new power balance between Europe and the Ottoman Empire facilitated Europe's growing presence in the East, contributing to an outpouring of orientalist analysis, art, and literature. These works were marked by a growing emphasis on the European observer's complete mastery over the details of Eastern life. Similarly, panoramas at mid-century depicted an East that could be completely surveyed, detailed, and known. These later panoramas purported to present not just topography, but the processes and distributions that distinguish regions also.

By the end of the panorama's popularity, surprising claims were made for its ability to see beyond topographical details to grasp the hidden nature of a place. In 1861, for example, *The Times* lauded Burford's panorama of the Bay of Naples, explaining that

there are aspects of soil and climate which neither engraving nor photograph can represent, but which, in great panoramas such as those of Mr. Burford, are conveyed to the mind with a completeness and truthfulness not always to be gained from a visit to the scene itself.[41]

From the heights of the panorama platform even features of soil and climate revealed themselves in a "completeness" denied travelers (and inhabitants) of the region.

This seemingly magical ability of the panorama view to grasp the totality of a region, while still revealing minute details lost even to observers on the ground, is especially pronounced in discussions of orientalist panoramas at mid-century. Burford's Cairo panorama of 1847 presented, according to the souvenir pamphlet, "a complete view of the city and suburbs, and of the surrounding country, to an immense extent."[42] A review of the panorama speaks of an amazing array of sights, ranging from "the great Libyan desert, in some parts bounded by the mountains of Libya and Upper Egypt" and "majestic pyramids of Dachoor, Sakkarah, and Geezeh" to the "narrow crooked streets [of Cairo] . . . crowded with a motley throng of Turks, Copts, Armenians, Arabs, Franks, and Jews in every variety of costume and completely embodying the vivid descriptions of the Arabian Nights."[43] This magical panorama presented Egyptian topography in its entirety as well as delineating the racial breakdown of the old city.

While the inclusion of the *Arabian Nights* as proof of the ethnographic accuracy of the panorama might surprise modern readers, it was perfectly logical in an age that interpreted these fourteenth-century tales as a record of the unchanging customs of the East. In fact, in 1839 when Edward Lane, the noted linguist and ethnographer, translated a new version of the tales, he presented it to the public as a travel guide to Cairo, Damascus, and Baghdad, and deleted sections that contradicted his experience of Arab life. The panorama not only catalogued the monuments and races of Egypt, it revealed the fantastic sensuality that Europe had ascribed to the East since the *Nights* were first translated in 1704. In addition to deserts, pyramids, Turks, and Copts, panorama patrons discerned females in the Cairo streets, "closely enveloped in black garments, their eyes alone visible" as well as the "wild and lascivious dances" of the "Ghawa'zee, or public dancing girls."[44] The panorama view recorded the entire surface of the East as well as its racial and sexual interior.

In truth, the Cairo panorama was simply a collage of the Egyptian imagery made available to British audiences. Like the comically abridged productions of "The Complete Works of Shakespeare" that provide all the famous quotes in one evening's entertainment, the Cairo panorama was filled with every familiar image of the East. If, as Jonathan Culler argues, "the proliferation of reproductions is what makes something an original,"[45] then the panorama was central in the creation of an "authentic" East that exceeded the grasp of the panorama. It was this very proliferation of Eastern images that convinced patrons that the "true" East lay elsewhere even as the panorama redoubled its efforts to insist that the East had been captured in its entirety.

This new sense that the growing number of British reproductions had obscured the authentic East inspired several Victorian artists to travel to the Levant. In fact, the artist who supplied the sketches for Burford's Cairo panorama of 1847, David Roberts, had been inspired to make his journey East because of assumed inaccuracies in the authoritative collection of Eastern images, *Description de l'Egypte*. The notice that prefaced Roberts's *The Holy Land, Syria, Idumea, Arabia, Egypt and Nubia...*, the first of two multivolume collections of Middle Eastern lithographs, explained that Roberts considered "the drawings of the French Commission in Egypt very incorrect." Roberts apparently knew the reproductions to be false before having seen the original. As proof that Roberts had uncovered the real that had been lost to successive reproductions, the notice continued to explain that Roberts had even penetrated Muslim spaces that no Christian had ever seen:

he even obtained permission to enter every mosque he desired to visit, a privilege never before given to a Christian, but to which one condition was attached – that in the instruments he used in making his studies, for he was allowed to paint there, he was not to desecrate the mosque by the introduction and use of brushes made of *hog's bristles*.[46]

The italicized detail provided evidence of Roberts's real encounter with Islam. With its implication that Muslims are strangely superstitious, the detail guaranteed authenticity by confirming Western bias.

While sketching in mosques, Roberts was obliged to dress in Middle Eastern fashion with a turban, to shave his mutton-chop whiskers, and to grow a mustache.[47] While the costume may have been a necessary expedient, it is worth noting that after his return, Roberts was painted in Middle Eastern dress by Robert Scott Lauder in three-quarter length to better show off his costume, making Roberts one of several Victorian adventurers who publicized their use of disguises when traveling in the East. By the time of the sitting, Roberts had presumably shaven his mustache and regrown his whiskers (he joked that he would have to borrow a mustache to complete the effect for the painting); nonetheless, Lauder's canvas shows him with shaven cheeks and a mustache, a scabbard and sword hanging from his waist, colorful sashes over his robes, and a turban. The painting speaks of Roberts's command over the intricacies of Eastern life and his ability to completely mimic the manners of the East. In this sense, Roberts reproduced the experiences of Edward Lane. Lane similarly complained of the careless nature of the *Description de l'Egypte* in his popular *An Account of the Manners and Customs of the Modern Egyptians* (1836). Lane was the first Victorian Arabist to narrate his experience of praying in a mosque, disguised as an Arab and completely fooling the unsuspecting natives – beginning a genre of Victorian orientalism that would culminate in Richard Burton's sensational account of his pilgrimage to Mecca. In this sense, Roberts's relation to the East can be seen as structured by a vocabulary of mastery prominent in Victorian orientalism.

Considering the publicity surrounding Roberts's name and the attention surrounding the release of his Holy Land lithographs (published in monthly installments between 1842 and 1849) it was quite a coup when Robert Burford convinced him to provide drawings of Cairo for the Leicester

Square Panorama. Even more fortunately for Burford, advance publicity for Roberts's new collection of lithographs, *Egypt and Nubia*, circulated in March 1847 at the time of the panorama's opening. Burford drew attention to Roberts's contribution; in advertisements, the announcement of "Mr Burford's New Panorama of Cairo" was immediately followed by the line, "made from drawings of David Roberts RA" in prominent type. The review in the *Illustrated London News* began by repeating this information and concluded by explaining that the costumes of the many different ethnic groups depicted were "principally taken from a collection in the possession of [Roberts]."[48] Through the figure of Roberts, the panorama suggested various tropes of Eastern mastery that were newly emerging: the delineation of ethnic types, the collection of implements and costumes, a critical familiarity with earlier orientalist works, and the use of disguises to pass for native.

Mastery of ethnic detail was closely allied with the mastery of a resistant geography. Not only did this panorama draw attention to Roberts's knowledge of the East, but England's control of an inhospitable geography. As the panorama pointed out, Britain had transformed the seemingly impossible journey from Alexandria to Suez into a common and comfortable trip. In doing so, Britain had transformed Egypt along a European model.

The immense importance of the overland passage through Cairo, established mainly by the energy of Lieutenant Waghorn, is sufficiently obvious, in the rapid communication with our eastern possessions. The effects of this intercourse are also very visible in the city, in the changes that have taken place during the last few years in the manners and customs of the inhabitants, especially in their treatment of foreigners. Order and security of property has been established, the laws have been more equitably administered, manufactories of all kinds have risen, and more useful institutions have been called into existence by the Pasha, than by any other sovereign of Egypt, or perhaps of the whole world. A system of education and schools has also been formed, of which not the slightest conception existed in the East.[49]

Mastery over the desert had put Britain in easy communication with her "eastern possessions." However, the effects on Cairo were much more profound. In the quote's telling progression, the control of territory leads to the proper "treatment of foreigners," which is followed by the institution of "order and security of property," ultimately concluding with the creation of manufactories and schools.

The "overland route," the proclaimed cause of these transformations, claimed an important place in the British imagination. From early in the century, considerable attention was directed to the easiest route to India.

The overland route was considerably shorter than a sea trip around Africa (this Cape route took five to eight months by sail and often as much as three months in the early days of steam) but the overland route was also considerably more dangerous. A variety of paths from the Mediterranean to the Red Sea had been attempted; all required several days of desert journey (during which travelers were easy prey for robbers) followed by a dangerous trip down the Red Sea. In the 1820s meticulous surveys of this waterway reduced the hazards of Red Sea navigation; however, the overland route did not gain popularity until Thomas Waghorn increased the safety and comfort of Egyptian land travel. Waghorn, a lieutenant with the Bombay Marine, began promoting a route that took travelers to Cairo by Nile steamer and then across the desert to Suez, where an India-bound steamship waited. Waghorn first attempted this route in 1829 and completed the journey in a mere forty days, despite being robbed and falling sick in the Egyptian desert. In the coming years, Waghorn created a chain of resting places and hotels along the desert portion of the voyage. Signal towers, which were set up along the route, sent semaphore messages to Cairo announcing the arrival of India steamships at Suez. In this way travelers could tarry at the more comfortable Cairo hotels or sightsee until the last minute before beginning the desert trek to Suez.[50]

In the process of facilitating travel and mail service to India, Waghorn became something of a cultural hero. Newspapers like the *Illustrated London News* devoted feature articles to his achievements[51] though few writers were as effusive as Thackeray when he ranked Waghorn's accomplishments above Napoleon's: "Nap massacred the Mamelukes at the Pyramids: Wag has conquered the pyramids themselves, dragged the unwieldy structures a month nearer England than they were, and brought the country along with them."[52] The English had taken possession of Egypt, pulling the periphery of empire closer to the center. It was fitting tribute, then, that Waghorn's death in January of 1850 inspired panorama artists to drag Egypt the rest of the distance to England. The *Overland Route to India* opened in March of 1850 at the Gallery of Illustration. The *Illustrated London News* described it as "superior to any work of its class hitherto produced in the country."[53] The *Overland Route to India* was also one of the more popular panoramas of the time. According to the *Athenaeum*, 200,000 people attended it in the first year of its exhibition.[54]

The panorama boasted an impressive combination of artists and orientalists. David Roberts was certainly the best known of the collaborators. Two of the other painters, Thomas Grieve and John Absolon, had begun their careers in the Covent Garden paint room (and both would ultimately exhibit canvases at the Royal Academy). A third painter, William Telbin, was well known as a principal painter at Drury Lane at the time when the actor–manager, William Macready, had done much to augment the historical accuracy of the décor. *The Times* assured its readers that the *Overland Route to India* had elevated the panorama "from a mere source of instruction to a work of art."[55] The panorama was complemented by a lecture by J. H. Stocqueler, an appearance that marked, according to Richard Altick, the first instance in which "the lecturer's presence... was as noteworthy as the panorama itself."[56] Stocqueler had spent twenty-four years in India as a journalist and wrote the *Handbook of India* as well as a guide to the overland route, and returning to London in 1843 he founded the East India Institute.[57]

The Overland Route to India organized a huge stretch of geography extending east from England to India; however, the Middle East was clearly the privileged region in this expanse. The moving panorama only presented the desert journey from Cairo to Suez, while stationary views showed scenes from the other legs of the route. According to text quoted in the *Illustrated London News*, the panorama depicted the sixteen-hour desert journey. On the way one encountered a range of desert sights: "Mussulmen [sic] cavaliers or a body of Egyptian soldiery," later a "camel-driver mourning over his dead camel," and, as night fell, one discerned "a cluster of Bedouins, smoking by the light of a fire which cooks their nocturnal meal." While these images suggest a strange and exotic East, there was no question that even this hinterland was firmly positioned within the British Empire: "at every eight or ten miles there are low brick buildings or stations." Even in the middle of the desert, the British Empire promised comfort for the British traveler.

Panorama audiences were invited to imaginatively engage the Orient through the experiences of adventuring Arabists such as Roberts and Waghorn – men whose knowledge of Eastern manners and terrains allowed them to penetrate prohibited or inhospitable spaces. Neither the mosque nor the desert (nor for that matter the harem) could escape the spectator's view. In this sense, the panorama offered its audiences both the pleasures of spectacle and surveillance. Foucault has famously argued in *Discipline and Punish: The Birth of the Prison* that the nineteenth century witnessed the development of a disciplinary apparatus in which new technologies of observation rendered the entire society visible to power (in contrast to the culture and architecture of antiquity, which was designed around public life and the presentation of limited objects to great multitudes). As Foucault explains, "Our society is one not of spectacle, but of surveillance; under the great abstraction of exchange, there continues the meticulous training of useful forces."[58] On the panorama platform, audiences could imagine the Orient as a boundless multitude taken in by a single glance, a web of behavior that could be penetrated and accounted for, and a storehouse of untapped resources. However, the pleasure of such imagined surveillance was deeply entwined in the desire for spectacle. Even in late optical entertainments, the recalcitrant Orient resisted enumeration and remained a beautiful surface, an incomprehensible conglomeration of striking objects.

War, as has been shown, shifted attention at the panorama to potential transport routes and the coordination of allied forces; however, here as well, images of the Orient could inspire a naïve fascination. Consider, for example, Leicester Square's Constantinople panorama quickly mounted at the start of the Crimean War. While the pamphlet for this 1853 panorama closely resembled the pamphlet for the Leicester Square's Constantinople panorama of 1846, the later pamphlet showered even greater praise on Britain's Ottoman allies: "The resources of Constantinople have been enlarged, many refugees from all parts, intelligent men and industrious mechanics, have made it their home; the educational and judicial establishments have improved, and manufacturing industry and the arts of life have progressed."[59] The panorama saw beyond terrain and architecture to reveal the peoples of the East, demonstrating that their potential was now being shaped in schools, courts, and factories, all thanks to intelligent and industrious men from the West who were bent on enlarging the "resources of Constantinople." Nonetheless, images of Constantinople still inspired a naïve fascination with Eastern beauty. The *Athenaeum*'s review of the panorama waxed lyrical: "As we gaze and dream of that gorgeous scene, the mystery of the Eastern question clears away. Who that has felt the north wind in his marrow would not yearn for those bright shores, that purple sky, those vine and orange bearing slopes."[60] No longer the site of complicated imperial struggles or Western-directed modernization, the Orient becomes once again the magically warm and verdant land that the panorama had long known it to be.

The idea that spectacle and surveillance are joined, rather than antithetical, pleasures and that both were offered by the nineteenth-century entertainment industry is actually implicit in Foucault's analysis. Foucault finds an architectural embodiment of the new disciplinary society in Jeremy Bentham's panopticon, an annular building composed of cells with a central tower affording a clear view into each cell. Significantly, Foucault notes that through the panoptic system, the disciplinary mechanism is democratically controlled: "any member of society will have the right to come and see with his own eyes how the schools, hospitals, factories, prisons function."[61] Foucault even suggests that the panorama inspired Bentham's idea of a structure that created total visibility but was itself open to any citizen's inspection. In a footnote, Foucault asks:

Imagining this continuous flow of visitors entering the central tower of the Panopticon, was Bentham aware of the Panoramas that Barker was constructing at exactly the same period (the first seems to have dated from 1787) and in which the visitors, occupying the central place, saw unfolding around them a landscape, a city or a battle. The visitors occupied exactly the place of the sovereign gaze. (n.317)

Earlier in the book, Foucault includes "the colonized" with "school children" and those "stuck at a machine" in a list of disciplined bodies (29). For a shilling, even pupils and workers could enjoy the illusion of occupying the seat of power and inspecting exotic life.

While Foucault is literally examining the surveillance of people rather than territories, his argument is entirely rooted in the examination of new strategies of demarcating space. As the editors of the journal *Hérodote* pointed out during an interview with Foucault, "With the Panoptic system we are no longer dealing with a mere metaphor. What is at issue here is the description of institutions in terms of architecture, of spatial configurations." Foucault himself acknowledged the importance of conceptions of geography to his work when he explained later in the interview:

The longer I continue, the more it seems to me that the formation of discourses and the genealogy of knowledge need to be analysed, not in terms of types of consciousness, modes of perception and forms of ideology, but in terms of tactics and strategies of power. Tactics and strategies deployed through implantations, distributions, demarcations, control of territories and organisations of domains which could well make up a sort of geopolitics where my preoccupations link up with your methods [of geographical research]. One theme I would like to study in the next few years is that of the army as a matrix of organisation and knowledge; one would need to study the history of the fortress, the "campaign", the "movement", the colony, the territory. Geography must indeed necessarily lie at the heart of my concerns.[62]

The shift to a disciplinary society was contingent on new systems of spatial organization and new conceptions of how such organization produced knowledge. The eye of power was not interested in bodies per se but the force that could be extracted from bodies, just as the eye of power was not interested in topography for its own sake but for the raw materials and strategic advantages it might yield. Such knowledge was contingent on the control of space. The useful body was generated out of the demarcation and control of the spaces bodies could inhabit along with the introduction of systems of surveillance specific to such spaces. In much the same way, the extraction of resources was dependent on the control of territories combined with new techniques of surveying. Control of the surface was only a means to control of the interior. As a French officer explained after the Algerian insurrection of 1845, if we "gather into groups this people which is everywhere and nowhere...[it] will perhaps allow us to capture their minds after we have captured their bodies."[63]

In this context we can see that the rise of the modern geographic imagination did not emerge as the servant of imperialism; rather its rise lay at the heart of the epistemological shift that made modern imperialism possible. This is not to contradict historians of geography like Brian Hudson, who argues that the academic study of geography that emerged in late-nineteenth-century Britain "was vigorously promoted at that time largely, if not mainly, to serve the interests of territorial acquisition, economic exploitation, militarism and the practice of class and race domination."[64] I am instead asserting that underlying the rise of geography as an academic field was a geographic imagination whose formation can be traced to the start of the century. It is not simply that this geographic imagination, like other humanist discourses, developed hand in hand with disciplinary society. Rather, the geographic imagination constituted the new sense of spatial control that *was* disciplinary society. The geographic imagination was not hatched by the academy or the military. It developed in a range of popular institutions, most notably entertainment venues like the panorama and other optical shows. Finally, I am asserting that the development of disciplinary power was entwined with new colonial realities. As Timothy Mitchell has remarked, "The panoptic principle was devised on Europe's colonial frontier with the Ottoman Empire, and examples of the panopticon were built for the most part not in northern Europe but in places like colonial India."[65]

JADED TRAVELERS

The new accessibility of Eastern regions ultimately undermined Britain's fascination with the East. With the growing number of colonial functionaries, soldiers, and correspondents traveling east, Europe became flooded with depictions that frequently contradicted the "gorgeous scenes" at the Leicester Square Panorama. More and more Eastern travelers experienced the frustration described by Gérard de Nerval, who searched Cairo in vain for settings suitable for Théophile Gautier's orientalist scenarios at the

Opéra Comique. "I really wanted to set the scene for you here," Nerval wrote Gautier in his description of a typical Cairene street, "but...it is only in Paris that one finds cafés so Oriental."[66] The increasingly detailed descriptions of Eastern life – ranging from examinations of customs and architecture to political structure – undermined the expansive and absorptive picture of the East available at panorama halls. It is not surprising, then, that Nerval and others preferred Europe's earlier draft of the Orient over the versions emerging from a new body of first-hand accounts. At venues like the Leicester Square Panorama one could read of Constantinople's 2,700 coffeehouses and its profusion of public fountains, but one certainly did not make out the layers of "ashes and dirt" of which Nerval complained.

At the same time that the panorama was mounting some of its last depictions of the East, a growing number of orientalist accounts focused on what they interpreted as the visible signs of the inherent decline of the Ottoman Empire. As Britain grew more confident that it saw through the Orient's beautiful exterior to fully grasp its "internal economy," the East of beauty and dalliance lost its claim on the "real." That East became a theatrical invention, rather than a theatrical representation. Poverty, ignorance, and intransigence became defining features of the theatrical East.

At one level, this new cynicism reflected tedium in the face of a growing body of orientalist popular literature and entertainments. As the *Illustrated London News* complained in 1851:

Every now and then a young gentleman returns from Greece or Egypt with a beard and a M.S. In a week or two, the new journal of Travels in the East is announced and a new "oriental traveller" takes his place among the "wise men" who have preceded him...It is a sad thing to reflect on, that, with regard to the East, Europe's honeymoon is over. We don't gather round the pilgrim to gaze with reverence on the shell in his hat – to touch his palm-branch – to listen to his wonderful stories. We ask him when he left Alexandria in the steamer, and we know that he left his curiosities at the Customhouse. We are acquainted with the "natural productions" of the places he has visited; we have caught leviathan and sent him to the Zoological Gardens.[67]

The following year, a reviewer in *Tait's Edinburgh Magazine*, would complain of the "daily Oriental productions" with "the same Arabs, camels, deserts, tombs and jackals that we journeyed with, rode on, traversed, dived into and cursed respectively, only a week ago with some other traveller."[68] The new power balance between Europe and the Ottoman Empire facilitated Europe's growing presence in the East, spurring an orientalist outpouring that apparently inspired impatience in some reviewers. Moreover, this new power balance also contributed to an emerging contempt for the "curiosities" and "natural productions" of what now appeared as an atavistic and decrepit power.

Perhaps in response to this impatience, some optical entertainments at mid-century incorporated humorous lectures. The most successful of these was Albert Smith's *The Overland Mail* which premiered at Willis's Rooms in 1850, two months after the *Overland Route to India* opened at the Gallery of Illustration. Smith hired Lyceum scene painter William Beverley to paint ten dioramic scenes (later increased to thirteen) illustrating the return trip on Waghorn's route from Suez to Boulogne. Smith delivered a narrative of the journey as the images appeared, impersonating travelers and natives and interspersing songs and anecdotes. The combination was a success; the show ran for over a year after which Smith took it on tour. Smith made it clear that he was an author and traveler, and his mimicry was intended to foreground his knowledge of Eastern manners and not his skill as a performer. In his first peformance he apologized for "the badness of his voice and the rigid limitations of his powers," disclaimers that reviewers described as unmerited.[69]

For audiences more comfortable in a salon than a theatre and who might listen to an Eastern traveler and expert but not an actor, Smith's amateur status was of paramount importance and reviewers duly noted it. *The Times* remarked that Smith performed with "a power of impersonation which is almost wonderful when we consider that the gentleman who affords the entertainment does not belong to the histrionic profession" and the *Morning Post* approvingly noted that "there is no attempt at changes of character nor of stage-like assumptions."[70] Smith's performance was conversational in tone, well-mannered, and moderately instructional. He never simply employed a prop, but instead explained the use of native objects slowly transforming himself into a native during the process (making the *Morning Post*'s description a fine distinction). At one point, for example, he demonstrated how to use an Egyptian water pipe and then became an engineer of a Nile steamer, who interspersed his yarns with long puffs. Even Smith's inclusion of songs was judged instructional and tempered. According to the above-cited *Times* review, "when a situation or a national trait becomes remarkably piquant he tells it in the shape of a song [and the song's effect] depends on the judicious utterance of the words." Smith did not present the East as much as he presented his mastery over the details of Eastern life. His mimicry was offered as the natural culmination of this mastery, and not a means for conjuring a region that might fascinate or entice in itself.

Smith cultivated the role of the no-nonsense English gentleman correcting romantic depictions of the East. As Smith explained in *The Overland*

Mail, "The absurdly false and over-coloured medium through which the majority of travellers have hitherto thought it essential to view the East will, I hope, soon be broken down. I have done my best to throw a stone at it."[71] This approach entailed humorous depictions of Egyptian squalor and demonstrations of the fact that the Egyptian peasantry would go to great lengths to earn the Englishman's money. In one scene – transcribed in the *Illustrated London News* – Smith impersonated an Egyptian attendant who offered to run up what the attendant himself reportedly called "Belzoni's pyramid" for a shilling.[72] The reference was to the Padua-born English adventurer, Giovanni Belzoni, who had opened the Second Pyramid at Giza and transported a remarkable quantity of antiquities to London (including the head of the 60-foot [18-metre] Thebes colossus), culminating in an exhibition at Leicester Square's Egyptian Hall in 1821.

Smith continued that this same attendant sold artifacts that he claimed to have found in tombs but were more likely "made in Staffordshire." Both the currency and the items for sale – from Staffordshire artifacts to a view from "Belzoni's pyramid" – were identified as English. Smith concluded the scene with the observation, "English money is most current; and, as proof of civilization, I took a bad sixpence in change when buying a handful of representatives of Osiris." The British had taken possession of both the monuments and symbols of ancient Egypt, and this appropriation of history had been accompanied by the proliferation of shillings. The scene at the pyramid revolved around scraps of English currency, which had become so common to Egyptian exchanges that it was even present in counterfeit form – an impersonation that provides a telling counterpoint to the cultural impersonations of Smith and the London entertainment industry. Even then the bad sixpence was reclaimed for the empire, "proof" of an economic penetration that Smith jokingly termed "civilization."

Smith presented himself as the quintessential Eastern traveler at mid-century. He was a leisured scholar–gentleman, thoroughly unsentimental and with an innate business acumen. He traveled under the protection of the British Empire through a world that had been opened for his inspection. He acquired knowledge effortlessly, adding to an already thorough store of facts and constantly subjecting newly encountered customs to his skepticism and wit. Whereas British travelers once followed in the footsteps of Childe Harold, they now followed the routes of W. M. Thackeray, Albert Smith, and the overland mail. Nonetheless, beneath the level-headed realism, there remained something of the "vagrant Childe" in Victorian travelers. Smith stood at the Hellespont where Byron himself had reproduced Leander's nightly swim, even if Smith only concluded that "there did not appear to be any remarkable difficulty about [the feat] – certainly nothing to make the accomplishment a matter of record."[73] Smith reproduced the romantic East even as he distanced himself from his creation. He searched out sights that were familiar from a host of earlier books and entertainments, as when he summoned up characters from the *Arabian Nights* in describing Cairo. Smith searched out an Orient of childhood stories and romantic corsairs, even if his ultimate goal was to mock this creation.

While Smith projected cynicism, the images that scrolled behind reproduced tropes of romantic orientalism. William Beverley's rich atmospheric effects were praised, and the Egyptian scenes were most often singled out (The Port of Suez; The Desert by Sunset; The Middle Station on the Desert; A Street in Cairo; The Kandjia, or Nile Boat; The Sphinx and the Pyramids; The Locks at Atfeh; The Frank Square at Alexandria). Beverley's treatment of "The Desert by Sunset" (with its "Caravan of Bedouins") seems especially indebted to earlier desert scenes. The scene, as described in the *World*, suggests awe before nature's expansive but indifferent majesty and conveys a sense of inescapable social isolation:

The painting of this wild and untenanted waste, with the glowing tints shed by the earlier sunset upon the distant horizon, and reflected by the few fleecy clouds visible amidst the expanse of blue, is of the highest order; and life-like as it is possible to conceive are the figures in the foreground, wearied with travel, still stealing onward upon their lonely journey.[74]

Smith attempted to demystify the desert with his clarification of "erroneous notions connected with it." At the same time, however, Beverley's dioramic view asserted a wild and lonely expanse in the romantic tradition.

At mid-century, the British read the world as a panoramic entertainment, even as the genre was beginning its decline. The *Athenaeum* declared, in 1850, that it was "an age of Panorama-painting."[75] The panorama's ability to organize and explain vast stretches of terrain made it central to the development of a popular imperialism; through the panorama, a wide public was able to imagine the empire. It presented a habitable and domesticated East while still suggesting exotic crowded cities and fantastic dry expanses (particularly salient for the inhabitants of a small and wet island). Panoramic depictions spread across the culture and became a primary means of understanding and celebrating the growing plentitude provided by Britain's ever-expanding trade and military influence. Goods, lands, people, even cultural practice, were pulled into the British orbit. It was all documented in panoramic views.

As interpretive frame, the panorama spread into other genres. Illustrated newspapers featured panoramic supplements to depict everything from royal processions to the goods displayed at international exhibitions. As early as 1830, portable panoramas were marketed to travelers headed to Constantinople and other Eastern destinations so that they could "detect every point of interest."[76] The panorama was an interpretive guide; it went before in order to reveal and clarify world geography. It is hardly surprising, then, that when Thackeray sought to describe his experience of approaching Constantinople, he had recourse to an optical entertainment:

Stanfield's panorama used to be the realization of the most intense youthful fancy. I puzzle my brains and find no better likeness for the place. The view of Constantinople resembles the *ne plus ultra* of a Stanfield diorama, with a glorious accompaniment of music, spangled houris, warriors, and winding processions, feasting the eyes and the soul with light, splendour and harmony.[77]

Constantinople resembled a painting of it in a Drury Lane pantomime, with sound and movement added. In a strange reversal, the success of the original was measured by its fidelity to the reproduction. Invariably, the productions of the metropole take prominence over those of the periphery even when it is the periphery itself that the metropole is fashioning.

CHAPTER 2

Fantasies of miscegenation on the romantic stage

As a burgeoning optical entertainment industry provided illusionistic images of distant lands, London theatres followed suit with increasingly realistic depictions of the "exotic" world. Considering the number of scene painters who doubled as panorama painters – such as David Roberts, Clarkson Stanfield, Thomas Grieve, John Absolon, and William Beverley – it seems likely that theatre and optical entertainments fed each other and that both fostered a growing taste for exotic spectacle. Exoticism in the theatre was facilitated by the same developments that helped spur the proliferation of optical entertainments. The greater ease of Eastern travel resulted in a growing number of first-hand accounts and images that were of use to both panorama and theatre artists. Moreover, changes in the technology and economics of printmaking resulted in the wide circulation of these images – both contributing to the fashion of exotic imagery in the theatre as well as providing scene painters with "authoritative sources." Finally, transformations in scenic technology and changes in the economics of the theatre facilitated the translation of such first-hand images into realistic stage-settings.

However, the assertion that the theatre began to produce realistic depictions of distant lands because it was now possible to do so masks the important question of what relation realism bears to exoticism and why both should become of interest to theatre audiences in the first place. Why did early-nineteenth-century theatre audiences crave a surfeit of detail in production, detail with little or no relation to narrative, when they had long been accustomed to think of stage decoration as an ornamental backing to the actors? Why this new interest in scripts that make reference to the manners and customs of distant places when previously characters often conformed to a presumed universal standard of nobility and decorum?

The answer has much to do with the emerging ambivalence to the visual and the correlated search for internal laws and processes. I will argue that the new realism of early-nineteenth-century theatrical orientalism was part

54

of a growing desire to see the image as a means to abstraction; specifically, scenic spectacle was often presented as an exploration of a racial essence. This is evident in the critical attention given in the nineteenth century to the theatre's detailed exotica, from scene painting copied from scholarly folios to experimentation with different shades of face-paint. Exoticized productions in the early-nineteenth century regularly invoked the authority of scholarly sources. More striking, though, the theatre also imagined artist–travelers who not only mastered the codes of native life but possessed a unique affinity for its essence. Genius did not simply describe the exotic, genius embodied the internal drives that distinguished the races.

This racial penetration figured in the celebrity of two of the most prominent men of the theatre in early-nineteenth-century Britain, both of whom blurred the boundaries between themselves and their exotic creations: Edmund Kean and George Gordon, Lord Byron. By examining Kean's exotic performances, the theatrical adaptations of Byron's oriental romances, and the theatre's (and Kean's) manipulation of the Byron myth, I hope to show that the theatre assuaged the anxiety that accompanied British fascination with exotic spectacle by imagining the stage as a space of racial examination – an exploration directed *beneath* darkened skin. Publicity materials invited spectators to imagine Kean and Byron penetrating the heart of the exotic in "real life" – joining native tribes or sneaking into harems. The theatre contained these fantasies of miscegenation within an emerging ethnographic discourse.

Such processes, I will further argue, were at work in much of the orientalist fare available to theatregoers in the romantic period. The theatre provided a vicarious identification with an "Eastern essence" within the tropes of orientalist mastery. This essentialism ultimately proved adaptable to practices that denigrated racialized peoples. By the end of the romantic period, the imagery that had been used as part of an imaginative engagement with the exotic was now used to justify military intervention in "barbaric" regions such as the Eastern Mediterranean.

EDMUND KEAN'S FACE-PAINT

Looking back on Edmund Kean's performance of Othello in "tawny" face-paint, the Victorian biographer, F. W. Hawkins, remarked that Kean "regarded it a gross error to make Othello either a Negro or a black, and accordingly altered the conventional black to the light brown which distinguishes the Moors by virtue of their descent from the Caucasian race."[1] Hawkins read Kean's performance in light of Victorian racial-evolutionary thought, namely that blacks were either the product of a distinct genesis or a splitting of the human tree at a point so remote in the evolutionary past as to virtually constitute a separate species. By contrast Semitic peoples, according to these views, constituted a more recent degeneration produced by environment. Whether or not Kean's performance portended the racist writings of John Lubbock and others as Hawkins's quote seems to suggest, I would like to propose that this Victorian biographer had in fact accessed a significant feature of racial representation in the romantic period: it functioned as both spectacle and means to abstraction. This was true whether racial representation prompted reflections on race and evolution, as was the case with Hawkins, or reflections on the nature of environmental determinism, as evident in the writings of William Hazlitt and other romantic critics.

Within romantic theatre, one discerns the emergence of a distinctly modern, and ultimately oppressive, conception of race. The theatre traced out the newly discovered scope of human diversity, generating both excitement and anxiety in fantasies of miscegenation. Race was both external marker and internal proclivities, drives, and desires. As such, it could be read as a determinant of human behavior and cultural achievement, as well as a record of environmental processes. Finally, I will suggest that at the same time that this new conception of race developed, a romantic strategy emerged whereby the artist purported not *to represent* the racially marked but *to embody* its internal mechanism. This artist or performer identified with their exotic creations, using the conceit of performance to manifest racially transgressive identities.

Attributing such a developed conception of race to the romantic period requires some explanation. The first recognizably modern definition of race did not appear until 1835 when the *Dictionnaire* described race as a multitude of men who originate from the same country, and resemble each other by facial features and by exterior conformity. Similar definitions did not surface in English-language dictionaries until much later. However, as several historians of race have demonstrated, the idea of race as a fixed biological category emerged as early as the late-eighteenth century.[2] Romantic critics in particular were instrumental in proposing, in the words of Ivan Hannaford, a "description of nations based on the assumption that innate mental qualities – temperament, character, inward sensation, and genius – may be revealed in literature and lineaments of the face."[3] Culture, no less than physical characteristics, was the product of racial type which was now defined by internal processes. One was Moor or Negro on the inside, and both physiognomy and culture were markers of this internal state.

I would like to further suggest that this conception of race as both external signifier and internal process is a feature of the often cited romantic ambivalence towards theatrical production. It is evident, for example, in the most famous anti-theatrical text of the romantic period, Charles Lamb's "On the Tragedies of Shakespeare, Considered with Reference to Their Fitness for Stage Representation" first published in 1811. When Lamb condemned theatrical production for bringing down "a fine vision to the standard of flesh and blood," he illustrated his argument by drawing attention to the "revolting" spectacle of miscegenation that results from the production of *Othello*. Lamb argued that imagination triumphs over the senses when *readers* of the play contemplate how Desdemona puts aside "every consideration of kindred, and country, and colour" for love. However, in production *viewers* are unable to bracket the fact of race, are unable to make what Lamb calls, that "beautiful compromise," and instead cannot help but "find something extremely revolting in the courtship and wedded caresses of Othello and Desdemona." Moreover, Lamb explained parenthetically, the spectacle is a historical error. The play depicts Othello as "a *coal-black Moor* . . . in the imperfect state of knowledge respecting foreign countries in those days, compared with our own, or in compliance with popular notions, though the Moors are now well enough known to be many shades less unworthy of a white woman's fancy."[4]

References to race do not necessarily mar a work's poetic value, according to Lamb, but when one is gripped by the spectacle of race there is no longer room for contemplation. The play's ennobling ideas are the product of race even as these ideas can only be grasped through the temporary suppression of the physical fact of race. How, Lamb asked, could this suppression ever take place in performance? I would suggest that Lamb's assertion that the play's troubling racial imagery was the product of Elizabethan ignorance points to a strategy of suppression that would be adopted by later practitioners. According to Lamb, the greater knowledge of his contemporaries made it possible to correctly place Moors in the hierarchy of race, "many shades less unworthy of a white woman's fancy." Potentially, then, racial representation could serve the examination of this hierarchy and its relation to geography, disseminating a more perfect "knowledge respecting foreign countries" in Lamb's above phrase.

Coleridge similarly objected to the spectacle of miscegenation generated in productions of *Othello*, though he asserted that the play's apparent racial confusion was the product of misinterpreting the text. Shakespeare, according to Coleridge, could not be "so utterly ignorant as to make a barbarous Negro plead royal birth" and besides, he continues, "it would be something monstrous to conceive this beautiful Venetian girl falling in love with a veritable Negro." Othello is a Moor, Coleridge explains, and if other characters depict him as a Negro it is only as a libel. If Shakespeare had in fact sanctioned blackface performance, it was only from the knowledge that "nothing could be made too *marked* for the nerves of his audience" and should not be thought to concern his "intentions as a poet for all ages."[5] Here again, the needs of production, which invariably pander to the tastes of the masses, are set in opposition to poetry's timeless value. The shock of miscegenation might titillate the pit, but such images ultimately obscured the "natural" antipathy whites feel for blacks. As such, Coleridge reasons, these images beg credibility in that they contradict the hierarchy of race, a position that apparently did not contradict Coleridge's abolitionist stance.

While a fixed hierarchy of race, as evident in Lamb's writing, limited imaginative engagement across race lines other romantics adopted the environmentalist outlook gaining precedence in ethnographic circles. According to one historian, the most prominent British writers on race prior to 1820 shared the belief that racial characteristics were acquired in response to environmental conditions and physical practices and then passed down the blood line.[6] This position did not preclude racist depictions; however, it was premised on a belief in human unity and the mutability of race. One hears this position echoed in Hazlitt's praise of Kean's performance of the Moor, Zanga, in Edward Young's *Revenge*: "He had all the wild impetuosity of barbarous revenge, the glowing energy of the untamed children of the sun whose blood drinks up the radiance of fierce skies."[7] For Hazlitt, Kean's performance succeeds not simply because he compellingly depicts an obsessive desire for revenge, but because he depicts an obsessive desire for revenge *specific to the Moors of Northern Africa*. In doing so, Hazlitt suggested, Kean makes manifest to the audience the environmental conditions that have produced the Moorish temperament. Kean's performance reveals both the impulses of Moorish "blood" and the fierce skies that have stamped its character. Racial representation places striking images on stage but, more importantly for romantics like Hazlitt, racial representation communicates larger historical processes and environmental conditions.

Kean's performances and the responses of his contemporaries demonstrate a growing fascination with the exotic and a desire, within strict limits, to identify across racial lines – though this identification was tempered by paternalism and ethnocentrism. Kean's list of exoticized roles was considerable. In addition to Zanga and Othello, Kean performed the Turkish Bajazet in Rowe's *Tamerlane*; the African prince Oroonoko in the play by Southerne; the Arab prince, *Achmet*, in John Brown's *Barbarossa*; the half-Turk, half-Greek Selim in *The Bride of Abydos*, which was adapted for Kean from Byron's poem; the Amerindian Omreah, in Twiss's *The Carib Chief*; the Inca leader, Rolla, in Sheridan's adaptation of *Pizarro*; and the disastrous title role in T. C. Grattan's *Ben Nazir the Saracen*. When one takes into account that some contemporary reviewers and later biographers commented on the "Eastern" or "Oriental" nature of Kean's Shylock, and Barabas from *The Jew of Malta* (a play that had fallen out of the repertory until Kean's performance), the number of Kean's racialized characters rises to eleven out of fifty-seven roles performed since his Drury Lane debut.[8]

The writings of Kean's contemporaries suggest that he attempted to bring racial and ethnographic detail to many of these roles, though I will only examine the reminiscences of T. C. Grattan, author of *Ben Nazir* and Kean's close friend. In an article published in the *New Monthly Magazine* shortly after Kean's death in 1833, Grattan noted Kean's use of racial markers, such as the "deep copper colour" of Kean's face-paint for Othello.[9] Tinsels depicting Kean in this role show Turkish tents in the background, giving a vaguely Middle Eastern feel to the scene (Fig. 2.1). Grattan, however, gave much more attention to the circumstance surrounding Kean's performance of *Ben Nazir* in 1827. Kean, he explained, was looking for a new role for his "regenerated" return to the English stage after being driven to an American tour because of his affair with Charlotte Cox. Kean turned down several new plays, one being *Alfred the Great* by Sheridan Knowles. Grattan described Kean's excited enthusiasm for *Ben Nazir*, and recalled visiting the actor at his residence soon after they had agreed upon a performance:

He was sitting up in his bed, a buffalo-skin wrapped round him, a huge hairy cape, decked with many coloured feathers, on his head, a scalping knife in his belt and tomahawk in his hand. He was making up his face for a very savage look. A tumbler glass of white-wine negus stood at the bed-side . . . and a portrait painter was placed before an easel at the window, taking the likeness of the renowned *Alanienonideh* [sic], the name in which the chieftain (most sincerely) rejoiced . . . I was announced by a black boy in livery. I saw Kean's eye kindle, somewhat, perhaps with pleasure at my visit; but more so, I thought, from the good opportunity of exhibiting himself in this savage costume. He gave a ferocious roll of his eyes, and a flourish of his tomahawk; then threw off his cape and mantle, and cordially shook me by the hand, producing from under his pillow the part of *Ben Nazir* written out from the prompter's book. (146)

According to Grattan, Kean explained that during his American tour, at Montreal or Quebec, he had gone mad for several days and joined a Huron tribe in which he was elected chief and renamed Alanienonideh, until he was carried back by pursuing friends and "treated for a considerable time as a lunatic" (146).

MᴿKEAN ᴀꜱ OTHELLO.

Published by M.&M.SKELT 11.Swan St.Minories London.

2.1 Tinsel of Edmund Kean as Othello

Grattan's account connects the myth of the self-destructive romantic genius to a new fascination with race. In his reminiscence, Grattan sought to attribute the failure of *Ben Nazir* to the fact that Kean paraphrased and excised large portions of the play. However, Grattan made this case by suggesting that Kean had become dangerously absorbed by his Indian identity. Grattan described Kean's costuming as the after-effects (or possibly the continuation) of delirium. He implicitly linked this alter-identity to Kean's continued alcoholism – the telling white-wine negus at the bedside. Later Grattan noted his concern on reading in a newspaper that Kean wore the costume when delivering an address at his benefit performance in a Dublin theatre, though friends assured Grattan that Kean "had no actual relapse of his Canadian complaint" (147). There is also the irrelevant detail that Kean employed "a black boy in livery," though given the context it seems to suggest a certain excess of racial mixing in Kean's presence. The scene culminates when the script for *Ben Nazir* is pulled from beneath the pillow, completing an enthusiasm that even the author of the play finds excessive. All of these details point to a potential loss of Kean's European self to a consuming racialized self.

The finished portrait was presented to the Theatre Royal, Drury Lane, an obvious place in which to commemorate Kean's cross-racial identification (Fig. 2.2). The caption on Storm's engraving describes the painting as "a faithful portrait of Mr. Kean, and a correct delineation of the costume of that warlike tribe who unanimously elected him a chieftain and a brother at Quebec on Saturday October 7th, 1826."[10] The caption indicates that at least some of Kean's contemporaries did not read his Canadian adventure as merely an instance of "playing Indian"; the caption instead asks us to believe that the Hurons instinctively recognized Kean as both a brother and a potential chief, as if he possessed some innate connection to the tribe. Kean reportedly stated that the honor the Hurons had conferred on him was better than the highest honors he had achieved during his entire acting career. (It is also interesting to note that Kean aided the African-American actor Ira Aldridge when he was in England.) The implication is that Kean's performance of racially marked characters was correct not simply because he got the external details right but because of a deeply essential bond. Kean and his contemporaries seem to suggest that he was uniquely able to embody the internal drives and desires of "warlike tribes" and "children of the sun."

Lord Byron, who similarly blurred the boundaries between himself and his Eastern creations, appears to have recognized Kean as a kindred exotic. In the aftermath of Kean's success as Richard III, Byron was asked to contribute verses on the subject of the actor's performance. Byron reportedly responded by quoting lines from the first Canto of his oriental romance, *The Corsair*, describing the poem's title character. In doing so, Byron implicitly linked the actor with himself, for that poem was significant in spreading the idea that Byron's characters were an extension of himself. In his dedication to *The Corsair*, Byron noted that if he was criticized for his Eastern heroes and held "no less responsible for their deeds and qualities than if all had been personal" it was probably because he was guilty of "the gloomy vanity

2.2 Edmund Kean in Huron costume

2.3 Print of Phillips's portrait of Byron in Albanian costume

of 'drawing from self.' " Byron's publisher was complicit in conflating the poet with his creations, commissioning book-size prints that depicted Byron's characters so as to resemble Byron. After Byron's death, the publisher also made available prints of the Phillips portrait depicting Byron in the Albanian costume he brought back from his Eastern travels (Fig. 2.3). Kean, then, would seem to be borrowing a strategy from Byron when the actor made use of visiting cards that listed both his European and Indian names with a portrait in the Huron costume on the reverse. Byron and Kean are also linked in their contribution to the romantic idea that genius's drive to excess – and here I include identification with the exotic – necessarily leads to destruction. Byron famously died supporting the Greek rebellion against Ottoman rule, and Kean collapsed during his last performance of *Othello* only to pass away weeks later.

BYRON–KEAN IN THE HAREM

In his mastery and engagement of the exotic, Kean played a role that Byron had developed. As we shall see, this process grew especially complex when Kean performed a character presumed to be based on Byron's own experience, Selim in Drury Lane's adaptation of *The Bride of Abydos*. In this and other exoticized performances, Kean perpetuated a gender coding that was central to Byron's oriental romances and was significant to the growing popularity of exotic spectacle in nineteenth-century theatre. Theatrical adaptations invariably featured lavish scenes in which European (or partially European) males sneak (or are sneaked) into harems. Beyond revealing Byron's fame and the degree to which this fame was associated with exotic sexual encounters, these orientalist adaptations suggest elaborate acts of displacement. Ambivalence towards Britain's continued slave trade and colonialism became occluded within a condemnation of oriental despotism, Regency London's culture of consumption was recast as an examination of oriental luxury, and concern over the perceived feminization of British culture was effaced by the spectacle of a transgressive oriental sexuality. The East was lascivious, idle, wasteful, closed to outsiders, and subject to tyrannous rulers. Whereas Byron used harem imagery in a critique of European power structures, the theatre often used such imagery to implicitly or explicitly laud British expansionism. In the process, the East was transformed from a threatening male power to a space of female segregation. The East was a harem daring abduction.

The idea that exotic cultures are gendered feminine in orientalist discourse has been an implicit, if under-explored, theme in post-colonial theory since the publication of Said's *Orientalism* (1978), and has received its most sustained analysis in Anne McClintock's *Imperial Leather: Race, Gender and Sexuality in the Colonial Contest* (1995). This gender coding is evident in a range of print media, but it grows especially complex in the theatre where male and female actors were enlisted in a project of conflating the real stage space with an imagined colonial space – both of which were strongly associated in the popular mind with the display of women.

Actresses in pink fleshings or draped in diaphanous material helped deliver the East to English audiences. While the theatre's eliding of the real within the represented is a feature of any production, it was especially complex in adaptations of Byron's oriental romances. The popular tendency to associate Byron with his characters, illustrations of these characters drawn so as to resemble the poet, and the Phillips portrait of Byron in Albanian costume, all served to underscore that the poet had in fact penetrated the Orient described in his poems. The idea that the poet had lived the staged events was further complicated by public knowledge of Byron's involvement in London theatre and his reported intimacy with the actress Charlotte Mardyn. These orientalist adaptations used the figure of Byron to evoke the experience of male entrance into closed spaces associated with female congregation: the harem and the dressing-room.

Byron was a visual, as well as literary, phenomenon and this iconography contributed to the belief that Byron drew from himself when creating romantic Eastern adventurers. While Byron's wandering Childe Harold made the poet instantly famous, it was Byron's oriental romances that truly made him the first celebrity writer. Shortly after the release in 1814 of *The Corsair*, Byron's third and most popular oriental romance, his publisher released book-size prints of the Phillips "cloak" portrait, reengraving it dozens of times until it became "one of the most recognizable images of the age" in the words of one literary historian.[11] The publisher also released illustrations of *The Corsair* in which the hero was drawn to resemble Byron. It was at this time that the first theatrical adaptation appeared, *The Corsair* at Sadler's Wells. Many such adaptations would follow throughout the nineteenth century, but the most hotly anticipated was Drury Lane's 1818 adaptation of *The Bride of Abydos* staring Edmund Kean and Charlotte Mardyn.

The venue and casting reflected the popular imagining of Byron's adventures in exotic realms like the Orient and the theatre. Byron had been associated with Drury Lane since 1815 when he joined the committee that oversaw its operations. He actively solicited scripts and was frequently seen backstage; one contemporary compared him to "a little dog behind the scenes, following [Kean] everywhere."[12] Moreover, Kean was a frequent guest at the poet's small dinner parties. Byron's association with Kean's costar, Charlotte Mardyn, was even more widely reported. Mardyn was rumored to have caused Lord and Lady Byron's separation two years earlier, a scandal that prompted newspaper debates and a flurry of pamphlets that continued well after Byron's departure from England.[13]

Publicity materials further invoked Byron's presence. The bills made no mention of the adapter, William Dimond, instead explaining that the play was "founded entirely on the Poems of Lord Byron." The bills continued:

"In the course of the representation, an attempt will be made to connect into a series of Dramatic Pictures, embellished by every aid of the Scenic Art, some of the most prominent characters and incidents, and descriptions of Lord Byron's Muse."[14] Byron's Muse stood center stage; the devices of the theatre were mere embellishments never threatening to obstruct the visionary verse with the basely visible. In this spirit the bills listed the scene titles with appropriate lines from Byron's poetry, as if the scenic spectacle only served to conjure in the minds of the spectators lines of poetry previously encountered. In point of fact, Dimond's adaptation featured very little of Byron's verse, cobbled together salient scenes from both *The Corsair* and *The Bride of Abydos*, and introduced stock melodramatic characters and incidents, resurrecting dead fathers and inventing a spectacular happy ending.

The production claimed a scholarly mastery of Islamic life, even as this scholarship served to license sensual spectacle. This, the production would seem to boast, was not mere speculation but a depiction of Oriental sexuality from one who had experienced the East first-hand. Eastern geography was depicted in scene painting, a variety of Arabic and Turkish terms were introduced into the script, and the published script gave an extended description of what was clearly intended as accurate costuming. The display of scholarship was consistent with "Lord Byron's Muse"; in the same year as the production, Byron had boasted that he had read "Knolles, Cantamir – De Tott – Lady Montague – Hawkins' translation from Mignot's History of the Turks – the Arabian Nights – All travels of histories or books upon the East I could meet with . . . before I was *ten years old*."[15] Byron's real authority, however, came not from his studies but his travels. In the notes for one of his oriental romances, Byron praised William Beckford's *Vathek* – a wildly erotic tale of Eastern sorcery – for its "correctness of costume," explaining that "those who have visited the East will find some difficulty in believing it to be more than a translation."[16] Apparently even the most lascivious depictions of Eastern opulence were borne out by Byron's experiences in the East – providing theatres with considerable liberty in their attempts to delineate Oriental manners.

The production's most repeated marker of authenticity was an image that strongly evoked the spectacle of Eastern sexuality for nineteenth-century theatre audiences: the harem. Included among the eleven settings in Dimond's script are "A Corridor of the Harem," "A Quadrangle of the Harem," "The Harem Gardens by Moonlight," "A Subterranean Chamber of the Harem," and "The Destruction of the Harem." The eighteenth-century mania for seraglio stories and abduction operas had helped transform the harem into an emblem of Islamic life in the European mind; after all, Mozart's *Abduction from the Seraglio* was the fourteenth such abduction opera staged in the second half of the eighteenth century.[17] However, Dimond's staging went well beyond this comparatively tame tradition, as evident in the stage directions for the scene in Zuliaka's apartment on the eve of her forced marriage:

Female slaves advance, joyously, some with musical instruments, others employ themselves in disposing strands of flowers. While the centre of the stage is occupied by dancers who pursue each other for the bridal veil and by turns possess it. Zuliaka in a glittering habit enters during their sports and reclines herself disconsolately. At the end of the dance the slaves dispose the veil into a canopy above her.[18]

Zuliaka is the prize at the center of the harem. She reclines, oblivious to the female dancers, musicians, and flower girls that surround her. Dimond evoked tropes that had only begun to emerge in orientalist painting and would come to dominate stage depictions of the harem: native instruments and music that intensify the sensualization of female bodies, sapphic play that reads as both innocent and provocative, a central figure who begins or concludes the dance reclined on a couch or litter, and scarves or a canopy that act as props in the dance but ultimately serve to frame the central figure – the languorous odalisque.

Audiences were invited to imagine Byron in this sensual and detailed East – the white man who rescues the brown Zuliaka from other brown men. Dimond's script repeatedly underscores the Greek ancestry of the rebellious hero, Selim, whose supposed father taunts him with lines like "Son of a slave! thy Christian mother's blood runs single in thy veins" and "thou Greek in soul if not in creed" (1.iii.). In the process, the script reverses the racial pairing that Lamb found so distasteful in *Othello*, making it that much easier to imagine Byron as the actual protagonist. This identification was underscored by the decision to cast Edmund Kean as Selim and Charlotte Mardyn as his beloved Zuliaka. Byron's friendship with and esteem for Kean was well known, and – as already noted – by comparing Kean to the hero of *The Corsair*, Byron implicitly compared the actor to himself. More significantly, though, Kean's affinity for passionate exotic characters made him especially suited to invoke Byron's persona as a visionary in sympathetic bond with the East. For both men, moreover, imagined transgressions were accompanied by equally public domestic disgrace. Even by 1818, audiences associated Kean with scandals that competed with the irregularities of Byron's own life. (Kean himself would be driven from England in 1820, after an affair with the wife of a Drury Lane committee member.) In addition, Kean's small stature and dark looks recall the frontispiece depictions of Byron's characters and the exotically clad poet himself, and at least one print of the actor appears to be modeled on the Phillips cloak portrait (Figs 2.4, 2.5).

2.4 Print of Phillips's "cloak" portrait of Byron

2.5 Print of Edmund Kean in cloak

The sight of Kean abducting Charlotte Mardyn, Byron's assumed mistress, from the stage harem summoned Byron's imagined escapades in the closed chambers of the Orient and the theatre. Both were gendered female in contrast to the knowing adventurer who retained masculinity despite an affinity with the exotic.

The stage became a vehicle for living the exotic. The production invited its audience to an imaginative engagement with a "real" East that existed beyond the wings but had been conjured on stage through the medium of the poet–traveler. In his preface to the published play, Dimond likened himself to an antiquarian that grafts new marble to a fragment of antiquity: "The interpolations of the Dramatist will, at a glance stand self-declared, like ordinary sculpture eking out some glorious fragment of the antique."[19] The poem is here revered as a remnant of a now absent poetic genius, but specifically a genius for affinity with the exotic. Greater stakes, then, were in place for the accuracy of scenic illustration. The complaints of *The Theatrical Inquisitor, and Monthly Mirror* that "The scenery was for the most part old, and arranged so strangely, as to display an utter ignorance of Oriental manners"[20] say as much about the new expectations for production as about the shortcomings of the Drury Lane paint room. Increasingly, productions would be censured for old scenery that revealed an "imperfect state of knowledge respecting foreign countries" (to reprise Charles Lamb's phrase).

THE IMPERIAL HAREM

As British military involvement in the Eastern Mediterranean grew more extensive, harem imagery was used to describe not only the relation between white men and brown women but also the relation between white nations and brown peoples. This was even evident in adaptations of Byron's most anti-imperial poem, *Don Juan*. Byron's popularity exploded across class lines with the publication of *Don Juan*. William St. Clair has identified fifty-one different editions of the poem published before 1828 (most of them pirated), estimating the number of copies in print between 126,000 and 158,000.[21] Given the poem's radical content, it is not surprising that the patent theatres ignored it. When it was adapted at minor theatres, dramatists either excised or transformed its political content; none of the three adaptations I know of follow Juan as far as the siege of Ismail. Samuel Chew explains that *The Sultana; or, a Trip to Turkey* (1822) opens with the shipwreck and Haidée episode, followed by scenes in which Juan is sold in the Constantinople slave market and then smuggled into the seraglio by the Sultana.[22] J. B. Buckstone adapted the poem as both a comic opera and a melodrama for the Adelphi in 1828, and it is the latter that I will address.

According to the published script of *Don Juan*, Buckstone's melodrama grew increasingly spectacular and sexual as the action moved East. The play began with a somewhat chaster version of the scene in Donna Julia's apartment, which was eventually followed by a sensation scene in which Juan's ship is struck by lighting and Juan and the sailors are seen tossing in the waves. As in Byron's poem, Juan is washed up on a Greek island, where he is found by the Greek girl, Haidée, and then sold into slavery by her father, Lambro. The script describes an elaborate slave-market scene in Constantinople, with "Merchants and inhabitants of both sexes . . . [and] venders of various articles" who "inspect" Juan and the other slaves. Haggling is interrupted by the Sultana's entrance: "Music is heard without. A general cry of 'The Sultana!' All draw back. A procession of female and other slaves advances escorting Gulbeyaz, who is borne in an elegant litter. Baba [the eunuch of the harem] walks by her side."[23] Later scenes include "Part of the Gardens of the Seraglio (Night)" and "A magnificent Pavilion attached to the Harem" with Gulbeyaz "seated on a superb throne, surrounded by a train of damsels."

While the narrative roughly follows that of the Eastern scenes in Byron's *Don Juan*, the events clearly have been adapted to the conventions of early-nineteenth-century melodrama. Buckstone, for example, provides Haidée with a blackface slave. Blackface has a long history in English theatre; however, Buckstone's character has a distinctly American feel, rejoicing at the assumed death of "old massa" for example. Buckstone also introduces an English tar, Will Johnson, in the slave-market scene. He is a familiar character-type whose speech is composed of nautical metaphors and patriotic speeches: "Cheer up, my hearty! The gale of fortune will turn before long. We shall be in another tack, give us but sea room and a tight vessel" (10). In the next scene, Johnson announces: "If any foul play is attempted towards the helpless and undefended, we'll soon show these black-bearded pirates what English tars can do in the cause of justice and humanity" (11). The role was performed by T. P. Cooke, who would later log a record four hundred performances as the lead in the nautical melodrama *Black-Ey'd Susan*. Juan has similarly been transformed into a hero of melodrama, announcing on two separate occasions, "My life I'll freely yield, my honour never." Juan is discovered in the harem and is about to be beheaded when Johnson breaks in with "a party of British sailors, armed with cutlasses." Johnson rescues Juan, whom he describes as "a Spanish vessel under Greek colours" that is now "under British protection." The Sultan is in the act of calling more guards when the back of the stage opens, discovering "the British ship in the Bosphorus, close under the walls of Seraglio; it fires two guns" (12).

The aptly named Johnson and his British Tars enter the harem while a British man-of-war enters the Bosphorus, the back of the theatre opening to welcome her liberator. The scene reproduces a familiar gender coding, though here Western male entrance into the feminine East is further conflated with the actual entrance of British gunships into the Eastern theatre of war. It is a strange and complex irony that Byron's attack on the mindless warfare of the *ancien régime* should be transformed into a celebration of the British victory at Navarino. A year before the Adelphi production of *Don Juan*, the British sank the Egyptian fleet anchored at Pylos (then Navarino) when the Ottomans refused to accept an armistice in the Greek War of Independence. Byron's own death in 1824 from fever in Missolonghi, where he was aiding the Greek insurgents, did much to intensify British philhellenism. In Buckstone's *Don Juan*, Byron's death becomes further support for a new *pax Britannica*, evidenced in Britain's growing involvement in the Ottoman regions. The British are protecting the "Greek colours," just as Byron had done in the final days of his life. However, Buckstone casts this protection in more expansive terms. The confusing layering of Spanish vessels under Greek flags under British protection would only seem to suggest that Britain oversees all maritime activity.

Byron's *Don Juan* was much more sanguine on the subject of national struggles. The Greek pirate and slavetrader of *Don Juan* – "Lambro, our sea-solicitor" – is anything but the romantic corsair of earlier works (III. 26). As Malcolm Kelsall writes, "[Lambro's] situation is such that this friend of freedom is now indistinguishable from the Sultan he opposes."[24] To quote *Don Juan*, "His country's wrongs and his despair to save her / Had stung him from a slave to an enslaver" (III. 53). The difficulty of distinguishing patriots from enslavers informs the entire work, a theme overlooked in Buckstone's adaptation – most glaringly so in the inclusion of Haidée's blackface slave. As a white, Juan's enslavement is an outrage that calls for a swift military response (hence the near-magical appearance of a British man-of-war at the back of the stage). No such liberation awaits the blackface character. Instead his misrecognition of his old master, Lambro, becomes the source for a comic scene of the black man's terror and supplication. Slavery continued in the British West Indies until 1833. If Buckstone's 1828 adaptation overtly lauded British imperialism, the play also covertly acknowledged the injustices that helped generate Britain's colonial wealth.

The use of harem imagery to attack Ottoman domination of Greece occurs in other plays from this period, most pointedly in William Dimond's adaptation of Mozart's *The Abduction from the Seraglio* produced at Covent Garden in 1827, only two months after the Battle of Navarino. Dimond introduced a range of melodramatic elements into the text, such as an Irish tar sidekick and the revelation that Constanza and Ibrahim (who replaces Mozart's Pacha Selim) are siblings separated at birth. However, the most striking transformation is Dimond's many references to the Greek War of Independence. In *The Seraglio*, Dimond returned to the harem imagery he had first employed in his adaptation of *The Bride of Abydos*. Whereas Byron's oriental romances imagined a revolt against entrenched power that invoked myriad injustices, Dimond used the harem imagery to attack oriental despotism generally and Turkish domination of Greece specifically. Dimond's inclusion of a loyal Irish sidekick signaled that liberation was not universally needed.

The harem tropes established in Dimond's *The Bride of Abydos* grew sufficiently well known to be parodied in his own adaptation of Carl Maria von Weber's *Abou Hassan* (Drury Lane 1825); however, this did not prevent Dimond from reprising such imagery when attacking Turkish domination of Greece. Like Mozart, Dimond depicted two European women – Constanza and Blonda – imprisoned in a harem, though Dimond transfered the action from a seraglio in an unspecified Turkish location to the seraglio of the Turkish governor of an occupied Greek island. While the Greeks plan rebellion, the women's fiancés plan their liberation from the seraglio. Posing as European artists interested in sketching Greek ruins, the fiancés encounter Greek partisans who are deeply touched by the artists' respect for antiquity: "Youth, you flatter the single pride which centuries of degradation have left to us. These monuments of former glory are to the poor bondsman the lonely evidence that his country was once free."[25] Soon after, the harem guard arrives on the scene intent on using the ruins to fill a ditch, clear proof of the necessity of Lord Elgin's act of preservation. As Dimond's adaptation makes clear, whether they are violating land, ruins, or women, the Ottomans will not stop until Europe intercedes.

While the European powers stymied Ottoman domination of Greece at Navarino, Constanza and Blonda undermined Ibrahim's control of his harem. Dimond gives considerable attention to their effect on the other women of the harem, introducing several harem slaves who demand greater liberty in response to Blonda's example. They have apparently become convinced by Blonda's argument that men are "mere playthings" for the mistress of the house, and are "designed especially like lap dogs and monkeys, for the amusement of our idler hours" (II.i). Dimond's adaptation attempted to paint a European-induced sexual liberation that parallels Europe's liberation of Greek territories. However, before it could do so it first had to assert that the confinement of European women in the domestic sphere was evidence of their considerable privilege and power. In contrast to the harems, bondsmen, and interned ruins of the East, Dimond presented an image of Britain in which women enjoyed domestic freedom, men enjoyed political freedom, and antiquities were properly displayed in illustrated folios and museums. The efforts of Elgin, Salt, and other antiquaries were apparently a better measure of British freedom than Peterloo or the Six Acts.

Harem scenes became common as female display became a more insistent objective of British theatre and here as well depictions of Eastern sexuality were informed by Britain's own sense of imperial power. Later in the century, the growing importance of the chorus girl in burlesque combined with the use of pink fleshings resulted in orientalist productions that bordered on the pornographic. The harem plays of the first half of the century were tame compared to the Edwardian ballets and tableaux vivants at theatres like the Alhambra and the Empire or compared to the oriental spectacles at twentieth-century follies. Nonetheless, then as now, the theatrical harem translated as the display (rather than the segregation) of women.

The harem dances that were minor interludes in plays like Dimond's *The Bride of Abydos* became prominent features of orientalist ballets popular in the thirties and forties. Once again the theatre turned to Byron. French romantic ballet, with its emphasis on picturesque and exotic settings, spread to London in the 1830s, creating a dance vogue that would continue until mid-century. The Islamic East was a frequent setting for such ballets. In 1837, the ballet *Le Corsaire* was staged at the King's Theatre (later Her Majesty's Theatre). Reportedly, at about that time the Lyceum brought out a "musical drama" also based on Byron's *Corsair* and entitled, *The Pacha's Bridal*.[26] In 1837 the King's Theatre also produced the ballet, *Sir Huon*, which was based on Christoph Martin Wieland's Oriental fairytale, *Oberon* (a poem that featured harem scenes in both Baghdad and Tunis). In October of 1844, Drury Lane produced its own dance version of *The Corsair*, which was followed in December by another dance piece, *The Revolt of the Harem*. In the same month, the Princess's Theatre produced the dance, *The Slave Market*. Her Majesty's Theatre adapted Moore's *Lalla Rookh* as a ballet in 1846. Covent Garden presented *L'Odalisque* in 1847. Joseph Mazilier's famous adaptation, *Le Corsaire*, which was first performed at the Théâtre Impérial de l'Opéra in 1856, was immediately remounted at Her Majesty's Theatre, and continues in the classical repertory. Furthermore, throughout the 1840s and after, harem ballets remained important features of melodrama and opera. There is an equally rich history of dance pieces with Indian settings, of which *La Bayadère* is the most famous.

These ballets mixed exotic settings with the romantic dance style, and combined Eastern costumes with the uncorsetted costumes and below-the-knee skirts of light drapery made popular by Marie Taglioni. So Mlle. Caroline Rousset could be seen to pirouette like a "spinning top" according to the *Illustrated London News* when performing in *The Slave Market*,[27] and an illustration for *The Corsair* of 1844 shows the Turkish Pasha in turban and robes while Gulnare wears a nineteenth-century romantic tutu (jacket illustration). It was just such a costume that caught the flame of a gas jet and killed Clara Webster when she was performing as Zulica, a royal slave in *The Revolt of the Harem*.[28] Whereas the settings and male costumes were exotic, the female dancers – in costume and dance style – were clearly European. Yet at the same time, they enacted roles the theatre had defined as characteristically Eastern; they became slaves and concubines. The pleasure of the theatrical harem (at least for the male audience) was the opportunity to imagine white European women assuming the position of the compliant and sensual Eastern woman. The theatre transformed the excess of the East into an excess of European women for the audience's benefit. Spectator pleasure revolved around the experience of proprietorship; the East's most intimate interior had been opened for the spectator's benefit. This subservience not only defined England's relation to the Eastern Mediterranean, but also defined the Englishman's relation to the English actresses on stage.

In the 1837 *Le Corsaire*, this pleasure of proprietorship was manifested in the scene painting in a rather revealing manner. The production included a number of scene changes and one of the more spectacular settings was Grieve's "Harem." The maquette for this scene features four sets of flats and a back scene (Fig. 2.6). The ogival arches, colored detailing, and plant life lend an exotic flair to a setting that is otherwise quite gothic. Though gothic features are apparent – heightened verticality, reduced wall surfaces, recessed lighting from stained glass, and multiple tiers of increasingly fine pilasters – the referent is not so much Chartres as Brighton; and it is through associations with Brighton that the set evoked English proprietorship. In 1803, the Prince Regent commissioned William Porden to design the Royal Stables and Riding House at Brighton. Porden's design combined gothic and Mughal features (possibly influenced by the then-current theory that the gothic was derived from the Saracens).[29] Grieve's harem design resembles the interior of these stables (Fig. 2.7), and it is worth noting that one of the pantomimes that the Grieves contributed to, *Harlequin and the Ogress*, included views of the Brighton Pavilion. The eclectic exoticism of the Pavilion reflected the nation's knowledge that it could extract the wealth of distant regions and master and reproduce anything the East might have accomplished. The Brighton Pavilion also reflected the Prince Regent's own "capacity for self-projection as an Eastern potentate himself,"

2.6 Grieve's maquette for harem scene in *Le Corsaire*, 1837

as John Sweetman has observed.[30] To lend a different spin to Sweetman's observation, George was as much the master of an excess amidst his horses, as the Caliph was amidst his wives. The harem became an image by which to castigate Eastern excess as well as laud British plenty.

The Corsair, a poem that initially allowed its public to imagine a transgressive familiarity with the exotic body, now offered the comfortably familiar. There was little threat at the 1837 *Le Corsaire* that audience imagination should be overwhelmed by the interracial caresses that Lamb found so revolting in productions of *Othello*. Instead, the exotic was delivered in architectural details that had already become associated with fancy and light entertainment. In the poem, the Turkish slave girl, Gulnare, seduces and kills the tyrannical Pasha in order to free the pirate Conrad, only to expire on his kiss – evidence that it is no small thing to reverse gender roles and cross racial boundaries on the same afternoon. Assuming that the climactic kiss was retained in the 1837 ballet, one suspects that Gulnare's tutu and the setting's resemblance to the Brighton Pavilion undermined any sense that the "real" East had been penetrated by a European adventurer.

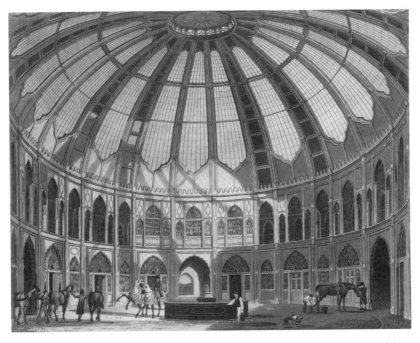

2.7 William Porden's Royal Stables and Riding House from John Nash's *Views of the Royal Pavilion at Brighton*

TOMB RAIDERS

The harem was not the only image used by theatre practitioners who depicted the East as a closed space of potential riches. One need only recall the underground palace of William Beckford's *Vathek* (1786) to recognize that marvels and dangers were imagined to hide deep in the East; crypts abound in the gothic orientalism popular during the romantic period. As far as I know, Beckford was not adapted to the stage until the Royal Coburg produced *The Caliph Vathek* in 1823. However, George Colman the Younger's adaptation of *Blue Beard*, with its deadly demon hidden in the "blue chamber" of a labyrinthine Turkish castle, was one of the London theatre's most popular afterpieces since its first production at Drury Lane in 1798.

Nineteenth-century British drama contains many more crypts (as well as harems) than can be discussed in this chapter; however, it is worth noting the plays of Edward Fitzball for their range of internment. Fitzball's adaptation of Robert Southey's *Thalaba* (Royal Coburg 1823) retained the poem's desert setting, sepulchre, enchanted cavern, demons, and incantations, adding a harem abduction scene as well as a blackface slave. Fitzball reduced the poem's complicated plot to a few episodes, in which he contrived to regularly feature the theatre's live elephant. Fitzball's *The Earthquake: or, the Spectre of the Nile* (Adelphi 1828) featured a scene in which the heroine is rescued from imprisonment in a pyramid – a device that would be used in other British plays before its use in *Aida* – and concluded with the villain being buried in an earthquake. In addition, the temple orgy in Fitzball's *Azaël the Prodigal* (Drury Lane 1851) featured scene painting based on the Assyrian monuments recently unearthed by Austen Henry Layard. Fitzball's other Eastern plays are: *Nerestan: Prince of Persia* (Sadler's Wells 1823); *The Fire-Worshippers; or the Paradise and the Peri*, which was based on Moore's *Lalla Rookh* (Surrey 1824); *The Maid of Cashmere* (Drury Lane 1833); a new production of *Thalaba* (Covent Garden 1836); and *The Desert; or the Imann's Daughter* (Drury Lane 1847).

While Fitzball had little recourse to authoritative sources or Eastern travelers, many of his competitors in the field of Eastern gothic did, and this is well illustrated by competing patent house productions opening on Easter Monday of 1824. Charles Farley's *The Spirits of the Moon; or, The Inundation of the Nile* at Covent Garden and W. T. Moncrieff's *Zoroaster; or, The Spirit of the Star* at Drury Lane vied for holiday crowds with competing images of the mystical wonders of ancient Egypt. The story lines of the two plays were quite similar. In both, sorcery was used to obstruct the natural succession. Both plays ended with marriages as the royal line (and the world by association) was set right. However, interest in these plays did not reside in their story lines, which *The Times* described respectively as possessing "little meaning" and "a mere vehicle for the introduction of some beautiful scenery, a pretty dance, and one or two tolerably good processions."[31] These plays capitalized on the possibilities of spectacle afforded by magical events and "correct" reproductions of ancient settings. Both plays included elaborate scenes in subterranean chambers and concluded with the villain sinking into the earth.

The action in *Spirits of the Moon* was propelled to dark depths. Magic was lodged within deep recesses that had to be broken into before their arcane secrets could be revealed, all at considerable risk. In addition to subterranean chambers, giant idols, Egyptian deities, and obscure omens, the play featured a giant eagle that descended and snatched a small child (like the giant roc of the Sinbad tale), a moving labyrinth of myrtle trees that magically disappeared to reveal the gardens of the palace, and a climactic scene in which the dead body of the usurper was gathered by the Idol Typhon who sinks beneath the stage as the Temple of Isis and Osiris appears.

Even when above ground the usurper shunned the sun for fear that his lack of a shadow would betray his evil bargain with the Idol. The secrets of his power were ultimately revealed in a subterranean chamber in which great wealth was stored, fulfilling obscure omens.

With its emphasis on penetrating ancient subterranean chambers and deciphering confusing omens, *Spirits of the Moon* serves as a fantastic parallel to the emerging science of Egyptology. Just as oriental romances invited audiences to imagine Byron at the sensual heart of the exotic, gothic orientalism conjured British adventurers at the East's occult core. As noted earlier, in 1818 the Englishman Giovanni Belzoni had found the entrance to the second pyramid at Giza, revealing that the structure was an elaborate crypt and not solid as previously thought. The Briton, Thomas Young, and the Frenchman, Jean François Champollion, were both deciphering the seemingly impenetrable hieroglyphs that covered Egypt's ancient structures. While the audiences at Covent Garden might not have read Young's recent *Discoveries in Hieroglyphical Literature* (1823) or examined the Egyptian Society's published facsimiles of hieroglyphs, many in the audience very likely knew what it was like to enter an Egyptian tomb. In 1821, Belzoni displayed his collection of Egyptian antiquities, gathered during three years of collecting, in London's Egyptian Hall (so named for its pharaonic-style façade). Most of the exhibition was devoted to reproducing the tomb complex of Seti I, with plaster replicas (one 20 by 14 feet [7 by 4 metres]) made from wax impressions of the bas-reliefs of the tomb and painted in colors copied from the spot.

Belzoni arranged these replicas so as to reproduce two of the tomb's chambers, in a room whose roof had been lowered and was lit by lamp-light so as to recreate his first impressions on entering the tomb.[32] Belzoni then supplemented this recreation with what *The Times* described as "a multitude of collateral curiosities – such as mummies, papyri, medals, and female ornaments."[33] As a whole, Belzoni's exhibition created an East of obscure mystery: a closed tomb that required forced entry, strange inscriptions that only a scholar could master, and a vast array of "collateral curiosities" that spoke of the East's fullness and disorder. Deep beneath the surface, the inscrutable meaning of the East resided. The theatre's frequent descent into ancient subterranean crypts was a physical corollary to the antiquarian desire to embrace the interred remnants of antiquity. In the theatre and the exhibition room, one could enter the tomb by lamplight. One could search beneath the surface and contemplate strange sights that only reluctantly yielded their meaning.

Playbills for *Spirits of the Moon* asserted that the scenery, painted by the Grieve family and others, was not merely a flight of fancy but was "taken

2.8 Grieve's sketch for unidentified Egyptian setting

from the best Authorities of ancient Egypt."[34] The production may have
reminded audiences of Belzoni's recent exhibition, particularly as the play
featured scenes such as the "Egyptian Hall," which *The Times* singled out
for special praise.[35] A Grieves watercolor depicting an Egyptian chamber
for an unidentified play shows certain similarities to the design of the Great
Hall of London's Egyptian Hall, the room in which Belzoni displayed his
antiquities – most notably in the shape of the rear portal, its use of wings as
ornamentation, and the slanting roof. While there is no evidence that this
particular watercolor was used for *Spirits of the Moon*, it does suggest that
the popular exhibition hall informed the Grieves depiction of pharaonic
interiors. However, Belzoni and the Egyptian Hall is not the only possible
reference; the very title of the play, *The Spirits of the Moon; or, The Inundation
of the Nile*, recalls Vivant Denon's metre-long Cairo panorama "pendant le
temps de l'inondation du Nil," which depicts the city in silhouette beneath
a bright full moon. Denon's influence on the Grieves is evident in another
of their watercolors, an unidentified Egyptian exterior that appears to be
copied from the illustration of Luxor from *Voyages* (Figs. 2.8, 2.9).

2.9 Luxor from Vivant Denon's *Voyage dans la Basse et la Haute Egypte*

The production featured multiple scenes of pagan worship, which may have passed as accurate recreations, given the bill's claim that the production relied on authoritative sources. Of course it is difficult to take such claims of accuracy seriously when the production blatantly mixed epochs, since the play depicted pre-Islamic Egypt yet also included views of Cairo, a city founded in AD 969. In this context, it is useful to recall that though John Philip Kemble contacted the antiquarian, Francis Douce, for information in staging Shakespeare's Roman plays, Kemble responded in horror to the suggestion that he depict republican brick rather than imperial marble. "Why if I did, sir," he reportedly exclaimed, "they would call me an antiquary."[36] In the theatre, historical accuracy was only useful if it enabled an *increase* in spectacle. While the antiquarian stage was quick to include new authoritative images of the East, it would never do so at the expense of proven crowd pleasers. This, perhaps, explains the inclusion of a moving panorama painted by John Henderson Grieve depicting "A caravan of Various Merchants, Halting on their March, after crossing the Deserts, and terminating with their Arrival at the Ancient Mart of the Great City,"[37] even though it served no plot function. (The panorama was given the impressive name "Polemporeremoporokinetikon.") *The Drama* rightly complained that, "brief as the real story was, there was an utter want of continuity in its parts." The paper also complained that the sense of an obscure past conjured in the scene painting was not equally evident in the text: "the language of these Egyptians resembled very closely that which is every day to be heard amongst the least educated portions of our own neighbours in and about this metropolis."[38]

Drury Lane challenged *Spirits of the Moon* with its own *Zoroaster; or, The Spirit of the Star* by W. T. Moncrieff. In an attempt to outdo Covent Garden's Easter Monday Egyptian spectacle, Elliston squeezed additional sights and tricks into *Zoroaster*'s thin story line. The production included a moving panorama painted by Clarkson Stanfield, the Eidophusikon, that was advertised as 482 feet (147 metres) long (presumably surpassing Grieve's Polemporeremoporokinetikon in the length of its canvas if not its title). When *Zoroaster* was later published, four pages were devoted to describing the various scenes of the panorama and Pietre van der Merwe argues that it took at least half an hour to be shown with its musical interpolations and stationary moments.[39] In *Zoroaster*, ancient sorcery similarly results in internment. Characters were magically transported to the center of the Earth, characters dropped suddenly through traps, an earthquake buried the palace, and once again a character was imprisoned in a pyramid and left to die. (This production also featured a battle between the armies of Egypt and Ethiopia, so *Zoroaster* anticipated two of *Aida*'s plot details.)

Despite the fancifulness of this and Moncrieff's other orientalist plays, the author made a show of his research. When critics attacked his *The Cataract of the Ganges or the Rajah's Daughter* the year before (Drury Lane 1823) for a "lamentable ignorance of Hindoo manners," the author responded angrily in the preface for the published play. Moncrieff cited Alexander Dow's *The History of Hindostan* (translated from the Persian of Firishta), Thomas Maurice's *Indian Antiquities*, and "M'Cormic" who wrote on "female Infanticide" for verification of the events depicted in his play. While *Zoroaster*'s image of imprisonment in a pyramid hardly strikes the modern reader as scholarly, this plot detail was in fact based on Belzoni's recent discovery. It was the scene painting, however, that most invoked scholarly authority. The first four scenes of Stanfield's panorama – The Great Desert by Twilight and Arab Encampment, A Caravan of Merchants, The Pyramids and the Colossal Head of the Sphinx, and The Great Temple of Apollinopolis – were all painted from Denon, a fact that was announced in both the playbill and reviews. *The Drama* described the panorama as "far surpassing any thing of the sort ever witnessed" and asserted that its depiction of "nature and art," particularly in the production's use of dioramic lighting, were "gradually depicted in the 'most natural manner imaginable.' "[40] The combination of highly realistic scene painting, illusionistic lighting effects, veiled references to Belzoni, and a publicized reliance on Denon combined to reassure audiences that an accurate recreation of the East supported the fantastic events depicted.

In *Zoroaster* and *Spirits of the Moon*, as in other Eastern gothic productions, assertions of antiquarian research were little more than window dressing for stage magic and magnificent scenery. However, it was vital window dressing in that it grounded flights of fancy in a larger project of knowing. These plays produced an inscrutable East at the same time as they referenced Europe's success at pulling back the East's shroud of mystery. They produced inaccessible crypts so as to celebrate the British men who had dared penetrate the occult East and transport its riches.

BRITISH BEDOUINS

Just as Kean had been drawn to the Canadian wilds, a number of British in the early years of the nineteenth century ventured into once inaccessible Eastern deserts (albeit with less theatricalism). Increased safety of travel in Ottoman regions combined with the difficulty of European travel during the Napoleonic campaigns prompted a growing number of Eastern voyages and inspired some Britons to venture into Levantine deserts. In the eighteenth century, a play like John Brown's *Barbarossa* could evoke Eastern wilds with the simple reference to the "Arab's wand'ring tent" (II.ii). Nineteenth-century theatre provided more detailed depictions and noted the authority on whom such details were based. In the process, the desert became a rich image in the romantic imagination whether or not a work was set in the East. When Byron's Manfred describes his own self-destructive nature, for example, he finds no more compelling comparison than "the red-hot breadth of the most lone simoom" that sweeps along the "barren sands" (III.i.128,130). Stage technology followed. By 1847, Edward Fitzball's *The Desert; or, The Imanns Daughter* at Drury Lane could depict a sandstorm burying characters alive, prompting the *Illustrated London News* to announce that "We have never seen anything better managed than the flying clouds of sand during the Simoom at the end of the first act."[41]

Romantic orientalism's new reliance on first-hand accounts is exemplified by Colonel Ralph Hamilton's *Elphi Bey; or, the Arab's Faith* (Drury Lane 1817). According to the *Theatrical Inquisitor and Monthly Mirror*, the play was based on an incident taken from the travels of Lord Valentia. More significantly, the journal explains that the antiquarian and Eastern traveler, Henry Salt, selected the incident and even "furnished the sketches from which [the production's] scenery has been prepared."[42] Salt accompanied Valentia on his travels and provided the illustrations for Valentia's *Voyages and Travels to India, Ceylon, the Red Sea, Abyssinia, and Egypt* (1809). Salt's other orientalist publications include *Views of St. Helena and Egypt* (1809) and *Voyage to Abyssinia* (1814), and he was appointed Consul-General in Egypt in 1815. During his tenure as Consul-General, Salt employed Belzoni to collect antiquities which Salt then sold to the British Museum at a large profit (most notably the colossal bust of Rameses II, which inspired Shelley to write *Ozymandias*). *Elphi Bey* was not Salt's first collaboration for the entertainment industry; the 1809 panorama of Grand Cairo at Leicester Square was advertised as "painted from Mr. Salt's Drawings taken on the spot for Lord Valentia."[43]

Elphi Bey featured a range of picturesque settings that were becoming familiar thanks to volumes by antiquarians such as Salt. Not only do the stage directions call for "A camp between Giza and the Pyramids which are seen in the distance" and "A platform in the citadel with a gateway partly overlooking the walls [with a distant view of] the ancient aqueduct and a reach of the Nile," but the script also specified camels and horses in the scenes of desert life. Scholarly authority and all the resources of the stage were marshaled to convince audiences that they witnessed authentic pictures of the East. The play paraded its correctness of costume, as when a comic servant, seeing an opportunity to rescue his compatriots from the usurping chief (a seemingly necessary plot device in these plays), announces, "To cheat such scoundrels as these does me more good than to feast on a young kid with cloves and raisins after that terrible month's fasting in Rhamazan."[44] Reviewing the published version of the play, the *Theatrical Inquisitor* suggested that the comic servant "must have been nearly unintelligible to the good gallery-folks, with his local references to a 'calishe,' an 'ibis,' a 'Santon,' and 'melons on a sand-drift.'" The reviewer also complained that simple stage directions had become an opportunity to introduce extraneous ethnographic detail, and requested "a plainer stage-direction than 'bending to Zeinaba, with their Salam, in token of obedience.'"[45]

This was not the first time that the *Theatrical Inquisitor* complained of the unnecessary introduction of Arab customs and transliterations. Three years earlier, the journal expressed the hope that the excessive exotic flourish of J. H. Reynolds's *Sophie* would "induce Walter Scott, Lord Byron, Southey and their imitators, either to abandon altogether the childish attempt to give effect by the introduction of foreign names and epitaphs, or, for the sake of consistency, at once to write their poems in the language of that country the manners and scenery of which they profess to delineate."[46] Regardless of the journal's opinion, "foreign names and epitaphs" continued to attract both "gallery-folk" and popular readers, as evidenced by the fact that John Murray (Byron's publisher) offered *Elphi Bey* in an octavo version at a mere two shillings and sixpence.

Elphi Bey painted a picture of noble desert Arabs, complementing the thin plot with a range of questionable details on the customs of East. As the subtitle suggests, the plot turned on "the Arab's faith," the Bedouin custom of aiding anyone who claims protection in their tents. As one sheik explained:

> ...the man whom most we hate
> Gaining our tents, defenceless and oppress'd
> Our faith preserves... (ii.iii)

This nobility is linked to the primitiveness of Bedouin life:

> Our lot the desert and the mountain heights.
> Rude are our habits – lose and uncontrol'd –
> But smiling independence glads our tribes
> By vigorous toil and manly courage fostered.
> (ii.iii)

City-dwellers are viewed with suspicion, as "men without hearts, enslaved by luxury" (i.ii). Here, simplicity and nobility emerge as nearly identical attributes, and are contrasted with the material values fostered in an urban setting. Through the desert sheik, audiences could temporarily reject the conditions of modernity.

The production did not apparently live up to the text's careful delineation of Arab customs and manners. The *Theatrical Inquisitor* complained that "the gentlemen of the chorus had the arms of Negroes and the faces of Europeans; some wore mustachios, and some neckcloths, and the same scene is placed at the back of the Arab tent of Chedid [a Bedouin sheik], which terminates a view of the abode of Elphi." The introduction of a wealth of detail into the text presumably made the inconsistency of the staging that much more glaring. As the journal explained, this concern over a few inconsistencies "may appear trifling, but so much of the successful illusion of the theatre depends on them that they become of first-rate importance, and should be attended to accordingly."[47] Antiquarian research had been lavished on doggerel and a shoddy production. A later review of *Elphi Bey* in the *Theatrical Inquisitor* complained, "To the science and research of Mr. Salt, *cum grano salis*, we award their attributed honours, and merely lament that so much erudition has been wasted upon frivolity."[48]

The stage desert maintained a tenuous link to the "real" desert through the erudition of the antiquarian traveler. Somewhere beneath the European mustaches, mismatching scene painting, and overly obsequious transliterations, there remained Henry Salt's encounter with the exotic. It was not simply that the Arabian desert was vast and impressive, or that the Bedouin preserved a primitivism that had disappeared in Europe, but that in encountering this desert or studying the Bedouin the traveler rediscovered a cultural authenticity threatened by European modernity, an authenticity somehow preserved in an architectural fragment or native costume. Here one discerns the romantic's peculiar relation to the exotic as well as the underlying romantic attitude of orientalist projects at the start of the century. Correctness of costume was precisely that, a costume. One did not simply enumerate ethnographic details; one wore them like the Albanian costume that Byron brought back from his travels and donned for Phillips's portrait. It was not enough to study the ancient past, it had to be unearthed and preserved in one's study or – slightly more generously – at the British Museum. The desire for detailed costumes, properties, and scene painting in theatrical orientalism is not simply evidence of a preordained march towards realism, but the crisis of authenticity that lies at the heart of romanticism. In a perverse way, the large-scale removal of Eastern antiquities was evidence of Europe's growing desire for an imaginative engagement with the exotic.

Antiquarianism's fetishization of architectural fragments reflects the same essentialism that informed the cross-racial performances of Kean and Byron. The essence of a people is thought to reside in the ancient frieze or native costume, and through its possession the antiquarian shows a special affinity for this other (more authentic) state of being. Consequently, the retrieved object or term could be presented in isolation with its significance intact; historically accurate costumes could appear in the most outrageous of orientalist spectacles without any sense of disjuncture. Given the prevalence of harem and crypt imagery in depictions of the East, and the widespread belief that fantastic tales like the *Arabian Nights* offered "a real presentation of the manners in Turkey" (as Lady Montague enthused),[49] it is not surprising that antiquarian research was lavished on magical tales filled with supposed Eastern sensuality.

In no production is the mixture of antiquarian research, harem imagery, and fantasy as striking as in *Oberon; or, The Elf King's Oath*, the Carl Maria von Weber opera with libretto by J. R. Planché which premiered at Covent Garden in 1826. Christoph Martin Wieland's poem *Oberon* enjoyed considerable popularity in Britain (via Sotheby's 1798 translation) and has been described as a primary influence on British romanticism.[50] *Oberon* was a reworking of the medieval French epic, *Huon de Bordeaux* (with the addition of a motivating quarrel between Oberon and Titania, the work's only connection to Shakespeare). Set in Charlemagne's court, Baghdad, and Tunis, and including Shakespeare's fairies, Wieland's poem combined various elements that would become popular in romantic literature, such as its medieval and oriental subject matter, its emphasis on a chivalric code, its exotic settings, and its magical occurrences. Considering this mix of popular features it is not surprising that there were at least four different stage adaptations of the poem between 1800 and 1826.

The first adaptation, *The Magic Flute; or, Harlequin Champion*, was an equestrian pantomime at the Royal Circus staged in 1800. (The production substituted an enchanted flute for Wieland's magical horn, but it has no other relation to the Mozart opera.) Advertisements for the production stressed its medieval setting, explaining that the production was "fixed during the Reign of Emperor Charlemagne" and that costumes were copied from "correct Drawings of the Costume of the Times." Among the many scenes listed in this advertisement were "a Turkish Cottage," "Exterior and Interior of the Sultan's Seraglio" and "a Mahometan Mausoleum."[51] This mix of medieval and Eastern settings was also evident in the second adaptation, Drury Lane's 1816 production, *Oberon's Oath; or, the Paladin and the Princess*. Drury Lane produced an additional version of *Oberon* in 1826, rushing out a hugely elaborate production weeks before the Weber and Planché opera. At both minor and patent theatres, exoticism and medievalism were a means to elaborate spectacle that simultaneously claimed a certain scholarly respectability.

Antiquarian research reached new heights in J. R. Planché's libretto for the Covent Garden *Oberon*. Planché is noted in histories of British theatre for designing historically accurate costumes for an 1823 production of *King John*, research that would eventually lead to his election as a Fellow of the Society of Antiquarians in 1829 and his publication of *The History of British Costume* in 1834. With *Oberon*, Planché branched into orientalist research; the published script included seven content notes explaining Arabic terms and customs, citing authorities such as Simon Ockley and Barthélemy d'Herbelot. Attention was given to both medieval and Eastern costumes. The elaborate description for Charlemagne's costume concluded with the explanation that it was taken from "a contemporary representation of that monarch receiving the consecrated banner from Pope Leo" as described in Montfauçon, Sherasmin's cap was described as "resembling the ancient Phrygian," and the Caliph Haroun was said to wear "the black burdah or gown of the prophet."[52] "Burdah" is in fact an accurate transliteration of the Arabic term specifically denoting Muhammad's outer garment. The script even aspires to a certain racial specificity, distinguishing between the black and white slaves and eunuchs. These descriptions bring the reader no closer to imagining what the costumes looked like, nor do they even refer to a single time period. Instead, they are intended to reveal Planché's deep immersion into distant worlds, inviting the reader to similarly contemplate the old and exotic fragments that Planché has unearthed.

These learned references complemented extravagant depictions of fairy magic. In a scene that culminates when Sir Huon blows on a magical horn to freeze his enemies, Planché pauses to explain that when the chorus speaks of the "shadow and the night" it is in fact a reference to the traditional banners of the Abbasid Caliphs. Planché's use of scholarly detail in the midst of fantasy was hardly an anomaly in the theatre of the day: in the following year an antiquarian production of *Cymbeline* prompted one reviewer to complain, "We expect to next see legitimate authority produced for the dressing of Puck, and authenticated wings allotted to Mustardseed."[53]

While tongue-in-cheek, the quotation in fact captures a salient feature of the antiquarian stage. The combination of fairies with historical, philological, or ethnographic research was not simply permissible on the antiquarian stage, this mix was in fact the essence of antiquarianism. At the heart of the antiquarian impulse was a flight from the present, a desire for an imaginative encounter with distant places and distant times as mediated through an individual detail or object retrieved from this longed-for beyond. The authenticity of a stage image was measured by its apparent remove from the features of modernity.

Oriental sex featured prominently in this vision of anti-modernity, and Planché's libretto was no exception. The story details how Sir Huon abducts and weds Reiza, daughter of the Caliph Haroun Alraschid, with the help of fairy magic. (Harun al-Raschid is the eight-century caliph who figures prominently in the *Arabian Nights*.) The libretto calls for the elaborate display of Eastern women, first when Reiza is discovered behind a "veiled portal," herself "veiled and richly attired," proceeded by a train of dancing girls, and followed by the slaves of the harem (ii.i). Later, the libretto grows more suggestive after Reiza has been imprisoned in the harem of the Emir of Tunis. Hoping to find Reiza, Huon is guided to the harem by a female slave. The "rich curtains" in the back of a darkened stage "fly open and discover a recess illuminated, in which Roshana [the Emir's neglected wife] is reclining, covered with a rich veil." Huon rushes forward and the veil is thrown off, revealing his mistake. He withstands Roshana's seductions and refuses her entreaties that he kill the Emir, despite her assertion that:

The passions of the daughters of Africa burn as fiercely as the sun which blaze over them. Two of the wildest rage within my bosom – vengeance and love. Nerve thine arm, Christian, to gratify the first – the latter shall reward thee beyond thy most sanguine wishes. (iii.iv)

When Huon still resists, Roshana claps her hands, summoning "a troop of dancing girls and female slaves, richly attired" who surround him offering him flowers and rushing to block his exit.

Planché's description of African passions burning like the African sun echoes Hazlitt's review of Edmund Kean's performance as one of "the untamed children of the sun whose blood drinks up the radiance of fierce skies" in Young's *Revenge*. Here, however, this appetite is not simply for "vengeance" but for what is euphemistically termed "love." The (repeatedly) veiled figure is illuminated against an otherwise darkened stage, forestalling the inevitable revelation of the odalisque who, by definition, is secluded from public view. The theatre brings "a fine vision to the standard of flesh and blood," as Lamb would put it. The spectacle of illicit caresses, which Lamb found so revolting in *Othello*, is dramatically staged in *Oberon*; by Roshana's own assessment, Huon would be "more or less than a man" if he withstood the temptation of the Eastern queen with her dancing girls and female slaves. Planché's fantasy of miscegenation was repeated in the numerous harem abductions of the romantic stage. Their mix of fantasy and research muted the potential to offend. More importantly for the acceptability of such scenes, it was a white *man* who caressed the exotic. The theatrical harem depicted Eastern women as lustful, indolent, violent, and – paradoxically – subject to male domination, creating a dangerous but titillating terrain for the Western adventurer. In *Oberon*, the Christian knight remains true to his Baghdadi love despite the wiles of the Tunisian Roshana, reinforcing a newly sharpened hierarchy of race that distinguished between Northern Africa and the lands of the Euphrates. To paraphrase Lamb, in matters of race ours is a more perfect state of knowledge respecting foreign countries.

The scene painters depicted the cities of the East in lavish and ornate detail, finding an architectural equivalent to the theatrical harem. In the synecdochic logic of the stage, Eastern women defined the East. The production featured sixteen different settings, all of them newly painted, according to the playbills, and twelve of which were set in Baghdad and Tunis. Thomas, William, and John Henderson Grieve – the painters under whose tenure Covent Garden would become renowned for its scenic beauty – painted the majority of these scenes. Their work was singled out for combining the picturesque with accuracy:

The scenery is extremely beautiful; it displays a great deal of happy invention, especially in Messrs. Grieve. The view of the port of Ascalon is one of the most grand and picturesque representations we ever saw. The distant view of Baghdad is also excellent. The scenes of interior palaces are splendid beyond description, while the colouring is so judiciously laid on, that the most gaudy scene is rich without being offensive to the eye. The hall and gallery in Almanzor's [the Tunisian Emir] palace is a beautiful piece of Eastern architecture.[54]

The Grieves sketches and watercolors give some indication what it means to present a "beautiful piece of Eastern architecture" that is "rich without being offensive to the eye." A pencil and wash of the port of Ascalon is notable for its grandeur and richly intricate detail. The city vista is composed of repeating sets of tapering towers topped with spired onion domes and buttressed by elaborate ogival arches, but nowhere does one spy doors or

2.10 Grieve's sketch for Ascalon in *Oberon*, 1826

windows (Fig. 2.10). One is struck by the elaborate ornamentation of the structures, by their magnitude, and – more than anything else – by their purposelessness. The imaginary Islamic city, like the harem, was delivered in its superfluity. It was an antiquary's haven – a land of minute, intricate, picturesque, and purposeless detail – splendid beyond description but never offensive to the eye.

Scene painting and performance styles in the romantic period employed a wealth of detail in order to prompt emotional investment in an imaginary space outside of modernity. In theatrical orientalism, such details served as nodes of contemplation, enabling fantasies of immersion into a feminine East. Eastern reproductions, from Moorish face-paint to renderings of pyramids, transported audiences and enabled identification with the exotic. This was a theatre of talismans not of material culture. The theatre was yet to discover that one could trace out patterns of behavior in the selection and arrangement of commonplace objects. Exotic details could still induce wonder. However, the pleasure and power of these details resided in the narrow zone between recognition and familiarity. Once Eastern products appear in shops like Liberty's, their status as commercial objects becomes too apparent; they lose their position outside of modernity as well as their power to transport. The process had already begun during the romantic period. With prescient cynicism, Byron himself alluded to the temptation to dash off "A Grecian, Syrian, or Assyrian tale; / And sell you, mix'd with western sentimentalism, / Some of the finest Orientalism!" (*Beppo* 51. 6–8). With the proliferation of travel narratives and the growing number of antiquities available in illustrated folios and exhibitions, the introduction of foreign names and epitaphs in dialogue and the use of exotic details in scene painting ceased to "give effect."

Which brings me to my final example of theatrical orientalism from the romantic period, a remarkable trifle that reveals a certain exhaustion with the simple accumulation of exotica on the London stage. A. L. Campbell's *The Demon of the Desert; or, The Well of Palms* (Sadler's Wells 1829) contained many of the elements of romantic orientalism: a smattering of Arabic and Turkish terms and names, a scene in a Cairo Bazaar, a preponderance of veiled women and female slaves, random exotic details in the scene painting (the stage directions for the opening scene call for "a few huts belonging to a Kraal, *or* some Pyramids" – my italics), differentiation between Arabs and "black Arabs," and a demon who makes frequent use of the theatre's traps and elevators to spectacular effect. The production even appears to have invoked Byron. One of the play's characters, "Haidee," was presumably named after the Greek girl who rescues Don Juan.

The hackneyed and inaccurate use of exotica in *The Demon of the Desert* – one Bedouin girl praised her "wandering life, free as the deer that bounds across the desert" – makes the play's parody of London's display culture all the more striking. *The Demon of the Desert* featured two English antiquity hunters who scoured the desert in search of "marble noses and agate fingers" and explored the bazaar collecting "extraordinary curiosities" for importation. The younger was trained by "one of the first professors in the kingdom," a philologist, expert in "Greek, Latin, Hebrew, Persian, Chaldean, Gentoo, Arabic, English, French, Spanish, Italian, Dutch, Welsh, Scotch, and Irish," and all sciences ending in "ology" until he was transported to Australia for being a pickpocket. The antiquity hunters found themselves in increasingly worse straits until threatened with death, the elder announced that "If ever I come antiquity-hunting again, I wish they may stuff me before I am dead, and shew me about as a living mummy."[55]

In *The Demon of the Desert* we arrive at the limits of romantic strategies for staging authenticity. The theatre amassed isolated details, such as obscure Arabic terms in the text or exotic monuments on the flats. However, as long as productions did not explore the cultural significance of such details, their interest was simply a function of their rarity. As more "marble noses" came onto the market, Eastern "curiosities" ceased to live up to their name. The sciences of collecting – whether focused on antiquities, languages, or other people's pocket watches – threatened to become mere pilfering at best and an unnatural fetish at worst. In such a light, the "scholars" who transported monuments from the East did in fact bear a resemblance to the individuals who were themselves transported east to Australia. The humor of the philologist in the penal colony was in part premised on the audience's recognition that useless objects had been exchanged for a useless body. The stigma of antiquarianism would only be dispelled in the theatre with the idea that an actor's interaction with an environment of details communicated larger meanings. Until then, the most one could do was wear an affinity with the ancient and exotic in the garnering of superficial detail, to make of oneself a kind of "living mummy." Without the concept of material culture the entertainment industry was incapable of staging the systems of exotic life. However, such an understanding did not emerge in the theatre until after it was disseminated in popular exhibitions.

CHAPTER 3

The built-out East of popular ethnography

Authenticity in romantic theatre resided, by and large, in language, painting, and costume; there was as yet no concept that an individual's interaction
with a surrounding environment could carry the marks of authenticity. The
idea of authentic *behavior* did not become prominent in popular entertainment until mid-century when a series of popular exhibitions promised to
reproduce Eastern environments and the characteristic behavior that tran-
spired therein. From rational amusements, such as "The Oriental and
Turkish Museum" of 1854 to seemingly crass amusements, such as the Arab
serpent-charmers who performed at the Regent's Park Zoo in 1850, entertainment venues promised insight into how Orientals went about their daily
lives. While these examples of display would appear to point in opposite
directions – one looking forward to museum displays of the representative,
the other looking back to fairground displays of the strange and exotic –
they actually shared a common vocabulary and a similar ambivalence towards Eastern bodies. Both exhibitions and human displays reflected a new
ethnographic world-view that transformed exotic bodies into documents
of cultural practice; both similarly reflected an imperial world-view that
interpreted these documents in relation to Britain's new military and economic interests; and both perpetuated older tropes of exotic display that
defined the East as an over-sensual odalisque. By placing the emergence
of what has been called "museum culture" in the context of contemporary
human displays, and within the tradition of theatrical orientalism, one sees
both a continuing ambivalence towards the perceived engrossing materiality of the exotic and new strategies for containing and even employing this
materiality.

HUMAN DISPLAY BEFORE 1851

The tradition of displaying exotic people in London extends well before the
Victorian period; however, the meaning of such display changed radically

in this period. From the middle of the sixteenth century onward, American and African natives were regularly featured in London exhibitions.[1] These peoples were invariably advertised as fantastic and unusual. Far from asserting the characteristic nature of the displayed peoples, showmen more often asserted that their natives were noblemen or paragons of savage conceptions of beauty. Moreover, the uniqueness of the displayed person was not attributed to their behavior or customs. The Inuit displayed by Captain George Cartwright in 1772 continued to attract crowds even after trading their skin dresses for broadcloth. The Tahitian youth, Omai, who was brought to London after Cook's second voyage, was lauded precisely for his ability to adopt European dress and social manners. Whether displayed peoples were presented as noble savages or as distinct species (as would increasingly be the case) they were valued for a rarity that was defined as immanent to their person. By the Victorian period, however, the objectives and strategies of display had changed. As Tony Bennett notes, collections in this period "were rearranged in accordance with the principle of *representativeness* rather than that of *rarity*."[2] No longer was the collection a place for displaying the wondrous. Instead, the collection served to reveal the structure of the natural world and social institutions through the careful manipulation of commonplace objects. In other words, the collection illuminated the rule and not the exception. As Barbara Kirshenblatt-Gimblett argues, nineteenth-century natural historians "were interested in taxonomies of the normal, not in singularities of chance formation."[3]

The example of Omai is a particularly interesting example of the eighteenth-century interest in exotic peoples because his story inspired a spectacular pantomime at Covent Garden in 1785. *Omai; or, A Trip Around the World* was path-breaking in its use of first-hand accounts as sources for the scene painting but also in its attention to what would be later called ethnographic detail. De Loutherbourg was said to have based his scene paintings for this production on drawings and prints by John Webber and William Hodges, who accompanied Cook.[4] Even more unusual at this early date, the printed libretto included thirty-two notes explaining native terms, geography, and practices. The pantomime opened with a character supplicating a native god with a food offering, and in a later scene, stage directions asserted that the singing and dancing depicted "the Manner of the Natives." However, the air that followed was anything but Tahitian:

> Give me thy paw, my bonny bonny bear
> And here come dip they muzzle;
> Tho' a good warm coat thy back doth wear,

> When tempests blow
> The drifted snow
> Oh that's the time for a merry sup.
>
> (II.ii)

Here, exotic markers frame traditional theatrical fare with the unlikely spectacle of islanders singing about "bonny" bears in winter.

Despite the implied claim of accurate depictions of Tahitians, the pantomime actually juxtaposed the noble savage (in repeated references to Omai's dignity) with familiar blackface imagery, as when Omai's Tahitian companion sings about his experience in London:

> But dis lady fine
> Call me ugly divil
> Guinea, glass of wine,
> Den so sweet and civil;
> In her spousy jump
> As of kiss I beg her,
> Give my head de tump
> Cry, get out dam Negar.
>
> (II.vi)

The inclusion of ethnographic detail appears motivated by the demand for spectacle rather than interest in the "manner of natives." The opening supplication, for example, not only produced a sudden blaze and the desired native god, but an allegorical depiction of "Britannia." Even greater splendor was evident in the closing procession of "Deputies from the different quarters of the globe that have been visited by Capt. Cook," all dressed in picturesque costumes. The procession seemed less interested in illustrating customs than the expansiveness informing Britannia's opening assertion, "Still my sons, by Cook's example taught, / Thy new-found world protect and humanize."

In this sense, *Omai* acts as a kind of imperial cabinet of curiosities. Details were not selected with the intent of elucidating their context but of providing a marvelous picture of the strange and varied worlds being "humanized" by Britain's sea exploration. The fact that this august project was seen as compatible with blackface performance reveals the profound ambivalence that accompanied such racial contact. Ambivalence would remain a constant feature of racial depictions in the entertainment industry into the nineteenth century, as the incompatible projects of glorifying British expansion and conjuring the innate nobility of primitives were further complicated by increasingly strong images of the exotic world as a space of sexual freedom or licentious immorality. In the Victorian period, new ethnographic, economic, and imperial interests would reframe such depictions, changing their meanings and objectives but without reconciling this underlying ambivalence.

Early in the nineteenth century, native peoples began to be displayed as performers rather than spectacles in and of themselves. This change reflected an emerging interest in what exotics *did* versus what exotics *were*. In responses to these performances, one can detect a slow transition from interest in the rare to interest in the representative. According to John Whale, "Troupes of [Indian] jugglers made frequent visits to London in the first two decades of the century" and scored "spectacular successes, playing to enthusiastic crowds in Pall Mall and in popular theatres such as the Olympic."[5] At this same time, some theatres began to publicize native performance as a feature of their orientalist productions. The Adelphi Theatre advertised a "Deema Dance" in its "new Divertisement called MAHOMET" and the Olympic Theatre announced that: "The celebrated Deema Dance will be performed for the first time during the Pantomime by a native Mahometan."[6] Despite the apparent concern for authenticity, there is no evidence that such performances were valued for any ethnographic information they might impart. Instead, the reviews of Indian jugglers cited by Whale exclusively focus on the novelty and mechanical skill of the performers.

By contrast, William Hazlitt's essay, "The Indian Jugglers," transformed the exotic performer into an object of aesthetic contemplation, an opportunity to compare acts of mechanical perfection with the imperfect productions of art. The essay passes from awe at the jugglers' precision, to shame for the absence of perfection in Hazlitt's own endeavors, to the realization that art's imperfectibility stems from the fact that "the more ethereal, evanescent, more refined and sublime part of art is the seeing nature through the medium of sentiment and passion, as each object is a symbol of the affections and a link in the chain of our endless being."[7] Finally, the essay concludes with a transcription of Hazlitt's earlier obituary for "John Cavanagh, the famous hand fives-player." The movement of the piece is successively further from the subject of its title, a process of abstraction that might be motivated by the Indian jugglers but is distinctly the province of writers like Hazlitt. The concluding transcription serves as "a test case for distinguishing the artist from the mechanic," in the words of David Bromwich. Bromwich explains: "The truth is that only Hazlitt's ability to see depth of art in the surface of mechanical skill . . . has made the question an interesting one. The practiced eye more than finds, it invents the glory of the things that concern it."[8]

Similarly, the use of authentic detail in romantic orientalism was often read as evidence of the poet's discernment. In doing so these texts also invoked the changing power dynamic that made such Eastern resources available for poetic manufacture. Nigel Leask notes that Francis Jeffrey's review of Moore's *Lalla Rookh* praised the poem for its judicious blend of exotic detail with appropriate poetic Western passions. Leask explains:

The standards being erected for oriental poetry in the Romantic period... depended upon the colonization of diverse or "primitive" cultural forms by a universalized (i.e. European) moral imperative, the literary analogue of the developing style of colonial and capitalist domination of non-European markets.[9]

Oriental material could potentially produce wonder if simply displayed, but the poet's objective was instead to mold and combine these naïve forms to produce – to elaborate on Hazlitt – an ethereal, evanescent, refined, and sublime artistic whole in which objects reveal human passions and the larger chain of being.

As Leask implies, such Eastern raw material was invariably marked by its "Easterness" and never became neutral fodder for artistic creation. This is apparent in Hazlitt's "The Indian Jugglers." According to John Whale, while the essay enacts "a familiar Romantic preference for the unseen over the seen, the visionary over the visual," the bodies of the jugglers, as a sign of the East, inevitably obtrude into the scene of Hazlitt's meditation; "he never quite cuts himself free from mimesis" as his analysis returns to the Indianness of the performers.[10] In a desire to differentiate the apparent success or failure in mechanical skills from the ambiguous validity of opinion, Hazlitt writes:

If the Juggler were told that by flinging himself under the wheels of the Juggernaut, when this idol issues forth on a gaudy day, he would immediately be transported into Paradise, he might believe it, and nobody could disprove it. So the Brahmans may say what they please on that subject, may build up dogmas and mysteries without end, and not be detected: but their ingenious countryman cannot persuade the frequenters of the Olympic Theatre that he performs a number of astonishing feats without actually giving proofs of what he says.[11]

Rather than citing this intrusion of Indianness as the collapse of contemplation, I would argue that it actually becomes the impetus for two opposing lines of imaginative reflection, both of which begin with mimesis but progress into abstraction: the nature of artistic creation and the persistence of superstition in Indian belief systems.

The implicit idea that native performance clarified cultural practice grew more explicit in reviews from the Victorian period. For example, the Moroccan tumblers who performed at the Victoria Theatre in 1843 were praised for their "national dances," according to a review in the *Illustrated London News*.[12] A print accompanying the review shows that the performers wore native costumes. The review catalogued their attributes as if the performers were being offered for sale: the twelve tumblers range "from maturity to boyhood: the majority are stoutly framed but two or three are slightly made; and all have extraordinary suppleness of frame and limb." Here were not simply marvelous feats but a balanced presentation of Moroccan physiology and manners.

Interest in the history of native performance and its relation to traditional activities and knowledge was a marked feature of the *Illustrated London News* review of the two Egyptian snake-charmers who performed at the Regent's Park Zoo in 1850. The paper gave considerable background on the performers, explaining that they were of the Rufaiah tribe, "who hand down the mystery of serpent-charming from father to son." These snake-charmers, according to the paper, considered Rufia as the "founder of their craft," and he "appears to be a Mussulman saint." From here the paper segued into native beliefs, explaining that the tomb of Rufia still exists in the vicinity of Busrah, that it is frequently visited by pilgrims, and that Rufia's spirit is said to control the many serpents that infest his tomb, forbidding them from injuring pilgrims. The paper gave due honors to its native informant; in addition to being the "father of the profession," the elder performer, Jabar Abou Haijab, was said to be "conversant with snake-lore from his earliest youth" and acted as a "collector" to the French savants during Napoleon's invasion. The native performer was transformed into a collector of "lore," communicating to his Western audience the traditional mysteries (handed down from father to son) as well as the specifics of religious practices and beliefs.

Only about half of the review was devoted to a description of the performance, and it then included informative comments such as the fact that the erect position the serpents take "is common to the Egyptian and Indian species" and provided a transliteration of the Arabic term for cobra. The description concluded with comparative analysis – "The practice of serpent-charming among the Arabs appears to differ essentially from that of the Hindoos" – and implied that the antiquity of snake-charming is documented in religious sources – "It is certainly as old as the time of Mohammed, and probably derives its origin from a period of the most remote antiquity." The paper's accompanying illustration was remarkably untheatrical and seems much less concerned with capturing the performance than with delineating the clothing and physique of the performers (Fig. 3.1).[13] This attention to costume was even greater in a later illustration

3.1 Snake-charmers at Regent's Park Zoo from the *Illustrated London News* 15 June 1850

when one of the performers reappeared in the pages of the paper in 1854, this time as the attendant for the Zoo's Hippopotamus.[14] In the 1854 illustration he wore a much more elaborate costume, with turban, vest, and sash. Without a skill to demonstrate, it would appear, clothing had to do more of the work of signaling the absent cultural context. Far from being striking in their own right, the behavior and appearance of natives traced out regional practices and beliefs.

The use of the term "lore" in the paper's review is salient, as only four years earlier, the antiquarian, William John Thoms, had coined the term "Folk-lore" in a letter to the editors of the *Athenaeum*. Thoms, writing under the pseudonym Ambrose Merton, wrote to suggest that the paper devote a regular column to folklore, or "what we in England designate as

Popular Antiquities, or Popular Literature."[15] In his letter to the *Athenaeum*, Thoms began by situating the study of "the manners, customs, observances, superstitions, ballads, proverbs &c.., of the olden time" as a typically anti-quarian project of rescuing what would soon be "entirely lost." However, on taking up Grimm's *Deutsche Mythologie* (1844), Thoms explained that the apparently "trifling and insignificant" details of popular antiquity, "when taken in connexion with the system into which [Grimm's] master-mind has woven them, assume a value that he who first recorded them never dreamed of attributing to them." Thoms became editor of the *Athenaeum's* new department of "Folk-lore" and in subsequent issues outlined, accord-ing to Richard M. Dorson, a folklore methodology that included "direct field observation, accurate reporting, communication of specific data, and then the comparative commentary by 'Merton,' if this were beyond the resources of the writer, tracing the custom or notion to its heathen lair with the aid of Grimm and the English antiquaries."[16] "Folk-lore" transformed the mere collection of popular antiquities into a rigorous science, a means of exploring the persistence and transformation of ideas and practices across regions and centuries. As opposed to the simple adulation of antiquity, the folklorist looked through fragments to grasp their larger value. In much the same way, the *Illustrated London News* suggested that the serpent-charmers at Regent's Park Zoo provided insight into Egypt's pre-Islamic past as well as the transmission of practices across the East.

The emergence of ethnology in this period also contributed to the new interest in human display. Though the term "ethnology" was probably coined in the 1830s, London's Ethnological Society was not founded until 1843. According to an early-twentieth-century account, the Ethnological Society formed out of a split within the Aboriginal Protection Society be-tween a "student party, which wished to study native races sympathetically" and a "missionary party, which wished to protect [Aboriginal] rights and bestow on them forthwith the privileges of European civilization."[17] This "student party" formed the Ethnological Society, and in 1846 the organi-zation obtained the status of a sub-section in the Botany–Zoology Section of the British Association. By 1848 it was sufficiently established to be-gin publishing its own *Journal*.[18] During this time, the Ethnology Society evidenced little interest in what we would now call "material culture," hav-ing retained the Aboriginal Protection Society's focus on philology. The Protection Society's primary intellectual mission, and one retained by early ethnologists, such as James Cowles Prichard, was to establish a common history of humanity in opposition to theories of polygenism through philo-logical research.

Despite the limited mass appeal of the Ethnological Society's philological focus, the idea of ethnology developed a wide currency at mid-century. The British Museum reorganized its collection of Natural and Artificial Curiosities as an "Ethnological Gallery" in 1845, in part as a response to suggestions by ethnologists such as Robert Latham and Ernest Dieffenbach.[19] Then, in 1850, the Ethnological Society succeeded in establishing a separate Section for Geography and Ethnology in the British Association. In this linkage, one can read an implicit reorienting of ethnology as an imperial science. Like geography, ethnology's data would be increasingly generated in the shadow of colonialism, in the diaries of soldiers and colonial administrators – and, as such, shared in the glory of empire. Moreover, like geography, ethnology began to reflect a new interest in the evolution of human populations. The single greatest impetus to the dissemination of this more popular ethnology came in 1851 when London staged the Great Exhibition of the Works of Industry of All Nations at Hyde Park in a giant glass and iron building commonly known as the Crystal Palace.

THE EXHIBITION YEAR

When the Great Exhibition presented Eastern crafts and raw materials to the London public, London's panorama halls and pleasure gardens responded with displays of actual Eastern people. The Exhibition might possess arabesque carvings, Egyptian cotton, Turkish ornamental arms, even India's famed Koh-i-noor diamond, but the Vauxhall Gardens boasted a real Algerian family in authentic Arab costume on a specially constructed divan. The various entertainments of 1851 transformed London into a comprehensive catalogue of an expanding world geography through the elaborate framing of regional resources. Entertainment venues ranging from the museum to the hippodrome announced the accessibility of the world's products as well as its peoples. In an age that increasingly defined regions by their industry and resources, this concentrated geography was demonstrated in a profusion of displays. These Bedouins and bales of cotton were valued for their ability to conjure distant places as much as they were valued for rarity or utility.

Entertainment venues competed to provide the most compelling reconstructions of exotic lands, enlisting ever-larger fragments of the "real" in increasingly realistic environments. This profusion of fragments conjured up growing portions of the globe – London housed the world. Native peoples became the preferred fragments of the real as the proliferation of human displays made evident the expansiveness of Britain's imperial and commercial domain. These humans were undeniably real, their behavior signaled more of their absent context than static objects could, and past sensual associations lingered in even the most serious of human displays. Entertainment venues adopted popular versions of the methodologies developing in folklore and ethnology, ultimately adopting the later term to describe their offerings. In the process, emerging disciplines were made to embrace the iconography of an older orientalism, and both were presented as the servants of an expansive imperial economy. Whether one went to the Great Exhibition or Vauxhall Gardens, the presence of exotic peoples seemed evidence of Britain's international dominance.

The increased interest in exotic people in the year of the Great Exhibition is evident in the exaggerated sense that London had suddenly become overwhelmed with foreigners from every corner of the globe. Newspapers regularly reported the presence of foreign dignitaries at the Exhibition. As Paul Greenhalgh explains in his analysis of the human displays at world's fairs, "the actual presence of peoples at exhibitions went back to 1851, when representatives of most nations of the British empire were constantly in attendance at the Crystal Palace."[20] Even before the Exhibition had opened, *The Times* announced that "the whole world is in our streets."[21] A sense that the spectacle of exotic peoples rivaled the displays at the Crystal Palace is evident in the memoirs of the artist Henrietta Ward:

From every part of the globe came representatives, many gorgeous in oriental robes. Dusky Indian Princes with turbans and jewels on their foreheads; sallow-faced Chinese Mandarins in silken embroidered dress; sedate little Japanese potentates with inscrutable faces; broad-faced, woolly-headed African Chiefs wearing bright colours; travelers from America, Australia, Canada and other countries mingling with Russians, Poles, Frenchmen, Italians and Austrians.[22]

With so much attention focused on the presence (and complexion) of foreigners, it is not surprising that Sir Arthur Hallam Elton would report that his children went to the Exhibition more interested in seeing foreigners than the actual displays.[23] Even *The Times* complained of a "dearth of Turks and Turbans" at the opening of the Exhibition.[24]

Like other nineteenth-century commentators, John Tallis described both products and peoples in his three-volume account of the Exhibition. Relating the days preceding the opening, Tallis seems to forget which were actually on display: "Now rapidly congregated on British ground the representatives of the different nations, with their respective productions and wares, who had been invited to take their place in the great industrial mart..."[25] In a revealing reversal, foreign people take their place in the "industrial mart," accompanied by productions and wares almost as an afterthought. Even before the Exhibition opened its doors, writers commented on the influx of foreigners that accompanied the goods shipped for display. Tallis quoted one writer as explaining that

not a packet showed its flag on Southampton Water that was not crowded with a living freight of dusky Spaniards, and duskier Portugese; of swarthy Moors, and swarthier Egyptians; of cane-coloured East Indians, and copper-coloured Tartars; of Mulattos, with complexions of a lively brown, and of Haytians, with countenances – such as Solomon loved – of a lovely black.[26]

Just as the British arranged their products and industry according to development within type, the races that streamed to London were similarly organized in progressively darker hues.

In this context, even banal occurrences involving foreigners at the Exhibition were seen to merit commentary. One report described an instance in which an Egyptian family, unaware of the entrance fee and unable to understand English, were allowed to see the Exhibition "on credit." The event was related in detail and the "family of Egyptian Arabs" were described as "consisting of a tall old Sheik, in oriental tatters; two or three women, jealously concealed in voluminous linen, by no means the whitest, and four little boys, who might have boasted that their faces had never been washed since their birth."[27] The report vacillates between an apparent contempt for the family and a desire to read the group as a meaningful document. This is an image of the patriarchal East, though one divested of nostalgic respect. The "tall old Sheik" precedes the women, whose ambiguous number is suggestive of polygamy and whose "jealously" concealing clothing suggests the female segregation of the harem. However, this sheik is in tatters, his family and their clothing is unwashed, and they are at best an amusing spectacle unable to understand the simple shilling entrance fee.

This simultaneous interest in and contempt for the various "races" visiting London informs the pages of Henry Mayhew and George Cruikshank's comic novel, *1851, or, The Adventures of Mr. and Mrs. Sandboys and Family: Who Came up to London to Enjoy Themselves and to See the Great Exhibition* (1851). The novel opens with the assertion that the Great Exhibition attracted "the sight-seers of all the world" and then presents a long list of attending peoples. Beginning with the exotic, the novel describes Africans arriving on ostriches, caravans from "Zoolu to Fez," as well as Inuit, Senegalese, Egyptians, East Indians, and indigenous people from New Zealand and elsewhere. The Exhibition's comprehensive displays are mirrored in an equally comprehensive attendance. In fact, from the novel it is not clear what constitutes a "sight-seer" and what constitutes a sight. One of the novel's attendees was a well-known object of display – the Hottentot Venus, a South African woman presented to Piccadilly audiences in 1810 – muddying the distinction between viewer and viewed.

After completing this confused litany, the novel then explains that St. Paul's and Westminster Abbey had been transformed into theatres for the exhibition of the "Black Band of his Majesty of Tsjaddi" along with "the Musicians of Tongoose; the Singers of the Maldives; the Glee Minstrels of Paraguay; the Troubadours of far Vancouver; the Snow Ball Family from the Gold Coast; the Canary of the Samoiedes; the Theban Brothers; and 'expressly engaged for the occasion,' the celebrated Band of Robbers from the Desert."[28] The Great Exhibition extends out from Hyde Park to consume the entire city. Even religious monuments become adjunct exhibit rooms, and the display of the world's industry is complemented by the display of the world's inhabitants. In the passage, "exotics" are presented as performers whose range of characteristics is all part of the act. Completing the list is the "celebrated Band of Robbers from the Desert," a reference to the tale of the forty thieves from the *Arabian Nights*, which was frequently dramatized in melodrama and pantomime. Here, as elsewhere, human display was simultaneously read as ethnograhic and theatrical.

The belief that London had been inundated with exotic peoples in picturesque costumes is evident in the novel's frontispiece. The illustration shows the Crystal Palace perched atop the globe as people from every region stream upwards. Arabs, Indians, Native Americans, and Africans all make their way up – suggestive of both the perceived internationalism of the Exhibition's visitors as well as the belief that the Exhibition would raise up the ruder nations (Fig. 3.2). However, as the image also implies, many in London also feared an influx of savages. George Augustus Sala's collection of xenophobic cartoons about exotics visiting the Crystal Palace, *The Great Glass House Opend: the Exhibition Wot's Gone*, depicted Haitians, American Indians, Chinese, and composite orientals such as "Kooli Khan" and "Dost Mahomed Khan" all engaged in disruptive behavior or cannibalistic acts. Typical was his image of a dark squat figure on a bus with drum and snakes. The caption reads, "Dreadful behavior of Ram Jam Jellybag (from Benegal) in a two penny omnibus. He insists on making two venomous serpents perform a polka. Flight of the passengers."[29]

Here an imagined human display is read in the light of theatrical orientalism, as an omnibus becomes the set for an exotic *pas de deux*. These theatricalized foreigners ultimately became the subject of theatrical productions. In *The Great Exhibition of 1851*, two characters take advantage

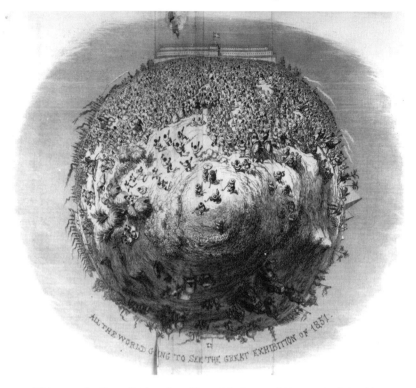

3.2 Visitors to the Crystal Palace from Henry Mayhew and George Cruikshank's
1851: or, The Adventures of Mr. and Mrs. Sandboys and Family

of the foreign influx to masquerade as a Prince of China and a Prince of
Egypt. *Apartments; Visitors to the Exhibition may be Accommodated* depicted
a London resident letting every nook in her home to a range of foreigners,
including a Yankee, a Highlander, a Native American, and a Frenchman.
Foreign visitors in the year of the Great Exhibition were read in the light
of theatrical tradition and then, in turn, provided the theatre with fodder
for new productions.

John Tenniel's cartoon for *Punch*, "The Happy Family in Hyde Park,"
sums up the strange mix of international cooperation and xenophobia
engendered by the Exhibition. The cartoon, which is reproduced in Jeffery
A. Auerbach's *The Great Exhibition of 1851: A Nation on Display*, shows
a group of well-dressed Europeans looking on as Prince Albert points out
dancing figures crowded inside the Crystal Palace. Closer inspection reveals
that the dancing figures are all exotics: a Chinese, an American Indian,

a Turk, and so on. As Auerbach explains, "They are alien 'others,' on display as in a museum case or circus cage, engaged in a bizarre and perhaps primitive dance."[30] The unity of Europe is here imagined through its mirror image – a vast uncivilized horde that, though entertaining, is best viewed from a distance.

Tenniel's cartoon divides the attendants at the Exhibition into two separate categories: those who look and those who are looked at. The division paralleled a similar division between industrial and non-industrial presenting nations. While discussions of the former focused on the relative merit of the manufactures and technology displayed, discussions of the latter often focused on what the displays revealed about daily life in the presenting nation. In short, they became ethnographic displays. The Tunisian Court, for example, received an award even though most commentators seemed to agree with the *Illustrated London News* that the objects displayed there were "more remarkable as matters of curiosity than for their intrinsic value or importance."[31] However, these same commentators were quick to praise the exhibit's "bazaar-like fittings." Often, however, this was a backhanded compliment. In Tallis's description (which appears to be an elaboration on the coverage published in the *Illustrated London News*) the exhibits at the Tunisian Court emerge as "such a stock as one might expect to see in a native old clothes' shop at Algiers or Cairo."[32] While his description suggests that a trip to the Tunis exhibit in some ways simulated a trip to the native shops of the East, it is not clear from the description that it was a trip one would actually want to make. In another compartment, the *Illustrated London News* found:

musical instruments, including a lute and a timbral; and strewed about in all directions are skins of animals, dressed and undressed; pieces of matting, parasols, fans, ornaments in gold and silver; claret bottles, filled, some with Begia snuff; and all sorts of odds and ends, mostly of the rudest description but all admirably calculated to afford illustration of the *ménage* and *convenance* of the North African tribes.

While at first overwhelmed by a seemingly endless array of objects, the paper is finally able to step back and assign a meaning to the display – it serves to illustrate tribal life.

The object most evocative of Eastern life, judging from the paper's description, was "a tent made of camel's hair cloth which stood in the middle of the room." It was a "perfect picture, low dark, dismal – a mere shelter for the mountain wanderer from the blast and the rain; in which saddles, saddle-bags, leather water-bags, clumsy arms, and other articles for immediate use, and adopted for prompt removal, were scattered about in admired disorder."[33] The description repeats a taxonomy of objects listed elsewhere in the article, but now these objects have been "adopted for prompt removal" such that even their disorder can be judged, with obvious condescension, as prompting admiration. Together with the tent they form a perfect picture of the rigors of nomadic life. *The Crystal Palace and its Contents* saw this object, not only as an illustration of "barbarism" but the "cause of its duration," explaining that the nomadic life renders "intellectual and social culture impossible."[34] From material culture, one could deduce both the patterns of Eastern life and the cause for its stasis.

The perception that the Tunisian exhibit successfully depicted native life was largely the result of its most prominent feature – native attendants. When the *Times* described the objects displayed in the Tunisian Court, its first entry was "Moorish attendants."[35] The *Illustrated London News* implied that the Tunisian Court was required viewing primarily because of its attendant, alternately described as a "good-natured Turk" and an "extremely picturesque and obliging native *custodien*."[36] As proof of the exhibit's worth, the *Illustrated London News* published a large image of the attendant surrounded by those objects "calculated to afford illustration" of tribal life (Fig. 3.3). In this context, the attendant emerged as a specimen of the North African tribes and the surrounding objects became props intended to heighten the realism of the human display environment. Most historians of exhibitions would agree with John MacKenzie that "the practice of bringing peoples from overseas seems to have begun in 1867, when the Parisians were served exotic products by those who allegedly produced them."[37] However, the native craftspeople and vendors of the Egyptian Bazaar at the Paris Exposition Universelle were preceded by the Tunisian attendants at the Great Exhibition.

Visitors experienced the Great Exhibition as two separate exhibitions: one industrial and the other ethnographic. Compared to the elaborate typological classifications of the British exhibits (which occupied half of the Crystal Palace's floor space), the foreign exhibits appeared paltry and unsophisticated. In the non-European courts, the displayed objects were valued less as examples of industrial achievement than as bearers of culture (or proof of untapped resources, as shall be discussed later). However, objects do not immediately disclose their value as cultural artifacts without a clear interpretive frame, and it is not surprising that few of the foreign exhibits attracted the interest of the Tunisian exhibit. In the absence of some kind of ethnographic marker, "exotic" objects became mere bric-a-brac.

THE TUNIS COURT

3.3 Tunisian Court from the *Illustrated London News* 31 May 1851

The distinctive arrangement of objects at both the Turkish and Tunisian exhibits was read as culturally significant because of its difference from the presentation style in other courts. Without such ethnographic markers, objects became little better than the British reproductions already available to consumers. Thomas Richards explains that one of the chief attractions of the foreign displays was supposed to have been the architectural styles of the various national exhibits, "but even these seemed familiar to the English, who after all had built their own French Gothic churches and French Renaissance hotels, Venetian Gothic museums, Grecian clubs, Egyptian houses, and Moorish baths."[38] In the absence of an ethnographic frame, the foreign displays became a disorganized and inferior copy of the British exhibit, their native styles imitations of the British reproductions already in circulation. It is not surprising then, as Richards notes, that a *Household Words* article surveying the displays at the Crystal Palace should be titled "The Great Exhibition and the Little One." Sitting in the shadow of the British courts, the foreign courts that attracted most interest were either those that displayed technological innovations challenging those in the British Machine Court (such as the McCormick Reaper in the American Court) or those exotic courts that prompted ethnographic readings through their difference.

Ethnographic displays in both the Fine Art and the Indian Courts further prompted visitors to read certain foreign displays as cultural documents. The Fine Art Court contained wax models of native North and South Americans and Mexican peasants in "proper costume and displaying their characteristic customs."[39] An even more extensive series of models was displayed in the Indian Court. These clay and plaster models featured elaborate reproductions of village life with rows of wooden houses and shops. One collection cited for praise included upwards of sixty groups purportedly illustrating the various castes and professions of the Hindus. The Exhibition complemented its complicated taxonomy of human produce with a taxonomy of humans. While the organizers of the Exhibition did not devise an ethnography section, commentators like John Tallis adopted this term as a heading when describing the Exhibition's collection of human models.

Such ethnographic readings were also facilitated by what *The Times* described as the Exhibition's "geographic solution" to the problem of assigning locations to the various presenting nations. According to *The Times*, the central transept was declared "equator of the world" and the nations around it constituted the "torrid zone."[40] While *The Times* clearly over-emphasized the precision of this geographic arrangement, it is true that Eastern nations were grouped, with India on one side of the transept and Egypt, Turkey,

Persia, Greece, China, and Tunis on the other side. The grouping of Eastern nations prompted them to be read together as a representation of " 'barbaric' civilizations of the East," as George W. Stocking, Jr., notes.[41] Whereas European industry was most often compared according to types of products, under headings such as "Pianofortes" or "Stained and Painted Glass," the displays of Eastern nations were often discussed en masse. *The Crystal Palace and Its Contents*, for example, devoted one section to "Productions of Aboriginal States" in which the publication actually lamented the fact that Egypt had tried to "confine their contributions too much to the results of civilized industry"[42] and so produced a misleading picture of Egyptian life.

While ethnographic human display was at most an implied entertainment at the Great Exhibition, it became a salient attraction at competing venues. In an attempt to attract Exhibition audiences, Robert Wardell of Vauxhall Gardens announced a new "instructive as well as amusing novelty," an Algerian family camped at the pleasure garden. A report in the *Illustrated London News* explained that "the World's Fair and the mighty expectations it elicited induced Youssoff [the head of the household] to visit London with his interesting dependants."[43] Here was an example of the streaming horde of natives depicted in Cruikshank's illustration for *The Adventures of Mr. and Mrs. Sandboys*. Though visitors to the Great Exhibition might not be lucky enough to spot one of the visiting exotics, they were assured of seeing an entire family at the Vauxhall Gardens for a small additional admission price.

The Algerian family wore "the Arab costume" and were displayed on a "gorgeous divan" specially constructed for their exhibition. As added proof of authenticity, the paper reported that the family professed Islam, though "divested of its fanaticism." Youssoff, the paper explained, had served fifteen years in the French army as a soldier and interpreter. Perhaps it was this Western contact, culminating in a trip to the Great Exhibition, that had civilized the family's religious beliefs. For the exhibitor, however, the native could only absorb so much civilization before losing value as an ethnographic object. This tension is evident in the paper's illustration of the family (Fig. 3.4). Youssof turns to the illustrator in half-profile, flanked by his demurely seated wife and their three children. It is a typical bourgeois family portrait, except for the elaborate "Arab costume." This is the comfortable ethnology of the pleasure garden; natives check any disturbing habits at the entrance and show their receptiveness to Western civilization while retaining the characteristic costumes that conjure up the East.

3.4 Algerian family at Vauxhall Gardens from the *Illustrated London News* 12 July 1851

The growing significance of ethnological performance in human displays is illustrated by the troupe of Syrian natives who performed as part of the Holy Land panorama at the Egyptian Hall during the summer of the Great Exhibition. The Middle East had long been a popular panorama subject and three panoramas of the Holy Land were on view that summer. In response to a competitive market, panorama managers had been incorporating live performance into their exhibitions in recent years. For example, the Egyptian Hall's Nile panorama of 1849 featured "characteristic musical illustrations" including "the famous boat-song, 'Hèy, hèy, hò, Hellèysa,' a barcarolle with which the boatmen of the Nile cheer their voyage."[44] Originally, the Holy Land panorama of 1851 at the Egyptian Hall was accompanied by Hebrew Melodies; however, as ever larger crowds flooded London, the Egyptian Hall turned to a more compelling illustration of Eastern life. The Syrian troupe that replaced the Hebrew choir clearly had greater ethnological value; as the *Athenaeum* explained, the attraction of the Syrians was simple – they "exhibit[ed] the manners and customs of their country."[45]

In a series of scenes and tableaux, the troupe recreated Arab marriage customs, including a musical performance on native instruments and a marriage procession, followed by a scene in a coffee-house. The *Athenaeum* was particularly impressed that "before the termination of each performance, one of the company of Syrians got up and explained, in very good English, the whole of the matter in hand."[46] It was probably this level of explanation that enabled the *Athenaeum* reviewer to explain the significance of the scenes, provide Arab terms, and include obscure historical details such as the fact that the wax tapers held during the procession replaced the oil lamps used eighteen hundred years before. Even the review in the *Illustrated London News* included transliterations of the Arabic names of the musical instruments in the performance.

Despite this attention to ethnological detail, human displays in the year of the Crystal Palace preserved a fanciful exoticism and sensuality that had long characterized the East as portrayed in West End entertainment. In describing the Algerian family at Vauxhall, the *Illustrated London News* alternated between stressing the quotidian nature of the Algerian family and presenting them as objects of wonder and desire. Their divan was "gorgeous," the Arab costume was "remarkable for its beauty and gorgeousness," and (in a rather suggestive tone) the paper concluded that "the crowds who nightly visit them" all assert that "the personal attractions of the females, with the extreme novelty of their appearance, render the exhibition very gratifying." The family is framed by a sumptuous setting, indication of both visual pleasure and authenticity. The divan, while clearly Wardell's creation, referenced the countless orientalist fancies of London's theatres and – paradoxically – may have gained authenticity in the process.

In much the same way that orientalist scholars derived legitimacy from what Said terms "the restorative citation of antecedent authority," orientalist entertainments rewrote and pieced together past performances just as "a restorer of old sketches might put a series of them together for the cumulative picture they might implicitly represent." Newly acquired images of the East were adapted to existing expectations. Said continues, "From these complex rewritings the actualities of the modern Orient were systematically excluded," especially when new details detracted from the sensuality of past representations.[47] The Algerian family's bourgeois configuration was not allowed to undermine their inherent sumptuousness; their gorgeous clothing and setting reveal that they are true Arabs. In the most telling move, the two girls (aged fourteen and sixteen respectively) and their mother were refashioned as "the females" whose "personal attractions" and "novelty of appearance" rendered gratification to the night-time viewer. This Westernized family was simultaneously an example of an Arabian harem. Contradiction was at the core of these orientalist displays in which the harem – the space that is, by definition, forbidden – lavishly invited the spectator's gaze.

The *Athenaeum*'s self-consciously ethnographic account of the Syrian troupe at the Egyptian Hall similarly conjured up a world of Eastern pleasures and excess familiar to British theatre audiences. The *Athenaeum* explained that bridegroom and mother wore "the richest silks of Damascus" and sat on "a well-furnished divan" as they awaited congratulatory visits. Their female visitors emitted a "gurgling shriek" as the group grew, until the musicians arrived, took their places on the ground, and performed. The *Illustrated London News* added that coffee and pipes were "amply supplied" to the guests throughout. The *Athenaeum* then explained that the scene was followed by a marriage procession, at the end of which the bride finally made her appearance with her attendants. The papers painted images of Eastern luxury; a beautiful setting and costumes combined with shouting women, music, pipes and coffee to reproduce images of Eastern excess that were common in the theatre. At the climax, she enters surrounded by her women – simultaneously chaste bride and odalisque.

These human displays evoked another important element of theatrical orientalism, the fantastic. Considering the huge popularity of the *Arabian Nights*, it is not surprising that the *Illustrated London News* praised the Syrian troupe for their creation of "a scene in a coffee-house, in which a dwarf tells a tale from the 'Arabian Nights'" all the while "taking whiffs from the pipes of the customers, by way of recompense." The *Athenaeum*, in typically contradictory terms, stated that the storyteller's "gestures and grotesque figure were admirable." The fantastic and the grotesque, as much as the gorgeous and luxurious, were expected features of Eastern displays. Consequently, a side-show fascination with the storyteller's "grotesque figure" could masquerade as critical assessment of the accuracy of an Eastern display and the presence of fantastic tales served as proof of authenticity.

The question is not whether the Syrian troupe or the Algerian family provided inaccurate depictions of general patterns of behavior in their respective countries; no doubt storytellers in Syria recited tales from the *Arabian Nights*. What is significant to my argument is that these performances facilitated certain established tropes of orientalist discourse even as presenters and reviewers framed these performances as examples of ethnographic display. As the *Illustrated London News* explained in their review of the Syrian troupe:

All this, it must be acknowledged, is as novel as it is genuine; and as we witness these native musicians, singers, and story-tellers in their Oriental costume, we feel that a real addition is made to the knowledge of the fireside tourist, who need not go far from his chimney-corner to behold the very persons and manners of which he reads in books of adventure and modern travel.

In orientalist displays, the "novel" and the "genuine" went hand in hand. Even as native performance was increasingly seen as a means of recreating distant places for the fireside tourist, these performances continued to be valued for their exotic playfulness – for their delightful mix of music, singing, and extravagant costume. This is the East as delivered in "both books of adventure and modern travel," genres that make differing claims to the "real" but that apparently present complementary images nonetheless.

Commentators on the Great Exhibition similarly invoked an East of fantastic and sensual excess when discussing the Eastern courts, often citing the *Arabian Nights* and oriental romances as illustration of what visitors could expect. For example, Tallis gave special attention to an apartment in one of the India courts that was furnished like an Indian palace, explaining that it "realised all that the Arabian Nights, and other romances, have detailed with respect to their gorgeous and costly luxury."[48] It was apparently unimportant that the *Arabian Nights* are set in eighth-century Baghdad and not India, nor that they give little attention to architecture or furnishings. The *Nights* authenticate the recreation of Indian architecture at the Crystal Palace, not because the text has any relation to the exhibit, but because the *Nights* had become shorthand for the strategies by which sensual and extravagant displays were contained within the safe parameters of "authentic" reproduction. As Tallis himself explained, "*Oriental* magnificence is still a proverbial mode of describing a degree of splendour and artistical richness, which is not found among ourselves."[49] In this manner, the excess and lavish display of an event such as the Great Exhibition was displaced onto an East of British invention.

Just as human displays combined a newer ethnographic vocabulary with an older romantic vocabulary of Eastern sensuality and fantasy, the Exhibition similarly reveals a dialectical relation between seemingly antithetical orientalist discourses. Visitors to the Exhibition frequently contrasted the unceasing progression of Western civilization and the perceived stasis of Eastern civilization; however, at the same time, commentators invoked images of Eastern excess in order to praise the bounty of industrialization. British manufactures were often arranged to illustrate progress and improvements over time. Leaving British manufacturers, visitors found that most of the contributions from the colonies were in the Raw Materials section, with the exception of the separate India courts. Even the Indian displays stood in marked opposition to the story of progress told in the manufacture and machinery sections. A writer for the *Illustrated London News* posed a common question when he asked why, in the Indian agricultural and manufacturing arts, "no advance should be made for centuries." Influenced by theories of environmental determinism, the writer turned to climate and geography to explain why "this people have made so little progress" and why "the great bulk of them are in the same condition, moral, social, and intellectual, that they were in 300 years ago."[50] The writer went on to argue that in India – as in Egypt, where the implements showed "curious coincidences" with those of India – a temperate climate resulted in few needs, geographic remoteness undermined trade, and the vegetarian diet undermined commerce. Outside of Europe, visitors encountered savage lands capable of producing little more than raw materials or the crudest manufactures. Even the relatively civilized peoples of the East (as they were represented by the British) were depicted as frozen in time, their limited industry demonstrating a "moral, social, and intellectual" paralysis.

As George W. Stocking, Jr., has demonstrated, this question of how to account for the perceived relative degrees of civilization possessed by the nations of the world would grow prominent in Victorian histories and ethnologies in the years following the Great Exhibition. It seems likely that the great array of objects displayed, from the Tunisian tent to Britain's mechanical looms, prompted speculation on the diversity of human accomplishments. In this light, it is particularly salient that Henry Thomas Buckle – whose influential *History of the Civilization in England* argued that the powers of nature accounted for the internal stagnation and waste of India, Egypt, Mexico, and Peru – conceived of the grand scope of his history of civilization in May of 1851. Earlier in that year he served as judge of a chess tournament held in conjunction with the Great Exhibition.[51] The Great Exhibition had an equally pronounced effect on the field of ethnology, disseminating the evolutionary organization principle to Victorian museums. To quote Stocking, "there is evidence to suggest that the two great ethnological collections of the evolutionary period – the Christy and the Pitt Rivers – were stimulated by the Great Exhibition." Christy began his study of primitive customs as a result of his visit to the Crystal Palace and Pitt Rivers began his collection at the same time and employed a system of classification by form that bears a clear relation to the Exhibition's judging categories.[52] Clearly a gospel of progress informed both venues of popular entertainment and scholarly disciplines; however, it may also be that venues of popular entertainment helped shape the idea of progress as it emerged in academic disciplines.

While the Exhibition proclaimed a commitment to "progress," and identified itself as a "rational amusement," its real attraction was an opulence and scale that bordered on excess. In highlighting these qualities, the Exhibition turned to tropes associated with the Eastern civilizations that appeared static or declining when framed within the Crystal Palace. In describing the opening of the Exhibition, Tallis employed the images of "oriental magnificence" that were supposedly absent from England:

And, unquestionably, neither Eastern fairy tale, nor Arabian Night's wonder, could surpass, or even emulate the gorgeous reality that greeted the delighted gaze of the assembled spectators, as the royal party and brilliant *cortége* advanced through the bronze and gilded gates that led into this hall of enchantment; fragrant exotics bloomed and shed their soft perfume around, [and] crystal fountains threw up their sparkling waters...[53]

Tallis painted an image of an opulent Eastern palace and not without cause; Owen Jones, who was responsible for the interior decoration of the Crystal Palace, designed the iron railing around the building in a Moorish fretwork and based his paint colors and application on the Alhambra. (Jones had published a study of the Alhambra seven years earlier.) Jones, in fact, had wanted to hang large carpets above the mezzanines and arched arabesque paintings over the central aisles, giving "the impression of a bazaar, and . . . further emphasis[ing] the impression of eastern atmosphere" in the opinion of one design historian.[54] It was perhaps Jones's design that prompted *The Times* to compare the Exhibition building to "an Arabian Night's structure."[55] In manufactures and cultural achievement, the East served as the static example against which British advances were defined. At the same time, however, the East provided the metaphors by which Britain assessed the plenty these advances reaped.

Framed within this lavish architecture, the Exhibition fetishized works of industry in much the same way that human displays and theatre fetishized Eastern women. The Exhibition imagined itself as an elaborate harem. Its array of commodities and machinery posited a world of impossibly endless availability. As Prince Albert said at the opening ceremony, "the products of all quarters of the globe are placed at our disposal, and we have only to choose which is the best and cheapest for our purposes."[56] In this fantasy world of availability, one need only select from a throng that simply awaits his choice. Britain turned to an East of its own creation for the imagery that would give a material form to this idea of availability. The Crystal

Palace, with its Moorish fretwork and Alhambresque coloring, was another of London's gorgeous divans and the personal attractions and novelty of the displayed objects similarly promised gratification. Islamic ornament and color were the raw materials from which Britain constructed its monument to surplus. In the process the Exhibition referenced the East appearing in its own foreign courts, as well as the East at pleasure gardens and theatres. Here theatre-savvy spectators looked past muslin veils and damask cloth to discover sweetmeats and coffees in the hands of convivial old Turks and alluring Algerians. Here then was the "real" East, more tangible than decorative patterns or color combinations, more engaging than a bale of cotton or a sack of dates. This was the East as Eastern body, a world that invited Western industry and intervention with the languid desire of an odalisque.

THE BUILT-OUT EAST

The *Illustrated London News* depicted the attendant at the Tunisian exhibit sitting cross-legged in the exhibit's inner room, surrounded by shelves of shoes, hanging bags, stacked rugs, and a tambour. When Wardell presented the Algerian family at Vauxhall, he found it necessary to construct an ornamented divan for their display. The imitation of exotic space in three dimensions was entering the entertainment lexicon. Certainly exoticism had been a feature of regency eclecticism. However, the vogue for hieroglyphs, lotuses, and crocodiles – especially in the years following Nelson's defeat of the French at Aboukir Bay – reflected a desire for novel (and in this case, patriotic) design features rather than constituting an attempt to recreate Eastern objects and architecture. Belzoni was probably the first to do so, when he employed modeled colored reliefs, lowered the roof, and dimmed the lights in recreating chambers of the tomb of Seti I in 1821. At mid-century such techniques were spreading. By 1842, the creation of side-walls for theatrical settings by angling the wings perpendicular to the stage was sufficiently common as to be described in an article on scene painting in *The Penny Cyclopedia of the Society for the Diffusion of Useful Knowledge.*[57] Practical scenery was also growing more common at this time, as will be evident from the plays discussed in the next chapter. Panorama halls and exhibition spaces, however, led the way in fully modeling exotic settings.

The most ambitious of these was the remodeled Colosseum of 1845. Since it was first opened in 1832, this panorama and pleasure garden had regularly added exotic environments, such as an Indian supper room and an Egyptian tent, to complement its main attraction, a London panorama. It had long been in financial straits but was invigorated by several new attractions in

1845. The rotunda was now encircled with a 300-foot (91-metre) frieze of the Panathenaic procession in the Elgin marbles, the grounds featured elaborate reproductions of the Arch of Titus and the Temple of Vesta, and its former marine grotto was redesigned as a replica of the caves at Adelsberg, filled with stalactites and stalagmites.[58] The *Illustrated London News* carried illustrations of several of the new attractions, including the reconstructed conservatory, now decorated in what the paper called "the Arabesque style" (Fig. 3.5). The arched portal was ornamented with designs that suggested Kufic-style script, a reference to the Islamic practice of adorning buildings with lines from the Koran. However, at the Colosseum the meaningless designs divested the practice of any religious significance and instead became simply an indication of the Eastern taste for ornament. In describing the new conservatory, the paper resorted to quoting a Washington Irving reverie on the heroic romances associated with the Alhambra, and then concluded: "here you may almost forget the working-day-world, amidst the murmur of sparkling fountains, and the beautiful forms and freshness of the colours of the embellishments."[59] The East was a world of leisure, its forms well suited to English sites of recreation.

Later architects would copy, or claim to copy, actual Eastern monuments, essentially assuring patrons that solid research buttressed their leisure activities. This was especially the case after 1851, the Great Exhibition having provided clear proof of the profitability of recreational learning. In 1854 work was completed on one such structure, the Royal Panopticon of Science and Art, an Institution for Scientific Exhibitions, and for Promoting Discoveries in Arts and Manufactures. According to the architect, Hayter Lewis, the structure was based on "the mosques of Zalaon and El Moyed" in Cairo, which were "copied with such modifications as are rendered necessary by modern European habits."[60] Whether or not Lewis based his design on existing mosques, the Royal Panopticon did help transform him into an Eastern expert. He made many trips to the Near East in later life and delivered lectures on Moorish, Persian, Cairene, and other examples of Islamic architecture.[61] Patrons of the Royal Panopticon could examine the achievements of Western technology in an Eastern pleasure dome; when they grew tired of examining the vacuum flask, pin-making machine, or the gas cookstove, patrons could relax by the central fountain or simply admire the building's elaborately ornamented keyed arches and enameled glass and slate mosaics.[62]

The Panopticon's project of intellectual improvement did not survive in the competitive entertainment industry, though its exoticism did. The building was sold in 1856 and reopened two years later as the Alhambra Palace and Music Hall. Reconstruction after a fire in 1881 added additional

3.5 Moorish conservatory at the Colosseum from the *Illustrated London News* 3 May 1845

Islamic motifs, including geometrical fret panels on the balcony fronts, honeycomb capitals on the lower columns, horseshoe arches supporting the ceiling, and keel arches over the promenade. An extensive redecoration in 1888 further intensified the building's Islamic ornament; a variety of surfaces were filled in with Moorish fretwork, the tiers were painted in a "mosaic effect," new "Alhambresque capitals" were affixed to all the columns, and stalactites were affixed to the ceiling of the first circle.[63]

Exotic structures could suggest both learned reproduction and fanciful invention. Though the latter would come to increasingly predominate in Victorian and Edwardian places of entertainment – most notably in the theatre architecture of Frank Matcham[64] – Eastern reproductions were an important site in which the entertainment industry explored the relation of objects and architecture to perceived patterns of life. Islamic structures were fast becoming the preferred style for the entertainment industry, but interest often followed the military. In 1841, during the Opium War, the Chinese Collection was exhibited in a specially built two-story pagoda bearing a gilded inscription in Chinese characters announcing, "Ten Thousand Chinese Things." In addition to an extensive array of art objects and manufactures, the collection featured life-size groups from every strata of Chinese society. Writing in 1867, John Timbs would recall seeing:

> a council of mandarins, and Chinese priests, soldiers, men of letters, ladies of rank, tragedians, barbers, shoe-makers, blacksmith, boat-women, servants &c., amidst set scenes and furnished dwellings. Here was a two storied house from Canton, besides shops from its streets; here were persons of rank in sumptuous costumes, artisans in their working-clothes, and altogether such a picture of Chinese life as the European world had never before seen.[65]

In 1854, in the midst of the Crimean War, London's pagoda was renamed the Oriental and Turkish Museum.[66] This new collection also featured life groups, the majority of which depicted contemporary Turkey, including scenes in a hammam (bath), kahoe (coffee-shop), barbershop, harem, and slave-bazaar.[67] *The Times* explained that the costumes came from Constantinople, and the *Illustrated London News* provided extensive commentary on the individual scenes in two separate articles – commentary that was presumably indebted to the "description and historical matter contained in the well-written 'Guide-book.'"[68] The *Illustrated London News* described the physical environment of the displays, noting – for example – that the close lattice of the harem permitted "a full view of the surrounding scenery" while also "permitting those from within to see without being seen." The paper then described harem etiquette in great detail:

A visitor is received according to her station in life, and after being announced is met by the lady of the house, with her suite, stepping down from the sofa, as may be demanded by the rank of the guest. The manner of salutation also varies; those of equal rank and age endeavour to kiss the hem of each other's garment, or only to exchange temenahs.[69]

The paper explained this "graceful mode of salutation" as well as the various circumstances in which it was used. The volume of detail in these descriptions reflected the increasingly thorough ethnographic writings that were generated as more and more British soldiers, functionaries, and missionaries took up stations in the Middle East. The ways of the East were being made known, and the entertainment industry counted on a popular desire for the fullest possible illustration of this emerging body of knowledge.

Three-dimensional ethnographic representations long preceded historical period rooms,[70] suggesting important differences in the manufacture of historical and ethnographic knowledge. While Augustus Welby Pugin designed a Medieval Court for the Great Exhibition, this was intended to popularize the Gothic Revival style and not to recreate a historical period. The fact that the Court was set in the manufactures section and that the *Eclectic Review* denigrated the Court as "felicitous copyism"[71] suggests that the room was judged for its contributions to design, and not for the accuracy of its recreation. The early development of the life group relative to the period room demonstrates a basic distinction between the ethnographic and historicist projects as defined by Michel de Certeau. According to de Certeau, from its earliest inception ethnology has been organized by four concepts – orality, spatiality, alterity, and unconsciousness – while historiography is organized around the opposing concepts of writing, temporality, identity, and consciousness. Historiography (pre-Foucault) credits its object, the written documents of Western activity, with a consciousness that is immediately apparent. Consequently, historiography "is satisfied with arranging [these documents], composing a single text from the thousand of written fragments in which already expressed is that labor which constructs time, which creates consciousness through self-reflection." By contrast, ethnography is primarily interested in what is *not* written, as ethnography attempts to "organize its data in relation to *unconscious* conditions of social life," as Lévi-Strauss writes. As a consequence, ethnography employs a spatial mode in that it creates "the synchronic picture of a system that has no history."[72]

De Certeau's delineation of ethnography's organizing concepts helps explain the conceptual basis of the life group. Ethnography attempts to uncover "unconscious conditions of social life," that is to say the unarticulated

3.6 "A Turkish Dinner Party" at the Oriental and Turkish Museum from the *Illustrated London News* 14 August 1854

systems by which people relate to each other and the objects around them. As these unconscious systems only exist in spatial relations (in the absence of writing meaning can only be implicit in the relation of people and objects) ethnography attempts to use its own language "to organize the space of the other into a picture of orality." Ethnographic writing is only successful in the degree to which it reproduces this space of the other – a goal much more effectively achieved in three dimensions. As Ira Jacknis writes, "Instead of communicating cultural integration by means of object juxtaposition and labels, to be synthesized in the viewer's mind, the life group was a presentational medium, allowing these cultural connections actually to be *seen*."[73] In "A Turkish Dinner Party," one of two illustrations of the Oriental and Turkish Museum appearing in the *Illustrated London News*, the posture of figures, the handling of objects, and the details of costume all suggest complex social patterns that would remain unarticulated had they not been captured in wax (Fig. 3.6).

As such, Said's observations on Edward Lane's monumental *An Account of the Manners and Customs of the Modern Egyptians* (1836) can be seen to describe the very substance of ethnographic field reporting. Said writes: "Lane's objective is to make Egypt and the Egyptians totally visible, to keep nothing hidden from his reader, to deliver the Egyptians without depth, in swollen detail."[74] Such reporting seeks to exclude no detail in the space of a human interaction, for only from such mute and seemingly extraneous details can an ethnographically "true" interpretation of social life emerge. In much the same way, the Oriental and Turkish Museum created a striking verisimilitude, prompting *The Times* to marvel: "The arms and legs of the males are rough with real hair, most delicately applied – actual drops of perspiration are on the brows of the porters; a real grassplot is laid out for the oxen to tread. In fact, the whole is less a copy of life than life itself brought to stagnation."[75] The ethnographic project depends upon freezing a moment in space and amplifying every detail down to the perspiration on a porter's brow. It depends on a certain erasure between the real and the represented; here "real" Turkish clothing and implements are complemented by a real grassplot to intensify the sense of reality clinging to a constructed setting. The result, as *The Times* aptly noted, was a sense of stagnation. Even though the museum sought to describe the Turkish Nation, "Past and Present," and its guidebook noted changes in dress, the Oriental and Turkish Museum like other nineteenth-century ethnographic displays created an overwhelming sense of cultural stasis.

THE SYDENHAM CRYSTAL PALACE

The month before the opening of the Oriental and Turkish Museum, London's attention was fixed on a project of architectural reproduction and ethnographic analysis that far exceeded anything the city had seen before. After the Great Exhibition closed in October of 1851 there was considerable debate over what was to be done with the Crystal Palace, with calls that it remain as a winter-garden or that it be transformed into a permanent industrial museum. When the House of Commons finally voted to remove the structure it opened the door for a group of private investors to purchase the building, which was reerected at Sydenham as a year-round pleasure garden, with multiple exhibition halls and a 4,000-seat concert room. In the process, the Crystal Palace grew from three to five stories and the floor area increased by nearly half as much again as the original.[76] A week after the opening, the *Illustrated London News* announced that the new Crystal Palace gave "appropriate illustration" to "geology, ethnology, zoology, and botany." The Crystal Palace displayed the races of man (in thirteen life-size groupings of "uncivilized" peoples), exotic plants, hundreds of stuffed animals, and models of prehistoric animals. The most prominent feature in the new pleasure palace was in the Fine Arts Department – a series of ten historical courts recreating a range of architectural styles including Assyrian, ancient Egyptian, Byzantine, and Medieval, and a reduced-scale reconstruction of portions of the Alhambra.

While the Sydenham Crystal Palace was primarily devoted to recreation and entertainment, it declared an adherence to the educational mission of its progenitor. It has been rightly said that the new Crystal Palace sought to educate, "not so much about industry as about the Beautiful";[77] however, it would be a mistake to read the courts as solely concerned with art and design. Instead, it is useful to examine them in the context of the ethnology section, which the *Illustrated London News* described as "one of the most conspicuous and attractive sections" of the new Crystal Palace.[78] Dr. Robert Gordon Latham, a doctor and philologist who was prominent in the London Ethnological Society and widely published, organized the ethnological exhibits at the Crystal Palace. Ethnology was classified with zoology and botany in the Natural History Department at Sydenham (as previously had been the case at the British Association), but the study of race clearly took precedent over plant and animal life. The guide to the Natural History Department devoted seventy-nine pages, written by Latham, to describing the ethnological exhibits whereas zoology and botany combined for twelve pages of description. The zoological and botanical displays served as background to, or were presented as context for, the racial models. As Latham explained, "the trees, plants, animals, and human occupants of the different portions of the earth's surface are grouped together – so that the allied sciences of botany, zoology, and ethnology illustrate each other."[79] Several of the groups were engaged in "characteristic" behavior; the Indian group depicted a tiger hunt with Indian rhododendrons, *Ficus elastica*, tea plants and other indigenous plants in the background and North American Indians were shown dancing near a display featuring a porcupine, elk, beaver, raccoon, opossum, and deer (82–83, 75).

Life groups had been displayed in London before the Sydenham Crystal Palace, but never had they been explicitly presented as examples of ethnological research, nor had there ever been an attempt to present a wide-ranging comparative racial analysis.[80] While the Oriental and Turkish Museum was organized around national customs, the guide to the Ethnology portion of the Natural History Court clearly defined a larger project. As Latham explains, "*Ethnology* means the science, not exactly of the different *nations of the world*, but of the different *varieties of the human species*" (5). Delineating the greatest range of "varieties" in the greatest detail possible was clearly the object of the ethnology section. Latham's guide described a great number of distinctive activities (from "initiation ceremonies" to "depilation") as well as thoroughly comparing physical characteristics.

On the one hand, ethnology emerged as the study of permanently fixed racial categories. Latham asserted, for example, that the Danakil are African but not Negro: "Their hair is longer than the negro's; their lips thinner; their colour lighter; their nose more aquiline"(39). Latham invariably explained that the models were fashioned from casts made by travelers or were copied from people exhibited in London. For example, the naturalist, Alfred Russel Wallace, recounts correcting the features and poses of models of a Guiana group soon after his travels on the Amazon.[81] On the other hand, ethnology emerged as the study of customs and material culture; the natives of Greenland were exhibited with a tent, its furniture and a canoe (78). As the *Illustrated London News* announced well before the opening of the Crystal Palace, the ethnology section would be the first museum "to show the models of different varieties of the human race, together with their national costumes, their domestic and agricultural implements, their armour, their dwellings, their modes of conveyance and other characteristic objects appertaining to them."[82]

The global scope of ethnology was evident in the geographic arrangement of the displays. Latham explained that:

The visitor is enabled to place himself in respect to the objects before him in the same relation as he would be to a map of the world. Here, the North lies in front of him, the East to his right, the West to his left. In like manner, the groups on his right belong to Europe, Asia, and Africa; those on his left to America.

North and South were not as strictly laid out; "as a general rule, however, the Southern parts of the two worlds (the old and new), are the parts nearest the entrance – and the Northern parts lie beyond them" (6). The Crystal Palace aspired to delineate the races of the world – and while Caucasians were absent from the displays, "the character of most European populations [being] sufficiently understood," they did constitute a base of comparison. "The extent to which [the display groups] differ from each other is manifest," Latham wrote. "Still more do they differ from such groups of Englishmen, Frenchmen, Germans, and other Europeans as may collect around them" (5).

Throughout the guide, Latham abstained from suggesting a significance to the practices he described, and the closest he came to speculating on their origins is his acknowledgement of "the re-appearance of similar customs in the distant parts of the world where, however, the physical conditions are alike," implicitly granting environment a determining role in the development of culture (71). Instead, Latham seemed intent on amplifying the startling differences manifest between display groups and most profoundly between the displays and the groups of Europeans in attendance. Consequently, the guide's description of a group of Mundrucus with enemy skulls on poles featured a lengthy and detailed description of how the Mundrucu prepare the skulls (71–72). Meaning resided in the *physical relation* of these strange bodies to the strange objects, plants, and animals that surrounded them. Latham's guide did not attempt to articulate this meaning, only to provide a depth of practice to the objects on display.

Ethnology's early focus on philology and racial analysis was being complemented by a growing interest in material culture. Three years earlier, the *Athenaeum* had decried the "extremely deficient" nature of the national collections of "Ethnography, including Archaeology in its more limited sense."[83] The paper complained that: "It is, in fact, quite lamentable to think how many tribes first visited by our ships have now either entirely disappeared from the human race, or have so modified their manners and customs as to render it impossible now to obtain specimens of their industrial arts in their aboriginal state." Ethnography was inseparable from the collection of the "industrial arts" of aboriginal peoples. This belief was evident in the fact that the *Athenaeum* supported the British Museum's creation of an Egyptian Gallery even though the paper recommended that the Museum be devoted solely to natural history and ethnography, with the fine art collection being removed to the National Gallery. Archeology was conceived of as a subset of ethnography rather than fine art; non-European remains were significant as examples of aboriginal industrial art rather than objects of aesthetic contemplation. The issue grew more complicated when examining antiquities of ancient Italic peoples; according to the paper, the removal of "Etruscan Vases and Bronzes, Coins and Medals" from the British Museum should be left for future determination as they were "to a certain extent ethnographical articles." In this sense, the architectural reconstructions of the historical courts at the Crystal Palace walked a line between fine art and ethnography. The reproductions of actual Egyptian statuary would presumably make the Egyptian Court no less ethnographic than the British Museum's Egyptian Gallery, while the Roman Court was, at most, ethnographic "to a certain extent."

Ethnographic and aesthetic rubrics were invoked when discussing non-Western productions, largely depending on the degree of civilization attributed to the region. This mix of ethnographic analysis and aesthetic valuation is most striking in Owen Jones's guide to the Alhambra Court.

Jones's respect for the productions of Islamic artisans fed into a broader treatment of Eastern life that approaches a form of cultural relativism that is normally said to have originated in the anthropological writings of E. B. Tylor or alternately Franz Boas. Jones was the Director of the Fine Arts Department at the Crystal Palace, so it is not surprising that one of the courts was a reproduction of the Alhambra's Court of Lions, Hall of Justice, and Hall of Abencerrages.

While the Alhambra Court was presented as historical, Jones offered his reproduction as evidence of the continuing craftsmanship of Islamic manufactures and their connection to the patterns of Muslim life. As such, Jones's Alhambra Court constitutes another attempt to translate Eastern life into three-dimensional space, continuing a strategy evident in such distinct entertainments as the Oriental and Turkish Museum and the Algerian family and divan at Vauxhall. In his guide, *The Alhambra Court in the Crystal Palace*, Jones explained that "the Mohammedans are the only race, except the Chinese, who still practise the art which grew up with their civilization." One need only look to "the many beautiful works displayed in the Exhibition of 1851" for proof that "the unvarying principles which they have held for a thousand years are still powerful amongst [Muslim artisans]."[84] Far from being simply a relic of the past, Jones read the Alhambra as an example of the great work produced as a result of the Muslim artisan's rooting in tradition, a rooting that was as strong in the nineteenth century as it had been in the fourteenth, according to Jones.

Jones asserted that it was not simply the Muslim artisan who was grounded in tradition but all of Islamic society. Throughout the guide, Jones suggested that architecture is the physical manifestation of a society's spirit. He began the guide with the assertion: "The several styles of architecture have uniformly been the result of religion, habits, and modes of thought of the nations which produced them, and may be said to be the material expression of their wants, faculties, and sentiments, under the influence of climate and of materials at command" (7). Jones even read pre-Islamic history in the continued traditions of Islamic architecture when he noted: "It would seem that the Arabs, in changing their wanderings for a settled life – supplanting the tent by a form more solid – had transferred the luxurious shawls and hangings of their former dwellings to the new, changing the tent-pole for a marble column, and the silken tissue for gilded plaster" (14). Religious beliefs were made manifest in Islamic ornament as well. According to Jones, "The mosques of Cairo and India, the palaces of Spain, show everywhere the calm, voluptuous translation of the Koran's doctrines" (14).

Jones's guide provided a complex theory of the relation of Eastern architecture to Eastern culture (even as the influence of a longstanding exoticism is evident in his assertion that "voluptuous" Eastern form embodies the spirit of the Koran). Instead of a troubling stasis, Jones saw enduring tradition. Rather than defining the Eastern environment as a cause of stagnation, Jones suggested that it was the source of the excellence of Eastern monuments. Where Jones did find fault was in the low level of craftsmanship and taste evident in *British* manufactures, which lacked the unity and consistency of the products of the East.

> The beautiful cushions and slippers of Morocco at the present day are adorned with the same ornaments, having the same colours, as are found on the walls of the Alhambra. It is far different with ourselves. WE have no principles, no unity; the architect, the upholsterer, the paper stainer, the weaver, the calico printer, and the potter, run each his independent course; each struggles fruitlessly, – each produces in art novelty without beauty, or beauty without intelligence. (16)

Jones's guide recalls a romantic primitivism, one that would reappear with greater force in Sir George Birdwood's praise of the "serenity and dignity" of the Indian craftsman.[85] For Jones, the work of the Eastern artisan manifested the "wants, the faculties, and the feelings of [a] people" (9). In this context, Jones did not simply provide the Alhambra Court as an architectural reproduction, but as evidence of an exemplary way of being in the world that was manifestly Eastern.

Given the considerable significance Jones attached to Islamic ornament, it is not surprising that he paid tremendous attention to the accuracy of his reproduction. Rather than creating an imaginative compilation of Moorish architecture, Jones chose to reproduce chambers of the Alhambra on a reduced scale. The centerpiece was a reproduction of the Court of Lions at half size, with columns, arches, and ornaments at full size. Where the dimensions differed, Jones provided scale diagrams in his guide so that the reproduction could be compared with the original. The ornaments were created from molds taken by Jones and "coloured in every minutest detail in exact accordance with the original."[86] According to Jones, these ornaments demonstrated "the exquisite curves in use by the Arabs and Moors."[87] Koranic inscriptions were also reproduced on the walls in gold, requiring ten pages in Jones's guide for translation. Even a southern climate was reproduced; according to a later guidebook, the Alhambra Court was enclosed within the Tropical Department, which was kept warm for its foreign birds and plants, and the undated *Royal Album of Crystal Palace Views* shows rich foliage in its illustration of the Court.[88] Here was a reproduction with a thoroughness never before attempted. Crystal Palace patrons were offered the East in its full materiality, curving, gilded, warm, and lush. This was not simply an Eastern space, but the East as space – carefully delineated and interpreted in a London suburb. The Crystal Palace celebrated Eastern harmony and lamented the loss of such graceful integration in the products of modernity, all the while astounding patrons with the marvels of Western reproduction technology.

The Sydenham Crystal Palace delivered the civilizations of the East and the past in three-dimensional courts and then surrounded them with models of "uncivilized" peoples. As early as 1855, Herbert Spencer would argue that a less stimulating environment could not only inhibit the rise of civilization but also result in mentally inferior peoples. It was just a short step from this position to John Lubbock's assertion that the customs of modern-day savages illustrated a primitive state that all societies pass through in their ascent to civilization. According to these views, as Peter J. Bowler explains, "savages are fossilized relics of human evolution in the biological sense as well as the social sense: they illustrate the 'missing links' in the ascent of humankind."[89] In this context, the Sydenham Crystal Palace emerges as a vast human hierarchy across time and space, Jones's praise of Islamic ornament notwithstanding. The Crystal Palace created a history of humanity that began with models of Australian aborigines – commonly thought, according to Latham, to be "the lowest form of humanity" and demonstrating a "*minimum* amount of intellectual power"[90] – and concluded with the courts of British manufactures. In 1851, the Great Exhibition mapped world geography in manufactures and raw materials. Race was an unexpected draw. Three years later, the Crystal Palace at Sydenham delineated both geography and the history of humanity in architectural reconstructions and ethnographic models. Race had become a central attraction.

CHAPTER 4

The biblical East in theatres and exhibitions

The entertainment industry's fascination with the Middle East was not simply generated out of interest in the manners and customs of modern Orientals but by the belief that the region preserved remainders of the biblical past. A range of British scholars in the 1840s sought to illustrate, if not verify, scriptural authority through detailed examinations of the terrains, architecture, and antiquities of the Holy Land. Works as distinct as James Fergusson's *An Essay on the Ancient Topography of Jerusalem* (1847) and Austen Henry Layard's *Nineveh and its Remains* (1849) shared the belief that sacred history could be uncovered in physical remains. The discoveries of such scholars inspired a range of panoramas, exhibitions, and theatrical productions purporting to reproduce the biblical East. The entertainment industry was not only a venue for disseminating this emerging geographic and archeological information, it was complicit in the creation of such information. Fergusson served as director of the Crystal Palace Company from 1851 to 1858 and designed and supervised the construction of the Nineveh Court; Layard was enlisted to write the guide for the Court; and George Grove, who founded the Palestine Exploration Fund in 1865, served as secretary to the Crystal Palace Company from 1852. Even a theatre practitioner, such as Charles Kean, could be seen in his day not simply as referencing archeological discoveries but as synthesizing emerging information into a coherent image of the biblical past.

Increasingly, the entertainment industry sought to transform topographical surveys into three-dimensional displays. From Holy Land panoramas to models of Jerusalem to elaborate reconstructions of ancient architecture, the trend was towards encompassing reproductions of biblical settings. Similarly, the theatre at this same time shifted towards built-out practical scenery, notably in several highly spectacular mid-century productions depicting Eastern cities in the biblical past. This is also the period in which the British Museum created individual galleries to display its growing collection of large Middle Eastern sculptures, friezes, and

bas-reliefs. Increasingly, theatres, exhibitions, and museums were all conceived of as three-dimensional display environments that employed archeological and ethnograhic research to reproduce and interpret the shape of
distant spaces, whether that distance was geographic or historical. The combination of artifacts across regions and periods, which was once licensed
by theatrical and curatorial artistry, grew less common at both theatres and
museums. As theatres and museums espoused the goal of educating the
masses, and as they increasingly promised accurate reproductions of exotic
places, display became less a matter of invention than a process of transcription. This was especially true in the depiction of biblical regions, in
which a disregard for accurate reproduction ran the risk of offending not
only scholarly sensibilities.

HOLY LAND TOPOGRAPHY

British victories in the Middle East during the Napoleonic Wars focused the
attention of scholars and showmen on the Levant, well before the later outpouring of British scholarship and entertainments in the 1840s and 1850s.
The first wave of Holy Land topography was generated after Napoleon's
defeat in the Battle of Acre, which was reproduced in the Robert Ker Porter
panorama, *The Siege of Acre* (Lyceum 1801). Fearing Muslim reprisals against
the Christian population of Palestine (who were suspected of having abetted
the French), Commodore Sydney Smith landed a detachment of soldiers
that then marched to Jerusalem. The British military presence generated
numerous depictions of the Holy Land, which in turn inspired a growing
number of civilian visits. The effects of this short-lived occupation included
Edward Daniel Clarke's descriptions of Palestine in his six-volume *Travels
in Various Countries in Europe, Asia, and Africa* (1810–1823) as well as John
Lewis Burkhardt's *Travels in Nubia* (1819), *Travels in Syria and the Holy Land*
(1822), and *Travels in Arabia* (1829). Such publications inspired even more
popular volumes, such as the Finden Brothers' *Landscape Illustrations of the
Bible* (1836). The work strove for a scholarly attention to detail. As Kenneth
Paul Bendiner has noted: "A book such as *Landscape Illustrations of the Bible*
was not just an attempt to evoke the general spirit of the place, it was meant
to provide the hard topographical facts of what various monuments and regions looked like. Its approach to the Bible was mildly scientific and highly
rational."[1]

The entertainment industry slowly responded to the growing interest in
Holy Land topography with a range of optical entertainments and realistic
scene paintings in the theatre. As noted in the first chapter, the Leicester

Square Panorama produced its first Jerusalem panorama from on-the-spot sketches by Frederick Catherwood in 1835. Shortly after this a model of Palestine measuring 18 by 9 feet (6 by 3 metres) was displayed at a room near Somerset House. A bible was set at the end of the table for reference.[2] It is interesting to note that Catherwood was also one of the antiquaries and architects who contributed sketches for *Landscape Illustrations of the Bible*; specifically, David Roberts based his depiction of *The Golden Gate* on a Catherwood sketch. Fellow scene painter, Clarkson Stanfield, also contributed illustrations to the publication. Despite such early familiarity with Holy Land topography, there were few opportunities for scene painters to depict such settings in the theatre. George Colman, examiner of plays from 1824 to 1836, zealously upheld the prohibition against any reference to scripture in drama. As a consequence, depictions of the Holy Land most often appeared in the minor houses, which were exempt from the examiner's authority until 1843. The Royal Coburg Theatre produced post-biblical melodramas such as *The Crusaders; or Jerusalem Delivered* (1820) and Astley's Amphitheatre produced equestrian spectacles such as *The Crusaders of Jerusalem* (1834), but it was difficult for the legitimate theatres to produce works that depicted religious sites or made reference to scripture. As John Russell Stephens notes, Colman was quick to suppress *The Prodigal Son* (1828) even though the New Testament parable was a relatively popular subject in the minor theatres.[3]

It was a complicated matter for the patent house to circumvent this prohibition. In 1833, Covent Garden presented *The Israelites in Egypt; or, The Passage of the Red Sea: An Oratorio, consisting of Sacred Music, Scenery, and Personation*. The music was taken from Handel's *Israel in Egypt* and Rossini's *Mosé* and the production was billed as "the Sacred Performances During Lent." The text was written by Micahale Rophino Lacey, whose *The Knights Templar; or, The Maid of Judah* (Covent Garden 1829) was subjected to numerous deletions by Colman, even though the play was set in England during the period after the Third Crusade.[4] *The Israelites in Egypt* featured four settings: Near the City of Memphis, The Palace of the King of Memphis, The Temple of the Egyptian Idol, and Passing of the Red Sea.[5] Martin Meisel has noted that the sketch and maquette for the last scene suggests that the setting was copied from Francis Danby's apocalyptic *The Delivery of Israel out of Egypt* (1825),[6] an indication that less than scholarly sources were consulted. Despite the sanction of the Bishop of London, Colman interdicted repetition of *The Israelites in Egypt* and made clear that all Lenten oratorios "to be represented in character and with scenery and decorations" would be excluded in the future, prompting the manager of Covent Garden, Alfred Bunn, to drop plans for another spectacular oratorio on a sacred theme, *Jephtha's Vows*.[7]

Topographical reproduction of the Holy Land would grow more common and accurate in the 1840s and 1850s, coinciding with renewed military involvement in the region and advances in scholarship. Rising military tensions in the Levant culminated in 1840 with Britain's second capture of Acre. Months before the capture, the Regent's Park Diorama produced *The Shrine of the Nativity at Bethlehem*. The diorama provided compellingly realistic reproductions by employing multiple scrims painted in translucent and opaque colors, which were lit from several lighting sources controlled by a complex system of screens and shutters. The Diorama's focus on the play of light across an illusory representation of space is evident in an *Athenaeum* review for "The Shrine of the Nativity." The paper described how during the viewing

the stream of daylight fades upon the stairs – the shadows creep along the floor, and all becomes night and darkness (save for the lamps at the shrine), until gradually the chapel is generally illuminated; and in the upper church, where the blaze of light is at once the most distant and brightest, a group of figures celebrating mass bow to the altar.[8]

Like other venues, the Diorama assured its audience that these illusionistic reproductions were taken from on-the-spot sketches, in this instance supplied by David Roberts who had only recently returned from his eleven-month sketching expedition in the Holy Land. However, the Panorama at Leicester Square was even timelier in its productions. As noted earlier, the Panorama reproduced the capture of Acre only three months after the event, along with a Damascus panorama in the smaller circle. Then, in the following year, the Panorama depicted Jerusalem.

Interest in the Holy Land grew more intense after the publication of *Biblical Researches in Palestine, Mount Sinai, and Arabia Patraea* (1841) by the American Edward Robinson. Robinson's considerable background in biblical and post-biblical literature allowed him to make convincing speculations on the true location of biblical sites, including the exact location at which the Israelites crossed the Red Sea. The book produced huge excitement throughout the USA and Europe, and in 1842 Robinson became the first American to receive the gold medal of the Royal Geographical Society in London.[9] It was in this context that David Roberts published his tremendously successful three-volume collection of lithographs, *The Holy Land, Syria, Idumea, Arabia, Egypt and Nubia from Drawings made on the Spot by David Roberts* (1842–1849). Volumes such as these, combined with the greater ease of travel that was possible in the Levant after the return of Ottoman control of the region, facilitated an even greater number of Holy Land depictions in the entertainment industry.

Topographical models were popular for a public that still questioned any encroachment onto scripture by the drama. In 1847, a model of Ancient Jerusalem was displayed at 213 Piccadilly. Aware that both accuracy and propriety might be in question, the *Illustrated London News* announced that prior to its display in London, the model had been inspected in other cities by "at least 60,000 persons, including 1,000 clergymen and 300 travelers in the Holy Land."[10] The growing familiarity with biblical geography was evident in the fact that, notwithstanding the approval of 300 Holy Land travelers, the *Illustrated London News* published a second review faulting the model's depiction of Jerusalem as a walled city. The paper argued that "there is no authority to show that the exterior wall was built in the days of the Saviour, but quite the reverse."[11] A competing Jerusalem model, entitled "the Jerusalem of Prophecy," was displayed at the Egyptian Hall. The Egyptian Hall model depicted the city in the present day and was roughly half the size of the Piccadilly model. In the following year, small models of the tabernacle and the encampment of Israel were displayed at 58 Pall Mall. As always, authenticity was prized; in its review of the Pall Mall tabernacle, the *Illustrated London News* noted that "even the water-vessels have been carefully copied from the specimens in the British Museum."[12]

Despite scholarship and piety, Eastern landscapes continued to suggest violence and sexual excess to many reviewers. The same *Illustrated London News* article that faulted the Piccadilly model for inaccurately including exterior walls began with a pean to the excesses of the East:

Jerusalem! The very work is a spell and talisman to conjure up from the grave of history the shades of the Twelve Tribes – the glory of the Temple with the Hundred Gates – the pride, pomp, and circumstances of Solomon, in all his glory – the Pharisees and Sadducces, both deadly hypocrites – the siege, the sack, the slaughter, and smoking ruin, by Titus Vespasian, one of the acts of "La Clemenza di Tito" – the preachings and sufferings even to the death most ignominious of the Apostles, and their Divine Master – the prophecies of Jeremiah and our blessed Saviour, fulfilled to the very letter – these and a host of other considerations, lend to the soul a sad yet sacred excitement when we gaze upon a picture or model of the "City of Peace." Miserable misnomer! for therein peace hath seldom been.

Jerusalem translated into a mix of pomp, slaughter, and salvation, producing a "sacred excitement" in audiences. The quotation presented a long string of historical images suggesting that the mastery implicit in recreating three-dimensional terrain and architecture was met by a similar mastery of historical events. The writer then added an opera, Mozart's *Clemenza di Tito*, into this medley of historical images, suggesting that the lines between the real and the represented were not so clearly drawn.

The choice of an opera as illustration of the "sack and slaughter" of Jerusalem reflects the somewhat greater latitude that the genre was given by the examiner of plays in depicting sacred sites (even if Mozart's opera is actually set in Rome, nine years after the capture and destruction of Jerusalem by Titus' army). For example, when Verdi's *I Lombardi alla Prima Crociata* was performed in London in 1846, the *Illustrated London News* gave particular attention to the production's panoramic view of Jerusalem, explaining that the scene near the Sepulcher of Rachel was "copied from a view taken on the spot" and that the small square tomb represented in the production was one "rebuilt by the Turks, probably covering the true place of her internment."[13] Edward Fitzball's *Azaël the Prodigal* – an adaptation of the Scribe and Auber opera, *L'Enfant Prodigue* – was approved for performance even though it paralleled the New Testament parable without specifically making reference to it. In the same month that *Azaël* was approved, a drama entitled *The Prodigal* was withdrawn from examination on official advice that it was "unacceptable."[14] However, in most cases even operas were prohibited from depicting scriptural or apocryphal incidents. As a consequence, theatre managers were obliged to change the names of characters in a variety of operas. As John Russell Stephens explains, *Mosè in Egitto* (1818) became *Pietro l'Eremita* for its Haymarket premiere (1822), and *Nabucco* (1842) became *Nino* for a production at Her Majesty's Theatre (1846) and *Anato* for a later performance at Covent Garden (1850).[15]

Theatre managers had much greater success with dramas set in biblical cities but steering clear of scriptural narrative. When Covent Garden withdrew *Jephtha's Vows*, Alfred Bunn – who was managing both Covent Garden and Drury Lane – decided on a production of Byron's *Sardanapalus* at the latter theatre. Bunn did not stress the fact that the play's setting, Nineveh, is described in the Old Testament book of Nahum, though certainly his audiences would be familiar with this fact. Instead, Bunn stressed the play's connection to the tradition of theatrical orientalism, using the playbill to draw attention to the newly painted "Royal Harem" – a term that Byron, with his concern for correct costuming, would never include in a play set in the seventh century BCE. Bunn seems to have been more interested in Byron's fame than his verse. Bunn's playbill announced that "At the end... in lieu of the Green Curtain, will drop, a view of Newstead Abbey, The Residence of the late Immortal Poet."[16] The *Observer* noted that in the foreground of the painting "Lord Byron is represented sitting in a boat on the lake reading."[17] The Eastern adventurer had been transformed into an aristocratic scholar who had created his image of the East from study and reflection.

Bunn, however, was not oblivious to the continued public interest in the scandals surrounding Byron. He offered the role of Sardanapalus's concubine to Charlotte Mardyn and kept the role open for the mysteriously absent performer until the day before opening night, when he hastily recast Ellen Tree. Mardyn had long ceased to perform by the time of Bunn's production; however, that seems to have little concerned him. William Charles Macready, who played the role of Sardanapalus, was of the opinion that Bunn's "nasty motives" for casting the former actress was to capitalize on the "suspicion...circulated of her connection to Lord Byron" and decried the fact that Bunn would attempt to "attract a house by any empirical advertisement, however disgraceful."[18] Bunn became convinced that the entire episode was the "humbug" of William Dimond, the playwright who had first adapted *The Bride of Abydos* for Drury Lane in 1818.

The design for the production was no less fanciful than Bunn's hopes of securing Mardyn. While there were some Mesopotamian artifacts and reproductions in London that could have served as sources for a "correct" production, they had not had a considerable impact on the popular imagination. Claudius Rich's Mesopotamian antiquities had reached the British Museum in 1825; however, the collection was split into groups according to the various categories within which the objects fell, and so created no coherent image of the region.[19] Rich's two memoirs, *Memoir on the Ruins of Babylon* (1815) and *Second Memoir on Babylon* (1818), excited scholarly interest but made little impact on entertainment venues (though the memoirs did inspire Byron's aside in *Don Juan*: "Though Claudius Rich, Esquire, some bricks has got, / And written lately two memoirs upon't" (v, 62)). Also available was Sir Robert Ker Porter's *Travels in Georgia, Persia, Armenia, Ancient Babylonia...* (1822); however, the theatre neglected this text as well until it was used as the source for the decorations and dresses in an 1839 revival of *Artaxerxes*.[20]

Instead, the most widely disseminated images of ancient Mesopotamia at this time were not from scholarly accounts but John Martin's *Fall of Nineveh*, which was issued as a mezzotint in 1829. In reviewing *Sardanapalus*, the *Athenaeum* asserted that the production's debt to Martin would be obvious to audiences, noting, "We believe we need not inform our readers, that the last scene is a copy by Mr. Stanfield, from Mr. Martin's picture of the 'Fall of Nineveh.'"[21] Stanfield may have been influenced by Martin's fantastic

Mesopotamia when painting the Eidophusicon for *Zoroaster* (1824) as well. As Martin Meisel points out, one of the images in the panorama was "The Destruction of Babylon" and only two years earlier Martin's *The Fall of Babylon* had been exhibited at the Egyptian Hall along with his new canvas, *Destruction of Pompeii and Herculaneum.*[22]

Popular indifference to archeological discoveries in Mesopotamia changed to fascination in the aftermath of Layard's excavations of Assyrian antiquities in what is now southern Iraq. Layard's description and transportation to London of several tons of antiquities produced a huge sensation, intensifying interest in archeology and helping to precipitate changes in museum display. Layard incorrectly identified his site as the biblical city of Nineveh, capital of the Assyrian Empire, a mistake that generated further interest in his antiquities. The first shipment of Layard's antiquities arrived at the British Museum in 1848 to great excitement. Interest in the antiquities was further intensified in 1849 by the publication of Layard's account of his excavations, *Nineveh and its Remains.* The book sold 8,000 copies in its first year of publication, and by 1851 an abridged form was selling on railroad stalls. Shipments of antiquities continued to arrive at the British Museum, resulting in the creation of separate "Nineveh Rooms" for their display. The *Illustrated London News* ran several articles on the artifacts during these years, and in 1853 marked the opening of a new "Nineveh Room" with a large foldout section illustrating the "antiquities from 'The Buried City of the East'" in anticipation of the Easter holiday (when crowds at the Museum were greatest).[23]

Nineveh excited particular fascination because it was often depicted as a city consumed by sensual excess until its swift collapse. In part this image was generated by the Old Testament depiction of Nineveh in the Book of Nahum as an evil city of great wealth inviting God's retribution. The idea that the Assyrian decline was a near instantaneous collapse was first disseminated in Byron's *Sardanapalus*, which compressed the long war between the Medes, Chaldeans, and Assyrians into a rebellion that desolated Nineveh in a single day. This image of the swift collapse of a decadent city, precipitating the fall of a great empire, was further disseminated in paintings such as Delacroix's *Death of Sardanapalus* (1828) and Martin's *The Fall of Nineveh* (1828). Britons could interpret Layard's finds as vindication of their belief in biblical history at a time when geological finds had begun to undermine the biblical chronology. Layard's excavations were thought to reveal "details of the appearance and character of places and people mentioned in the Old Testament," as one historian writes.[24] Moreover, as illustrating a story of Eastern decadence and collapse, these antiquities bolstered British confidence in the superiority of their own culture and justified their presence in the declining East.

The theatre was quick to respond to public interest in Mesopotamian antiquities, incorporating elements of Layard's finds into several productions depicting the ancient East. While not specifically dramatizing scripture, two notable productions used these elements to produce convincing images of the biblical past: Fitzball's *Azaël the Prodigal* (Drury Lane 1851), and Charles Kean's production of Byron's *Sardanapalus* (Princess's 1853). The scene painting and mise-en-scène for both of these productions evoked contemporary research on the East, providing a wealth of realistic details suggestive of or directly copied from artifacts that had been transported to London. These productions also reflected contemporary theories on the decline of ancient Eastern civilizations. More significantly, one can discern in the theatre's adaptation of orientalist research both a debt to and an influence on display strategies at exhibitions and museums.

These two productions reflect different parameters for the combination and arrangement of exotic imagery, and this distinction parallels a significant shift in display strategies at exhibitions and museums. The combination of artifacts across regions and periods, which was once licensed by theatrical and curatorial artistry, grew less common at both theatres and museums. As theatres and museums espoused the goal of educating the masses, and as they increasingly promised accurate reproductions of exotic places, display became less a matter of invention than a process of transcription.

Azaël and *Sardanapalus* depicted the biblical past in scenes combining built-out scenery, flats, and elaborately orchestrated mise-en-scène all inspired by Layard's excavations. In the process, both productions demonstrate the Victorian conviction that current excavations verified scripture and provided a window onto the biblical past. They also reveal the Victorian belief that artifacts and ancient texts could be used to illustrate the unchanging manners and customs of exotic peoples. As Eastern civilization supposedly had not progressed since antiquity, it followed that Eastern manners and customs were similarly frozen in time. By piling scholarly detail into the surrounding environment, these productions suggested that the character types in these plays – standard figures from oriental romances such as the false prophet, the voluptuary, and the odalisque – represented the unchanging nature of Eastern peoples.

The theatre's depiction of a decadent East also reflected the popular dissemination of the degenerationist theory of human history to account for the high level of civilization of ancient Eastern cultures as evidenced by the excavations of Layard and others.[25] While these excavations seemed to verify the Old Testament's account of ancient cities, they also undermined the chronology of biblical scholars, which limited human history to 6,000 years. The degenerationist theory of human history reconciled contradictions between the biblical and archeological records. In this model, God endowed humankind with a natural propensity for civilization and the primitivism of non-Europeans was the product of degeneration. As George W. Stocking, Jr., explains, there was little time in the biblical chronology for civilizations "to have raised themselves from savagery." However, "there was plenty of time available for nineteenth-century savages to have fallen from an originally higher state."[26]

In addition, the fall of ancient civilizations may have been linked, in the popular mind, with the theory that the earth had formed through a series of catastrophes followed by divine creations. Unlike their European counterparts, many British scholars attempted to reconcile geological evidence with the Mosaic record. Such reasoning provided pre-Darwinian Victorians with both scholarly and religious justification for their fascination with ancient cataclysms.[27] The stage responded to current trends in scholarship when it illustrated biblical tales with stage designs either inspired or copied from recent excavations. Moreover, the depiction of these ancient cultures as licentious and depraved was consistent with theories of degenerationism – enabling theatre practitioners to preserve romantic depictions of the East's sexual excess while appearing to conform to a new disciplinary rigor. Finally, the tried and true practice of the closing conflagration could be used to illustrate the popular view that ancient Eastern civilizations collapsed with spectacular speed under the weight of their own decadence.

"AZAËL" AND THE RESUSCITATION OF THE ANCIENT EAST

Drury Lane's *Azaël the Prodigal* follows the biblical story of the prodigal son, depicting ancient Judea and Memphis in a range of elaborate sets, detailed scene painting, and spectacularly choreographed scenes. Reviewers praised the production for its archeological accuracy. It was, apparently, not only "one of the most elaborately gorgeous exhibitions ever placed on the boards"[28] but a careful examination of life in the biblical East. "All is correct, down to the most minute particular," the *Athenaeum* explained. The *Illustrated London News* praised the production for its "Egyptian costume," and its range of "orthodox 'properties'" which included "sphinxes… monster vases, glasses, lamps [and] ancient musical instruments," and the *Era* praised the production's "characteristic scenery and dresses."[29] Spectacle was reclaimed as edifying display, as when the lavish opening desert scene was deemed a justified representation of the biblical East. The *Athenaeum* explained that the opening included "all the accessories of Eastern magnificence, female attendants in oriental costume, travellers and camels, and whatever else is proper to realize the idea of a patriarchal encampment." As the *Era* explained, *Azaël* demonstrated "how rationally edifying a gorgeous spectacle could be made." The significant point is not whether or not these properties were in fact authentic but rather that their level of detail (down to the "most minute particular") combined with their tremendous range assured reviewers that they saw an accurate reproduction of the ancient East.

These details invariably revealed an Eastern taste for grandeur and sensual pleasure. From the first scene, the simple desert "habitation" of both Scribe and Fitzball's scripts is transformed into a giant pavilion filling the entire stage. The maquette shows rich draperies and pillows, and giant vases and pitchers.[30] This set was then filled with camels, travelers, and female attendants "in oriental costume," with stone tablets discretely placed against a down-stage right wing. A humble encampment was transformed into Eastern magnificence, an architectural enactment of excess paralleling the masses of female attendants. The pious tribal chief of both scripts becomes an Eastern voluptuary in his harem (despite his possession of what appears to be the ten commandments). As the action is transported to Memphis, the scenes grow even more lavish. The maquettes feature a brightly decorated interior with winged sphinxes as well as a cavernous interior of colonnades reaching back in minute perspective like one of John Martin's fantastic canvases (Fig. 4.1). At the same time, the inclusion of design motifs disseminated in British publications on ancient Egypt gave the impression of authenticity. The capitals and central wing ornamentation of *Azaël's* colonnades resemble those of the Temple of the Isle of Philoe, as illustrated in Belzoni's popular account of his Egyptian excavations.[31] Sumptuous stagings that purported to recreate the biblical East escaped reproach.

This architectural excess and staged sensuality attained an unprecedented peak in *Azaël's* scene of temple debauchery. The *Illustrated London News* reported that the scene began with a pantomime, groups of "priests and dancing almées...being first viewed in animated action in their orgies, and afterwards gazed upon, when, worn out with wine and revel, they are extended in deep sleep on the steps and ground."[32] The *Athenaeum* explained that these "secret orgies in honor of the god Apis" took place in "full temple costume" and constituted "the crowning effort of the piece."[33]

4.1 Grieve's maquette for the temple scene in *Azaël the Prodigal*, 1851

While noting the success of the staging, the *Athenaeum* was also conscious of the scene's potential to offend. The paper described the temple scene as "shown with all its grandeurs and mystical rites, voluptuous and picturesque to the extreme point of tolerance." Such sensual excess was clearly dangerous material for the Victorian stage, and had to be carefully managed. Drury Lane's *Azaël* carefully linked orgy scenes to an Egyptian paganism that was documented in the Bible and duly punished. The sex scenes in *Azaël* could be justified as a careful examination of the dissembling and depravity of the false Eastern religions, as verified by scripture and scholarship. This aura of scholarship enabled a respectable entertainment to approach "the extreme point of tolerance" – this was not base sexual fantasy but a careful examination of Oriental manners.

A sense of imminent decline permeated *Azaël*'s magnificent scenes of pagan excess (the *Era* review described these "profane idolators" as a "dissipated and voluptuous people"), and this sense was further intensified by the production's architectural sources. The winged sphinxes excavated by Layard and reproduced in *The Monuments of Nineveh* possibly inspired the repeated depiction of winged sphinxes in *Azaël*,[34] reminding audiences of the inevitable collapse of decadent Eastern empires. If nothing else, Nineveh was on the mind of the reviewer for the *Illustrated London News*, who surveyed the tremendous range of elements marshaled in *Azaël*'s temple scene and concluded that "the whole is like a resuscitated Nineveh."[35]

This was both the Nineveh of Layard and that of John Martin. Earlier in the review the temple scene was compared to "one of Martin's monstrous conceptions." Victorian audiences would not have seen a contradiction. Layard's discoveries were interpreted in the light of Martin's apocalyptic imagery, not as a refutation. Martin offered a vision of human history structured around the violent cataclysms that lingered in many geological and archeological accounts. In this sense, the story of Oriental excess and collapse complemented the pre-progressionist model of history that persisted until the acceptance of the Darwinian account. In combining Assyrian design motifs with a Martinesque excess, *Azaël* simply confirmed that Memphis adhered to an accepted picture of ancient Eastern cities – they were the magnificent pinnacles of decadent empires, spectacularly perched before instantaneous and inevitable collapse.

While *Azaël* gave the impression of a debt to recent scholarship, much of its imagery was in fact borrowed from earlier productions. The fact that the script calls for dancing "almées" is an indication that Fitzball drew more from theatrical orientalism than scholarly works such as Wilkinson's well-known *Manners and Customs of Ancient Egyptians*. Almée is a transliteration of the Arabic word for a female singer, which entered into the English language in Byron's description of the Pasha's entertainments in *The Corsair*. The term was subsequently employed to refer to slave girls in many melodramas and ballets depicting the Islamic East, but it was decidedly not a term dating from or associated with ancient Egypt. The slip is telling, for *Azaël*'s principal dance scene – with its elaborate play of scarves framing a central dancer who is praised for her "light, licentious steps, and her languishing, seductive movements" – recalls earlier harem plays (ii.i). However, such theatrical borrowing did not diminish the play's aura of accuracy; no reviewer complained of the conflation of Islamic harem and ancient Egyptian temple. The harem, as symbol of Eastern sensuality and excess, was apparently accepted as a timeless feature of Eastern civilization.[36]

One sees similar theatrical borrowings in *Azaël*'s scene painting, which periodically mixed ancient and Islamic ornament. Judging from the maquettes, *Azaël* included a spectacular panorama of Memphis with a central pyramid featuring Islamic keyhole arches (Fig. 4.2). Even though *Azaël* purported to recreate the biblical past, the combination of almées with

4.2 Detail from Grieve's maquette for the Memphis setting in *Azaël the Prodigal*, 1851

ancient rites and pyramids with Islamic design escaped notice. The use of repeated imagery augmented the sense of authenticity, even when its use created combinations inconsistent with contemporary scholarship. A surfeit of vaguely familiar detail signaled the "real," regardless of whether the details originated in fanciful or realistic productions. *Azaël* overwhelmed spectators with the fullness of its spectacle, filling the stage with "sphinxes, monster vases, glasses, lamps, and ancient musical instruments," not to mention troops of almées in elaborate costumes right up to the lappets on their "Egyptian caps" as described in the published text.

Azaël's connection to orientalist study was not limited to its use of detail, its copying of antiquities, or its characterization of the East. *Azaël* carefully sculpted and combined such orientalist material in three dimensions at the same time that museums and exhibitions were moving towards the in situ display. *Azaël* stands out among productions that used built-out scenery and mise-en-scène to reconstruct historically and geographically remote regions, a trend – I will argue – that paralleled emerging practices at exhibitions and museums. Reviewers of *Azaël* were not simply struck by the production's use of elaborate and (supposedly) accurate scene painting, costumes, and properties; they were struck by how these elements were combined to recreate the exotic past. It was, according to the *Illustrated London News*, "the mise-en-scène of [the temple scene] which would alone ensure popularity for this spectacle."[37] The maquettes indicate that the scene featured a great practical staircase (or possibly, a series of ascending platforms fronted with paintings of steps). According to the *Illustrated London News*, these steps occupied "the entire breadth of the stage, and [rose] to the 'slips.'" During the spectacular orgy pantomime, groups of actors were placed on the steps and ground and surrounded by an extensive array of Egyptian properties. The *Athenaeum* commended the scene because the "groupings" of the priests and priestesses were "rich, varied, characteristic and finely disposed."[38] In other words, the placement of objects in the stage space was both representative and artful. The production succeeded because the assembly of its elements embodied the essential decline immanent to the East while still captivating audiences.

Critical response to the temple scene consistently figured the stage as a space of assembly; Drury Lane manifested the East through the careful manipulation of its parts. As such, theatrical orientalism shared the strategies of historical recovery that Richard Schoch has delineated in *Shakespeare's Victorian Stages: Performing History in the Theatre of Charles Kean*. Schoch argues that in Kean's Shakespeare revivals, "the diverse fragments of theatrical performance 'reassimilate' to evoke the presence, material continuity and oneness of the past."[39] As noted earlier, the *Illustrated London News* marveled at the range of properties and costumes displayed in *Azaël's* temple scene, concluding that "the whole is like a resuscitated Nineveh." Beyond suggesting associations between the production's design and Layard's excavations, the quotation also reveals central assumptions about the objectives and ontology of stage performance. It was the "whole" of the scene that the reviewer commented on: performers in historically accurate costumes performing characteristic actions, surrounded by an extensive catalogue of Egyptian reproductions, and carefully placed in an elaborate built-out ancient temple. This "whole" did not simply reproduce a single setting; it "resuscitated" an entire historical and geographical milieu. The Victorian stage attempted to create complete worlds out of excavated fragments.

It is in this new practice of constructing worlds out of fragments – modeled properties and built-out scenery – that the theatre shows its affinity with emerging museum practice. As Kirshenblatt-Gimblett has argued, the systematic arrangement of nineteenth-century museums was intended to rescue the "ethnographic fragment" from trivialization, allowing it to stand in for broader cultural practice or a historical process:

Plants and animals arranged according to the Linnaean classification affirmed the goodness of the divine plan in Charles Willson Peale's museum in Philadelphia during the eighteenth and nineteenth century. A. H. L. F. Pitt Rivers preferred to arrange his series of weapons according to formal criteria, from simplest to most complex, to tell the story of mankind's inexorable evolution through stages of racial and cultural development.[40]

The arrangement of objects revealed lessons that transcended the meaning of any isolated artifact. Similarly, in productions like *Azaël*, theatrical art was newly conceived of as a process in which meaning was produced through visual synecdoche; scenic fragments were bundled together so as to illuminate the fullness of the geographically and historically distant.

In this sense, nineteenth-century theatre, no less than the nineteenth-century museum, reflected a new way of conceiving of knowledge. Just as the nineteenth-century human sciences, according to Foucault, conceived of existence as structured by invisible "transcendentals" (such as the force of labor, the energy of life, and the power of speech), theatres and museums offered objects as a means of tracing out exotic life or a racial essence. The significance of objects did not reside in their specific forms, but patterns evidenced in the succession of forms or in their independent historicity and use. According to Hayden White, Foucault's modern *episteme* implicitly embodies a shift towards synecdoche. White writes: "This 'grasping together' of the parts of a thing as aspects of a whole that is greater than the sum of the parts, this ascription of wholeness and organic unity to a congeries of elements in a system, is precisely the modality of relationships that is given in language by the trope of *synecdoche*."[41] White's characterization of the modern *episteme* provides a useful vantage point on both Victorian stage and museum practice. The belief that both setting and mise-en-scène

can embody "characteristic" features of, and teach lessons about, the ancient and exotic provides a clear example of this synecdochal logic. *Azaël*
combined set pieces, built-out architecture, modeled properties, and flats –
all masquerading as archeological fragments – in order to reconstitute the
biblical East and illustrate that region's inherent decline.

   Such tropological analysis has been particularly useful to historians
of museum culture, and their findings shed light on theatrical practice.
Stephen Bann has applied White's analysis of Foucault to discover a strategy of synecdoche at the Musée de Cluny in which "the object from the past
becomes the basis for an integrative construction of historical totalities."[42]
Drawing on Foucault, Eilean Hooper-Greenhill's analysis of modern museums notes that museum organizers no longer think of their holdings as
"simple visual pieces" but instead use natural objects to explore "analogy and
succession." She similarly makes synecdoche central in the creation of museum knowledge when she writes: "the link between one organic structure
and another is no longer the identity of several parts, but the identity of the
relationship between the parts, and of the functions which they perform."[43]
Tony Bennett has argued that museums in the modern age sought to reconstitute the unity of "Man," creating a totality from fragments embedded
in disparate histories.[44] Kirshenblatt-Gimblett also practices tropological
analysis in describing in situ displays as "metonymic."[45] John Elsner has
explained how synecdochal logic coexisted with an antiquarian desire to
create complete idealized worlds out of fragments. Elsner writes that the
Model Room in Soane's Museum "reinvents the collection not just as a
synecdochic cult of the fragment (where the parts, and the casts of parts,
evoke the wholes from whence they derive), but also as a series of *representations*, whereby antiquity is imagined as an ideal realm of miniatures." As a
group, Elsner explains, the models "imagine an ideal Neoclassical world."[46]

   Elsner's comments have particular relevance for the study of theatrical
practice, for objects on stage are never simply an evocation of an absent
totality, but instead demand attention as a crafted whole – a single world –
in their constitution of a coherent stage picture. *Azaël*'s properties suggested the wonders that exist far beyond the stage, revealing through their
arrangement exotic life and its immanent decline. However, *Azaël* also demanded attention for its own imaginative combinations, claiming a space
for its own artistry. As such, it is useful to compare *Azaël*'s scenographic
method with that of Belzoni, whose illustrations of Egyptian antiquities
put in circulation the imagery that would eventually feature prominently in
Azaël's scene painting. As noted earlier, Belzoni transported his collection
of antiquities to London in 1821, and staged at the Egyptian Hall what *The*

Times described as a "magnificent *representation* of the great monument which he first discovered in Egypt – the tomb, or more properly speaking, sepulchral palace of Psamnuethes, the Egyptian King and conqueror" (my italics).[47] Belzoni had wrongly attributed the tomb to the biblical pharaoh Psamnuethes or Psammis (rather than Seti I) on the basis of Thomas Young's misidentification of a hieroglyph. Like later archeologists, exhibitors, and theatre practitioners, Belzoni looked to Eastern antiquities for corroboration of biblical narratives and then sought to reproduce this proof of divine history in three dimensions.

According to *The Times*, the exhibit was composed in two main parts: a 51-foot (16-metre) model of the tomb complex, and two plaster replicas (one 20 by 14 feet [6 by 4 metres]) made from wax impressions of the bas-reliefs of the tomb and painted in colors copied on the spot. According to one of Belzoni's biographers, these reliefs were arranged so as to reproduce two chambers of the tomb complex, and they were lit by lamp-light in a room whose roof had been lowered so as to recreate Belzoni's first impressions on entering the tomb.[48] Moreover, this room had been previously remodeled in the pharaonic style, with Egyptian-style portals and columns banded with lotuses, Hathor heads, and hieroglyphs.[49] Belzoni employed modeled and painted walls that were surrounded in turn by modeled columns and portals all theatrically lit so as to recreate the experience of entering an ancient tomb. Belzoni then supplemented this recreation with what *The Times* described as "a multitude of collateral curiosities – such as mummies, papyri, medals, and female ornaments" which were "placed in cases around the room."[50] Belzoni did not simply present the antiquities that he confiscated. Rather, as the *Times* article indicates, he created a "representation" of the entire environment of which his antiquities were an integral part.

Audiences at Belzoni's exhibition experienced the ancient, rather than simply observed isolated antiquities, but it was the ancient as a generalized essence rather than a network of specific practices, objects, and architecture. Belzoni's exhibition represents a break from the eclecticism that marked the Egyptian Hall's general holdings, in which spectators might pass through a mockup of a basaltic cavern to discover a panorama of a rain forest backing an Indian hut, as well as models of animals ranging from an elephant to seals.[51] However, it would be incorrect to conclude that Belzoni had created a historical period room in what had formerly been a "cemetery of bric-a-brac" (to adopt the 1889 phrase of George Brown Goode, director of the US National Museum).[52] The Egyptian Hall's (admittedly haphazard) use of modeled scenes already marked a significant departure from current exhibition practice. More importantly, while Belzoni's arrangement of antiquities and modeled reproductions was designed to create the sensation of entering a tomb, it was not designed to literally recreate a specific place, or for that matter, a specific period. Belzoni's "multitude of collateral curiosities" was the product of three years of collecting and as such represented materials from several sites and different historical periods. This mixing from multiple sites and periods distinguishes Belzoni's exhibition from later nineteenth-century exhibitions in which the placement of objects was determined by original position, typology, or the evolution of forms.

As *The Times* makes clear, Belzoni's ability to create the sensation of entering a tomb was as much evidence of artistry as scholarly rigor. *The Times* explained, "Every eye, we think, must be gratified by this singular combination and skilful arrangement of objects so new, and in themselves, so striking." It was not that information was generated in Belzoni's "combination and skilful arrangement of objects," but rather that it *gratified the eye*. Belzoni's exhibition straddled the transition from the cabinet of wonders to such modern-day exhibition forms as the in situ display and the habitat group. Like later exhibitions, Belzoni's created a synecdochal relation between the displayed object and a larger concept, here the ancient East as a space of wealth and mystery. However, the ancient East as figured in the Egyptian Hall was a general style, an imaginative combination across periods that created the sense of historical and geographical distance, and not a network of specific monuments and customs. The collection was judged by aesthetic as much as informational criteria. The displayed objects were not valued purely for the meanings generated in their presentation and combinations, but were praised as new and striking *in themselves*. In this sense, Belzoni's exhibition marks a point of transition, straddling the shift from "rarity" to "representativeness."

Drury Lane's *Azaël* similarly marks this point of transition. Like Belzoni's exhibition, *Azaël* employed built-out properties and a wealth of detail to create the impression of immersion into the authentic East. At both Egyptian Hall and Drury Lane, this aura of authenticity masked an inherent eclecticism and the elevation of artistic over historical criteria. Belzoni's scholarship "gratified the eye" just as *Azaël*'s mise-en-scène was praised as both "characteristic and finely disposed." If *Azaël* borrowed imagery from archeology, Belzoni borrowed his method from the theatre. His use of modeled, painted walls and controlled lighting expanded on early experiments in the theatre, even as his ancient environment far outpaced the possibilities of the contemporary stage. In this context it seems particularly telling that before remaking himself into an Eastern explorer, Belzoni performed in pantomimes at Sadler's Wells theatre as well as at Astley's Amphitheatre and the old Royalty Theatre.[53] Belzoni the actor saw the performative potential of antiquities – that objects could be used to recreate place and, in the process, imbue place with idea (whether that idea was the mysterious obscurity of an Egyptian temple or the decline immanent to Oriental luxury). However, at both Belzoni's exhibition and *Azaël*, the exhibitor's imagination shaped the recreation of place. By contrast Kean's *Sardanapalus* promised exact transcriptions of place, and as such paralleled an emerging museum practice. In the eclectic style of *Azaël*, the depiction of Egyptian antiquities could feature elements inspired by excavations in southern Iraq. For Kean, by contrast, archeology set clear guidelines for theatrical design.

"SARDANAPALUS" AND SCIENCES OF THE HUMAN RACES

At mid-century, Assyrian antiquities became repeated design elements for theatrical orientalism. Even plays that depicted an East far removed in period or geography from Nineveh incorporated Layard's antiquities into the design, such as Samuel Phelps's production of *Pericles* (Sadlers Wells 1854).[54] Without a doubt, however, Charles Kean's production of *Sardanapalus* in 1853 was the most renowned and archeologically rigorous evocation of Nineveh. I will argue that Kean's extensive documentation and his innovative use of the stage space in mounting one of the great dramas of the romantic period reveal the dialectical relation between the exotic East of poets such as Byron, Moore, and Southey and the new scholarly East of emerging disciplines. Kean spectacularly depicted the excess of ancient Assyria, relying on familiar images of theatrical orientalism and oriental romances. At the same time, Kean sought to ground his production in contemporary scholarship. He included numerous citations in his characteristically long playbill, but even more strikingly, he carefully reproduced both the form and arrangement of the artifacts at the British Museum on the stage of the Princess's Theatre. Kean then filled his theatrical period room with actors wearing purportedly accurate costumes, gesturing in purportedly Assyrian fashion, even donning make-up and beards so as to reproduce Assyrian physiognomy as purportedly recorded in artifacts.

Kean made clear in his playbill note that the Assyrian excavation, and his production by association, served to illuminate the biblical past. It was not simply any ancient city that had been "brought to light," but "the Nineveh of Scripture... the Nineveh in which the captive Tribes of Israel had labored and wept."[55] Piety, no less than scholarship, informed the mounting of *Sardanapalus*, and audiences could rest assured that they did not witness a mere imaginative creation but the carefully researched reproduction of the biblical past. Kean's incessant literalism and extensive cutting of the text effaced the romantic conception of Eastern lands as a metaphor for the alternately creative and destructive impulses of the poetic imagination. London, after all, was flocking to the Nineveh of the British Museum, not the Nineveh of Byron's soul.

While *Azaël* was praised for "resuscitating" Nineveh, the suggestion that theatre and archeology could together exhume and reanimate dead worlds became explicit in the excited reception of Kean's production. As the *Illustrated London News* enthusiastically announced, under Kean's direction *Sardanapalus* had become "the medium of placing on the boards the disinterred glories of ancient Nineveh."[56] Kean's scientific necromancy was well timed; three months earlier the British Museum had opened a separate gallery, dubbed the Nineveh Room, solely devoted to the display of Assyrian antiquities. In his playbill, Kean stated that "the sculptures now in the British Museum have been rigidly followed" and countless reviews concurred with the *Illustrated London News's* assertion that Kean reproduced these artifacts "with the most perfect accuracy of detail." In the playbill, Kean explained that a primary objective of his production was to "present to the eye the gorgeous and striking scenery, that has been so unexpectedly dug from the very bowels of the earth." He had simply sought to illustrate what others had "disinterred" and so join the ranks of an illustrious band of grave-robbers. However, Kean did not simply wish to reproduce artifacts, but "to convey to the stage an accurate portraiture and *living picture of an age* long since past away" (my italics). Rather than displaying dead artifacts, Kean provided a comprehensive view onto an entire age as it lived and breathed, separated from audiences by a mere proscenium arch. The production was, in the words of the *Era* review, further proof that Britain had "learned to annihilate space and time."[57] If trains, telegraphs, and steamers weren't already proof of this technological conjuring, according to the *Era,* Kean's reborn Nineveh was.

As was the case in Drury Lane's *Azaël*, the mise-en-scène for Kean's *Sardanapalus* was as responsible for creating a sense of accuracy as the actual objects depicted. Moreover, the similarity of Kean's design to the layout of the British Museum suggests the strong relation between the theatre's new scenographic logic and methods of display being pioneered in museums and exhibitions. Kean not only copied the form of Assyrian antiquities but their placement as delineated both in Layard's *Monuments of Nineveh* and at the British Museum's Nineveh Room. In the fifth act, designer J. Dayes placed colossal bulls around a rear portal, essentially reproducing the arrangement of these sculptures as depicted in the second plate of Layard's book (Figs. 4.3, 4.4). In doing so, Kean used a technique that had already been

4.3 Daye's setting for *Sardanapalus*, 1853

4.4 Throne Room from Austen Henry Layard's *The Monuments of Nineveh, From Drawings Made on the Spot*

employed at the British Museum. The *Illustrated London News* for 26 March 1853 depicts a similar layout at the Nineveh Room and explains that the antiquities were arranged in apartments according to their original placement. Audiences familiar with Layard's illustration, the British Museum's Nineveh Room, or its depiction in the *Illustrated London News* were more likely to view Kean's production as a reproduction rather than a fanciful invention. In both the museum and the theatre, the placement of objects signaled the authentic reproduction of exotic space.[58]

The theatre's growing emphasis on scenic fullness, its nascent practice of modeling unified environments, and its assertion that such practices were organized according to the discoveries of scholarly research corresponded with similar developments in museums. Individual rooms for regional artifacts had existed at the British Museum since the South Seas Room was reorganized in 1808 to "illustrate particular Customs of different Nations."[59] However, it was the growing number of large Eastern antiquities that prompted the proliferation of galleries devoted to specific regions and periods. According to Edward Miller, between 1834 and 1851 the space devoted to Egyptian antiquities increased from 1,773 square feet (165 square metres) to 9,044 (840) and the space devoted to Assyrian antiquities increased from 218 (20) to 2,736 (254) – even as Layard's finds continued to pour in.[60] It was not simply the number of artifacts but their size that provided museum-goers with a new sense of the relation between the museum gallery and exotic space. The colossal frieze placed against the wall became part of a museum environment rather than a displayed object. This sense of environment was intensified by the apparent permanence of the positioning; smaller objects could be transported from one gallery to the other with relative ease, whereas a ten-ton winged bull was not likely to be moved from the Nineveh Room. The Nineveh Room did not simply frame sculptures and fragments, it was composed of these fragments. In the process, the room itself ceased to be a neutral space for display and became instead a representation of ancient Assyria.

This new emphasis on the display environment was accompanied by an equally strong interest in racial categories. Two months before the opening of *Sardanapalus*, the *Illustrated London News* announced that an ethnology section figured prominently in the plans for the Sydenham Crystal Palace, and that there visitors would see "models of the human race, together with their national costumes, their domestic and agricultural implements, their armour, their dwellings, their modes of conveyance, and other characteristic objects appertaining to them."[61] Charles Kean similarly presented apparently researched racial models surrounded by reproductions of native implements and dwellings. The actors, no less than the walls, demonstrated complete fidelity to the archeological record. The costume notes that conclude his published acting edition explain, "All of the characters excepting Myrrha, have swarthy complexions and curled and bushy black hair, and, excepting the Eunuchs, long and bushy beards."[62] Myrrha, as a Greek, was apparently exempt from brownface and served, in her contrast, to underscore that a distinct and different race was depicted. This was race as preserved in the archeological record and available to the earnest researcher; the bearded faces of Layard's Assyrian bulls were reproduced in Kean's scene painting and in the faces of his actors. Even actor physicality conformed to the archeological record; Kean mimicked the angular body positions that characterized the figures of ancient drawings and reliefs. In his desire to capture the respectability of the museum, Kean transformed his stage production into an animated artifact. As in a *tableau vivant*, success was measured by the ability of the living to conform to images of the dead.

Both the *Athenaeum* and the *Illustrated London News* criticized Kean's specific physical choices, while embracing their underlying racial essentialism. The papers asserted that Kean, with his angular positions, had confused the deficiencies of ancient painting with reality. As the *Illustrated London News* explained, "The action of Oriental people does not justify this assumption [of angular body positions]; their manner having a general sweep and roundness which the rude artist, however, was incapable of imitating." Though strictly speaking Kean's stage picture might be incorrect, it was excusable according to both these papers. The *Illustrated London News* noted that Kean was prompted by "the laudable desire evinced to conform to the pictorial authorities, for the purpose of promoting the utmost possible vraissemblance," and the *Athenaeum* explained that Kean's "literal copying of angularities... add[ed] to the remote oriental character of the scene."[63] It was not that Kean was incorrect to suggest that a people conformed to a specific physicality, and that this physicality could be captured in reliefs and then reproduced on stage; the problem was simply that Kean had gotten the physicality wrong. Kean's posture was inaccurate because present-day Oriental people (apparently all of them) demonstrated a "general sweep and roundness" that remained unchanged since ancient times. Moreover, this inaccuracy ultimately produced a remoteness that embodied the "oriental character" with greater fidelity than was possible by mere ethnographic accuracy. Kean got the essence right, even if he had arrived there through error.

As in other orientalist productions, playing the exotic was a sexually evocative act. In noting the skin color of the characters in his acting edition,

Kean explained that the "bare feet and arms" of the dancing girls were also "coloured." At the most immediate level, this insistence that race be represented in face-paint served as a marker of authenticity. At the same time, however, the stipulation that makes the marker evident – the nakedness of feet and arms – indicates how charged "blacking up" was for actresses on the Victorian stage. Kean's costume notes further explain that the dancing girls wore white merino dresses "without under clothes," suggesting that the costumes fit closely enough to make anachronistic petticoats impossible, but also suggesting how sexually potent divergence from conventional female dress was for Victorian audiences. It has been argued that simply stepping on stage tainted the Victorian actress with an indecorous visual availability;[64] the act was that much more striking when brownface and costume suggested the limitless availability of the imagined harem.

Kean's large troop of dancing girls was a major component of the spectacle, but despite the production's implied ethnographic accuracy, *Sardanapalus* (like *Azaël*) was indebted to the sensual displays of an ongoing tradition of theatrical orientalism. This is evident from the opening scene in which Sardanapalus first entered on his "gilt chariot drawn by two cream-coloured steeds" and preceded by a host of court figures. Given Kean's relentless copying of artifacts, the chariot was presumably based on one of the many bas-reliefs featuring chariots illustrated in *Monuments of Assyria* and currently on display at the British Museum. However, the specific design of the chariot could not possibly command attention in the midst of the preceding spearmen, musicians, nobles, officers, eunuchs, standard bearers, and "troop of Dancing Girls, who advance with joyous and characteristic movements" before running to the back, "clapping their hands and gesticulating joyfully." The dancing girls also appeared in the banquet scene of Act III and again performed a "characteristic" dance as Sardanapalus – crowned with roses and surrounded by his fanbearers, cupbearer, and Myrrha – watched from a dais.[65]

The *Illustrated London News* explained that the dance was "Bayadère" and that it was not only "picturesque" and "striking" but also "characteristic."[66] The term "bayadère" refers to a dancer and singer in a Hindu temple and the bayadère was already becoming a common figure in theatrical orientalism. By 1858, the bayadère was familiar enough to inspire Théophile Gautier's libretto for the ballet *Sacountala* (which in turn inspired the libretto for the better-known 1877 Marius Petipa ballet *La Bayadère*). It would appear that in the mind of the reviewer, Kean's choreography recalled earlier orientalist productions, though these productions did not depict the period or region of *Sardanapalus*. At the very least, the use of the term suggests that the reviewer saw no distinction between Indian and Assyrian dance; the one could substitute for the other as both were Eastern. Despite this disjuncture, the script's assertions of "characteristic" movement was echoed by the reviewer's judgment. Neither Kean nor the paper stated of what the dance was "characteristic" – presumably Assyrian entertainments though theatrical orientalism is more accurately the reference.

The conflation of races implied by the review might seem like merely a mistaken word choice; however, it actually parallels a significant strain of racial thinking at this time. No less an authority than James Prichard would cite Layard's excavations as evidence of "the almost juxtaposition, or the existence in adjoining districts, during the earliest epoch of history, of the three greatest Asiatic families of nations." Speaking before the Ethnological Society of London in 1848, Prichard argued that philological study of the various forms of cuneiform inscriptions unearthed by recent excavations was on the verge of verifying the speculation of the eighteenth-century orientalist, Sir William Jones, that the three principal races of man – the Indo-European race, the Shemite or Assyrian or Syro-Arabic race, and the Tartar or High Asiatic race – were concentrated in a common point at the earliest dawning of history.[67] Of course there is no reason to think that the *Illustrated London News* writer, or Kean for that matter, was familiar with Prichard's address. The point is that a prominent strain in ethnological thought looked to Assyrian archeology for information on the racial origins of humans and believed it had discovered a striking concurrence across Eastern nations. While Prichard's search for the proof of human unity was radically distinct in complexity and intent from Kean's racial essentialism, the point remains that for all the archeological record was seen as a key to understanding race.

According to Kean, Byron's text no less than the Layard's antiquities revealed the essence of Assyria. While Kean consistently repeated that British archeology had made his production possible (and by extension, his architectural and racial mimesis), he also claimed that the essence of Assyria had already been delineated in the play. In his playbill note, Kean recreated the poet as an orientalist scholar and patriot. Kean presented the play text as a careful examination of Eastern manners and customs and an illustration of sacred history (though Kean acknowledged that he had corrected a minor geographical error stemming from an inaccuracy in Byron's ancient source text). If the play had remained unperformed for years, it only demonstrated that "it has been impossible to render Lord Byron's Tragedy of 'Sardanapalus' upon the Stage with proper dramatic effect, because until now, we have known nothing of Assyrian architecture and costume." Byron emerged as a careful researcher ahead of his time, knowledgeable of the history and essential nature of the East even if the limited archeology of his day made scenic illustration impossible. Fortunately for theatre audiences, archeology had flowered.

Not only did scholarship complete the poet's promise, but the poet had given purpose to scientific inquiry. Kean explained that the "rescued bas-relief" of Nineveh "could not find dramatic illustration but for the existence of the only Tragedy that has reference to the period of which they treat." A British poet and British scholars had rescued Eastern artifacts from idle internment, giving them a proper home and productive life on the British stage. Through the play, artifacts were made to speak their meaning, a meaning that the poet–scholar had been able to intuit through a combination of research and genius. It would appear, then, that the *Era* told only half the story when it announced that "Mr. Kean has exhumed from the dust of comparative oblivion Lord Byron's splendid tragedy of Sardanapalus."[68] Byron himself had been exhumed and placed next to the disinterred glories that proved the accuracy of his vision.

Throughout his playbill note, Kean suggested that he performed a national duty by staging *Sardanapalus* and, in the process, again associated his production with museum practice. Kean implied that his production of *Sardanapalus* was prompted by his desire to familiarize the widest possible audience with both Byron's neglected play and Layard's important discoveries. It was clearly a patriotic project; Kean explained that he considered himself "fortunate in having been permitted to link together the momentous discoveries of one renowned Englishman with the poetic labours of another." The triumvirate of English scholar, English poet, and English actor had pulled the shroud from a once unknowable East, reproducing the "real" past of a "real" region of great religious and political significance to Britain. As Kean pointed out, Layard himself had examined the production and approved this "search for truth."

The entire project had been motivated by Kean's knowledge that "scenic illustration, if it have the weight of authority, may adorn and add dignity to the noble works of genius." The patriotic tone in Kean's playbill note and its claims for the production's educational value and uplifting potential suggest additional points of contact between Kean's *Sardanapalus* and museum practice at mid-century. From the time that the Whigs came to power in 1832, there had been a concerted effort to make museums and national monuments more accessible and appealing to the London public. Institutions such as the British Museum were reimagined as a means for integrating ordinary citizens into the nation's cultural life, rather than a private preserve of the researcher. *Blackwood's Magazine* summarized the function of this new museum when it asserted, in 1842, that:

Exhibitions, galleries, and museums, are part of popular education in the young and the adult: they stimulate that principle of inquisitiveness natural to man, and with the right sort of food: they instil knowledge, drop by drop, through the eye into the mind, and create a happy appetite, growing with what it feeds on . . . They are schools in which the best and only true politeness may be taught – politeness that refines the manners by ennobling the heart.[69]

Knowledge is transferred "through the eye into the mind" and ennobles the heart, just as "scenic illustration" reveals the truth of the ancient past and adds dignity to the works of national genius. In other words, both the museum and the theatre teach through "object lessons" to adopt the phrase that George Brown Goode would use later in the century.[70] Objects teach as a result of their arrangement in a museum or on a stage, and the object's full significance is further elucidated through instructive labels or scholarly playbills. Both the artifact and the stage property stand in synecdochal relation to a larger totality, and it is the job of both the curator and manager to illuminate this connection.

In Nineveh, Kean could claim such edifying goals while also exploring the full scenic possibilities offered by an ancient Eastern city: extravagant congestion, intense sensuality, and – above all else – cataclysm. In doing so, Kean attached a distinct lesson to his collection of stage-objects; Eastern excess led to swift collapse. In his closing scene, Kean provided a scene of destruction that managed to awe Victorian audiences well-acquainted with conflagration scenes. (Reportedly, even the investigators from the fire insurance companies who watched from the wings retreated from the burning spectacle, though they ultimately declared the production safe.)[71] In the closing moments of the play, Sardanapalus and Myrrha recognize their certain defeat and assemble a large pyre in a private chamber of the palace. There, surrounded by giant sculptures of winged bulls (Kean's relentless symbol of authenticity) emperor and slave prepare for immolation. Sardanapalus ascends the pyre and Myrrha fires it. Then, as Kean explained in his stage directions, "Myrrha springs forward and throws herself into the flames; the smoke and flames surround and seem to devour them – the Palace bursts into a general and tremendous conflagration – the pillars, walls and ceiling crumble and fall – the pyre sinks – and in the distance appears a vast panoramic view of the Burning and destruction of Nineveh."[72] Kean combined flat scenery and the built-out pyre, a stage floor elevator, extensive pyrotechnics, a large panoramic view of the burning city, and "authentic" stage properties to produce and destroy the East. A vast exotic geography was systematically mapped and torched, as Britain showed its mastery of Eastern regions and the objects, peoples, and history therein. Poet, archeologist, and actor joined in the common project of excavating, animating, and leveling the exotic world for British audiences. The compatibility of Byron's sweeping vision with Kean's version of emerging disciplines and museum practice demonstrates the compatibility of the East of romantic writers and the East of the mid-century human sciences. Kean presented a world of fantastic exoticism even as he purportedly dispelled a cloud of mystery. All of the stage's resources were pooled in this endeavor, further demonstrating the rightful ascendancy of the technological West over the ever-ancient and sensual East.

The cinders and smoke of Kean's Nineveh must have been particularly salient proof of British dominance for audiences that remembered Britain's pummeling of Acre when Muhammad Ali refused to relinquish Syria in 1840. Like so many other scenes of Eastern cataclysm, the bombardment and capture of Acre drew enthusiastic crowds to entertainment venues like Burford's panorama. Whether British entertainment examined colonial warfare, medieval or contemporary Islam, or the ancient East of Memphis or Nineveh as depicted in *Azaël* and *Sardanapalus*, audiences discovered a lawlessness that called for retribution. The excess of ancient Oriental tyrants, like the transgressions of those of the present day, invariably invited destruction. Eastern cataclysm makes for great entertainment, as evidenced in plays, panoramas, and American television broadcasts.

THE BIBLICAL SYDENHAM

The desire for authentic detail in built-out settings reached its apogee in the historical courts at the Sydenham Crystal Palace, most notably evidenced – for this discussion – in the Egyptian and Nineveh Courts. In his guide to the Egyptian Court, Owen Jones explained that the Court was composed of "the reproduction of various Egyptian monuments" based on his own drawings and measurements made on the spot.[73] Casts were taken of the 90-foot (27 metre)-long sphinx at the Louvre for use in creating the Egyptian Court.[74] Two colossal figures in the transept reproduced the 60-foot (18 metre)-high statues that adorn the Temple of Abu Simbel, the heads molded from casts taken in Egypt by Joseph Bonomi.[75] Next to the Court, the Crystal Palace's Egyptian Museum housed two reproductions of the Rosetta stone (and Jones's guide included a line-by-line English translation of the inscriptions). The directors of the Crystal Palace even obtained permission to transport one of the ancient obelisks known as Cleopatra's Needles to Sydenham, though the monument was not actually transported until 1878 and was then mounted in its current position on the Thames Embankment.[76] The Nineveh Court made much more extensive use of monuments in the British Museum and the Louvre. According to the guide every portion of the Court was adorned with casts: the exterior façade was "almost entirely copied from existing remains" at the Louvre, and the Central Hall, Inner Chamber, and exterior walls were all lined with casts of the sculptures and bas-reliefs at the British Museum.[77]

Both the Egyptian and Nineveh Courts made recourse to noted experts and travelers. In addition to his own drawings, Owen Jones cited the published works of Jean-François Champollion (best known for his contributions to deciphering Egyptian hieroglyphs) and Sir Gardner Wilkinson (author of *Manners and Customs of the Ancient Egyptians*). In fact, Wilkinson would write a companion volume for the Crystal Palace's Egyptian collections in 1857. Jones explained that the execution of the sculptures was effected by Joseph Bonomi, whose ten years in Egypt enabled him to reproduce "that peculiar character of sculpture, which those who have visited Egypt will at once recognize." According to Jones, Bonomi's work recreated a distinctive beauty that "most published works, and hitherto attempted reproductions more especially, have failed to give."[78] With Fergusson designing the Nineveh Court and Layard writing its guide, Sydenham's list of celebrity–scholars was considerable.

The accuracy of the Nineveh Court was of particular importance since Layard presented it as an illustration of sacred history. He began his guide by noting that the collapse of Nineveh took place "six hundred years before Christ" (7). He then went on to cite the numerous instances in which Nineveh is mentioned in the Old Testament, concluding that excavations "most completely corroborate the events recorded in the Bible" as well as the Bible's descriptions of "the extent and power of the Assyrian empire" (9). According to Layard, everything pointed to these excavations as the site of the biblical Nineveh, demonstrating the literal truth of the sacred accounts. For example, Layard explained that his own survey of the apparent extent of the ruins confirmed Jonah's assertion that the city of Nineveh was so extensive that it took three days to traverse. While this might seem like an unusually large city, Layard explained that this was a product of polygamy and female exclusion "which have prevailed at all times in the East" and require larger dwellings than in the West, producing cities of greater area (9). Layard, who had no training in cuneiform, frequently interpreted inscriptions in the light of scripture. He saw reference to the Assyrian King

who "carried away the ten tribes" in inscriptions on sculpture and specu-
lated that Ezekiel's vision of four creatures with four faces was a reference
to "the four sacred types of Assyrian sculpture" (55).

Layard created an image of the biblical past that was tied to ideas
of Eastern decline and British ascendancy, an image equally present in
the Egyptian Court and in the productions of *Azaël* and *Sardanapalus*
discussed. Repeating an increasingly common misperception, Layard described Nineveh as falling after a "short siege" and then quickly disap-
pearing without a trace. (In fact, Nineveh was sacked in 612 BCE after
years of war and the empire did not fall until 609 BCE.) Moreover, Layard
strictly adhered to the Old Testament account of Nineveh as a depraved
city subject to God's retribution. He explained that the close relation of
Jews and Assyrians explains why "the Jews were so frequently in danger of
being corrupted by the superstitions and idolatrous worship of their neighbours." He went on to explain that "at a subsequent period . . . the Assyrian
army was destroyed by a pestilence sent by God to punish the pride and
arrogance of Sennacherib [an Assyrian King], who was murdered by his
two sons as he was worshipping in the House of Nisroch, his god." Soon
after this, Layard concluded, "Nineveh must have perished" (7–8). While
Owen Jones's guide to the Egyptian Court avoided biblical references, it too
created an image of Eastern descent when it explained that "the artistic character [of Egyptian sculpture] was constantly in a state of decline from the
earliest known examples, through the Ptolemaic period of the Roman" (5).
Both guides then provided detailed discussions of the European research
involved in the reconstruction of the East, presenting Britain, with its
scholarly achievements, as a foil to the imperial collapse under analysis.

British progress was defined against Eastern decline; however, at the same
time Great Britain invoked these decadent civilizations when lauding the
grandeur of its own accomplishments and the breadth of its empire. The
Sydenham Crystal Palace was implicitly compared to the monuments of
the pharaohs when a dedication in hieroglyphs was inscribe on the façade
of the Egyptian Court:

In the 17th year of the reign of her Majesty, the ruler of the waves, the royal
daughter Victoria lady most gracious, the chiefs, architects, sculptors, and painters
erected this palace and gardens with a thousand columns, a thousand decorations,
a thousand statutes of chiefs and ladies, a thousand trees, a thousand flowers, a
thousand birds and beasts, a thousand fountains (tanks), and a thousand vases.
The architects, and painters, and sculptors built this palace as a book for the
instruction of the men and women of all countries, regions, and districts. May it
be prosperous.[79]

As in all minstrel acts, the inscription adopted the voice of the primitive while carefully marking the distance between imitator and imitated. The British could reproduce the monumental architecture of the East and mimic its dedications while remaining free of the "superstition and idolatrous worship" that Layard and others attributed to the East, and which was thought to account for its rapid decline. Whereas ancient Egypt built magnificent tombs, modern Britain built "great books for the instruction of all." As the *Illustrated London News* explained at the time of the opening, "The Directors are bold enough to look forward to the Crystal Palace of 1854 becoming an illustrated encyclopedia of this great and varied universe, where every art and every science may find a place, and where every visitor may find something to interest, and be taught through the mind of the eye to receive impressions, kindling a desire for knowledge and awakening instincts of the beautiful."[80] Britain's illustrated encyclopedia would only grow more full with the passage of time, a marked contrast to the fate of Nineveh and Ancient Egypt.

While from our vantage point it might be clear that the nationalism and prejudices of theatrical orientalism contradicted its claims of objectivity and scholarship, it would be a mistake to conclude from this fact that the theatre shared only superficial connections to the developing museum culture. Both the theatre and the museum attempted to recreate the totality of distant places through the careful manipulation and combination of fragments, whether these fragments dated from the ancient past or the present day. As such, these venues posited an East ever-declining under centrifugal forces and celebrated Britain for its ability to gather and restore an East that would otherwise be lost. The East was constituted in its own remains; it was always in decay, and the process could only be momentarily arrested in British museums and theatres. With the help of archeology, *Azaël* resuscitated a world that had died long ago. As digging continued, not only were the glories of Nineveh disinterred, they were given a safe home at the Princess's Theatre. The simmering Eastern Question, and the growing importance of the Eastern Mediterranean in European affairs, ensured continued excavations and pyrotechnics in both London and Eastern theatres. It would be worthwhile to consider this entertainment history today when witnessing new broadcasts of "self-inflicted" cataclysm in the modern Mesopotamia, also known as Iraq.

CHAPTER 5

The geography of imperial theatre

While mid-century theatrical orientalism illustrated the collapse of biblical empires, late-Victorian theatre presented an East in which European powers struggled for the preservation and extension of modern empires. The eventual acceptance of humanity's extreme antiquity in the second half of the nineteenth century undermined the belief that the mosaic record detailed human history, as well as the hope of early ethnographers that philology could be used to trace the history of the human races to a single genesis. The key to human history had not been excavated in biblical cities as expected but in Brixham Cave in Devon (where human artifacts were found with extinct animals). However, the key to humanity's future clearly lay in the Eastern arena. From the conflict in the Crimea to the reconquest of the Sudan, Britain repeatedly engaged in Eastern battles in the name of protecting British citizens, British honor, and – invariably – Britain's access to India. The theatre responded by depicting colonial warfare or its milieu in genres ranging from melodrama to pantomime and ballet. The theatre of the late-Victorian period was more likely to depict monuments of the colonial infrastructure than those of ancient civilizations. Eastern excess still resulted in spectacular scenes of cataclysm but audiences now cheered British gunboats rather than burning Assyrian antiquities.

The late-Victorian period saw Europe's rapid production of geographic knowledge, and the theatre transformed this information into three-dimensional stage environments. A dizzying quantity of place names and descriptions became the substance of a comprehensible theatrical landscape. The challenge was to place the spectator in the exotic terrain, to provide a readable view from the ground without sacrificing the claims of mastery implicit in geography's view from above. Managers promised engaging Eastern landscapes that simultaneously clarified the wider colonial geography. All the resources of the stage – from script to publicity materials to lobby exhibitions – along with images from romantic poets and illustrated dailies were commandeered for the project. Whether a production placed Ayesha the Desert Queen in a landscape of dunes and simooms or the British Camel Corps before the Suez Canal (and often productions combined such contrasting features) the stage revealed a wider geography. As British involvement in the Eastern Mediterranean grew more extensive, transportation and communication systems became prominent features in theatrical orientalism. Increasingly, productions depicted the technology that made colonial space accessible while asserting that Britain's economic security and the good of her subject peoples depended on this continued accessibility. The theatre did not simply map the East but tied it tightly to Britain.

RACE AND THE GEOGRAPHIC IMAGINATION

The theatre was a principal space for the creation and dissemination of the modern geographic imagination. It was not simply that the theatre rallied support for Britain's imperial wars or that in doing so it familiarized audiences with distant regions; the theatre adopted an emerging conception of geography that was informed by the growth and popularization of the discipline at a time when new racial theories were coming to the fore. Once the handmaiden of geology and biblical scholarship, geography emerged as an autonomous discipline with a popular following in the last quarter of the century. At the British Association, the subject was combined with ethnology in a separate section (E) in 1851 and was intended as a public draw, featuring programs with famous speakers such as the missionary David Livingstone and the explorers Richard Burton, John Hanning Speke, and Sir Samuel White Baker. It was not until 1878 that geography commanded its own section.[1] Soon after this, geography began to enter the academy – primarily, according to Brian Hudson, "to serve the interest of imperialism in its various aspects including territorial acquisition, economic exploitation, militarism and the practice of class and race domination."[2] Not only did the new geography provide business and military interests with needed maps and surveys, geography's application of Social Darwinism to the study of the relation between environment and human populations legitimated, according to Richard Peet, "the conquest of some societies by others."[3] A repeated concern for geographers of this period was the analysis of how physical environment affected culture, civilization, and, in the words of one early geographer, "the mental processes of its inhabitants."[4] Geographic study accounted for the low levels of civilization and mental inferiority thought to exist outside Europe. The new geography explained why white men necessarily ruled the darker races.

This interest in the relation between environment and the perceived hierarchy of the races paralleled similar developments within anthropology. By 1862, the Anthropological Society of London had split from the Ethnological Society, abandoning the latter's interest in constructing a proof of monogenesis and instead focusing largely on the anatomical and physiological characteristics of the different races. By the time the two organizations were amalgamated in the Anthropological Institute in 1867, archeology and physical anthropology had replaced philology as a central concern in the study of race.[5] The different perspectives contained within the Institute, according to George Stocking, Jr., were "encompassable within a broadly evolutionary perspective – in which traditional questions of racial genealogy could find a place alongside those of a more strictly sociocultural evolutionary character, and both were enveloped in a pervasive aura of racial and cultural hierarchy."[6] Within this context, social evolutionist theories developed that extended Lamarck's theory of the acquisition and inheritance of physical characteristics to larger social organizations. As Stocking explains in an earlier work:

Social evolution was a process by which a multiplicity of human groups developed along lines which moved in general toward the social and cultural forms of Western Europe. Along the way different groups had diverged and regressed, stood still, or even died out, as they coped with various environmental situations within the limits of their peculiar racial capacities, which their different environmental histories had in fact created. The progress of the "lower races" had been retarded or even stopped, but the general level had always advanced as the cultural innovations of the "superior" or "progressive" races were diffused through much of the world.[7]

According to this line of thinking, European domination of savage and barbaric peoples was a clear blessing, their only hope of cultural advancement. It was an unavoidable fact that certain mentally inferior racial groups would "die out" as a result of their inability to adapt to a changing environment. The most that Europeans could do was preserve remnants of these groups' material culture.

The imperial theatre of the last quarter of the century reflected these new currents in Britain's understanding of exotic peoples and places. These productions repeatedly pitted European morality and armaments against the savagery and primitive technology of colonized peoples. While some natives showed themselves accepting of the domination of the superior race, there was always a sufficient atavistic contingent to motivate spectacular scenes of colonial warfare. In these plays, even the relatively civilized people of the Eastern Mediterranean demonstrated a perverse hostility to British domination and a recalcitrant attachment to slavery and other barbaric practices. Invariably the British triumphed, despite being vastly outnumbered. Their victory was as much dependent on expert river navigation, lightning-fast troop deployment, and superior communication technology as on the hero's valor; British armies conquered foreign terrains as much as native peoples. In this sense, imperial theatre did not simply depict a foreign geography, it celebrated geographic knowledge and the technologies that supported it. The theatre's own authority depended on its claim to this geographic knowledge. Authenticity no longer resided in the recognizable artifact or monument, as it had in romantic theatre, but in the impression that the troop movement depicted on stage resembled the troop movement described in newspapers. The theatre, no less than the conservative opposition, campaigned on the mastery of a foreign geography and the peoples therein.

While the new geography of imperial theatre is evident in scores of productions in the late-Victorian period, the stakes for this spatial representation were especially high in the years culminating in 1885. Three years earlier the British began what proved to be its long occupation of Egypt out of fear that the country's Minister of War, Ahmad Urabi, and a nationalist faction, were taking control of the country. On 11 July 1882 British warships bombarded the city of Alexandria, eventually reducing it to rubble. With the help of Gatling machine guns, the British took the city after a week of fighting. By September, British troops had taken Cairo. In the aftermath of the British withdrawal from Afghanistan (1881), the annihilation of British troops at Majuba Hill by Afrikaners (1881), and continuing tensions in Ireland, the seemingly effortless invasion of Egypt became a much-touted victory in the popular theatre.

British attention became fully riveted to the region in 1884 with the news that the popular Major General Charles Gordon had been sent to arrange for the evacuation of Egyptian troops from Khartoum. The city had been officially under Egyptian authority since 1842 and was now under siege by the forces of Sudan's self-proclaimed "Mahdi" (the religious leader sent to complete the work of the Prophet). Gordon delayed evacuation until it became impossible, and so throughout 1884 newspapers carried daily reports of the progress of a 7,000-man British force as it made its way up the Nile and across the Sudanese desert to relieve Gordon and his forces. The fall of Khartoum and the death of Gordon and his men at the hands of the Sudanese rebels with the relief force only days away produced an unprecedented public outcry. Gordon memorials were unveiled throughout England, Gordon Boys' Clubs opened, dozens of poems and songs eulogized the fallen hero, and the theatre mounted an avid defense of imperialism in a series of highly successful military spectacles and dramas. Even ballet, music hall, and pantomime responded to the increased attention to the Middle East with literal depictions of Gordon or more general paeans to the British presence in the region. "War teaches us geography," one journalist wrote twelve days after the fall of Khartoum.[8] In its sustained focus on colonial warfare, the theatre taught a new geography that extended beyond place names to include an ideology of race and empire.

"FREEDOM" AND FREE TRADE

Under Augustus Harris's management, Drury Lane became the home of imperial theatre. Soon after taking over the lease in 1879, Harris began his policy of opening the Drury Lane season with a spectacular melodrama depicting an expansive geography.[9] The first of these, *The World* (1880), followed its hero from the diamond mines of Australia back to England. In the following year, Harris turned to what *The Times* would later describe as "the function of Drury-lane," that is "practical illustrations of the latest war in which this country may have been engaged."[10] In the climactic scene in *Youth* (1881), a falsified telegraph message put British forces in Afghanistan in an indefensible position against vastly superior numbers. The soldiers prepare for their last stand (the colonel wrapping himself in the colors with the instructions, "let them cut you to pieces before they have a stitch of this flag")[11] when suddenly the hero miraculously returns with reinforcements after an assumedly impossible mission through enemy lines. Such jingoistic material proved highly popular. As Michael Booth points out, between 1881 and 1902 six of Drury Lane's autumn melodramas depicted British battles in colonial wars – a military world tour covering Afghanistan, Egypt, the Sudan, Burma, and South Africa.[12] Other, non-military melodramas featured civilians overseas, and (as will be discussed later) references to colonial wars were inserted into several Drury Lane pantomimes.

The British invasion of Egypt in 1882 inspired two militaristic productions. First Harris revived *Youth*, transferring the seat of the conflict from Afghanistan to Egypt. In advertisements for the production, Harris published excerpts from a letter from Sir Garnet Wolseley, who had led the British forces that defeated Urabi at Tel al-Kabir, stating: "Dear Sir, You are quite at liberty to announce my entire approval of the military scenes in 'Youth,' which are represented with a vividness and reality quite startling."[13] Harris quickly followed this production with *Freedom*, a play set entirely

in Egypt and depicting both the rise of a clearly misguided Egyptian nationalism and its swift defeat by British soldiers in their zeal for liberty.

Freedom revealed the true motivation of the Urabi forces: a desire to
preserve the slave trade (vigorously repressed in *Freedom* by the British)
and to swell Eastern harems with the daughters of British financiers. As
the powerful Araf Bey (whom both the *Times* and *Dramatic Notes* assumed
to be based on Urabi) explained to the British: "Slavery is sanctioned by
our sacred books, and the interference of foreigners has stuck in the Arab
throat. Egypt for the Egyptians is the secret murmur now – and all the
laws, which in your zeal for liberty you may manufacture, will not weigh
a feather in the scale against the sanction of the Koran, of Allah and the
Prophet!"[14] Moreover, Araf Bey was implicated in the slave trade and used
his authority to protect the sadistic slave-trader Sadyk whom Araf Bey used
to lead a nationalistic uprising.

Araf Bey's true motivation for starting the revolt was to create a situation
amenable to his abduction of Constance Loring, daughter of a British
banker. Defying Araf Bey was Constance's fiancé, Ernest Gascoigne, captain
of Her Britannic Majesty's gunboat, *Arrow*. Ernest made his appearance on
stage preceded by twenty-nine girls and eight children in ragged clothing,
whom he had recently liberated from Sadyk's slave ship. When the English
Consul made no protest against Araf Bey's claim of the slaves, the women
fell "at ERNEST'S feet – forming tableau – crying 'Save us!' " prompting
Ernest and his sailors to draw their cutlasses while announcing: "These
girls were slaves, they are free! England has decreed it, and in England's
name I speak" (ii.ii). The British defiance only served to further inflame
the Egyptian mob, and Araf Bey successfully launched a rebellion, killed
Constance's father, and imprisoned her in his harem, before all was set right
by Ernest and HMS *Arrow*.

The choice to make a British banking family the victim of the apparently
widespread Arab slave trade was a salient example of the play's displacement
of colonial guilt onto colonial subjects. It was hardly a secret that international finance had helped create the crisis that culminated in the British
occupation. Egypt had borrowed heavily under the Khedive Ismail, and by
1876 Egypt's foreign debt was £91 million.[15] In 1880, the Commission of
Liquidation (composed of representatives of Germany, Austria–Hungary,
France, Great Britain, and Italy) drafted a Law for the Settlement of the
Debt that set Egyptian debt service at levels expected to consume two-thirds
of expected government revenues.[16] In this context, Lord Cromer explains
that even in Britain "a strong body of public opinion existed which was
hostile" to the interests of the bondholders.[17] However, once the occupation

was in place, jingoistic sentiment necessitated that Egypt alone be responsible for creating a perceived state of anarchy forcing British intervention.
It was not that British bankers had produced instability in Egypt, instead it
was Egypt that robbed British bankers of their daughters. This was not an
occupation for crass financial gain; Loring was much less concerned with
his bonds than the one thing that, as he stated, "is dearer to me than all the
property in this world – dearer than my own life" (i.i).

The love of a father for his daughter was clearly a sentiment foreign
to the Egyptian mentality, according to *Freedom*. The sale of women was
ubiquitous in the play, and it was especially prominent whenever nationalist
sentiments were expressed. Only moments before Araf rallied his angry
mob, for example, two characters are shown conducting business: "I have
some plump maidens on my books, whose fathers will part with them,
for a consideration. My own terms are modest, simply 25 percent on the
transaction." The scene took place by the tomb of Saladin, the twelfth-
century Egyptian leader who captured Jerusalem from the Crusaders. Araf
chose the site for obvious reasons, and he painted his revolt as a similarly
inspired nationalistic uprising and religious campaign: "The pashas who
rule Egypt have pandered to these infidels, until they now usurp all offices
of profit. So, having muzzled us with stifling debt, they flash before our
eyes the noose they've spun, to strangle here the holy faith of Islam" (ii.i).
It would be a convincing argument if the audience was not already aware
that Araf's true goal was a white woman and not a nationalist government,
or if they had not just heard his partisans discussing the sale of women.
Moments later, Araf and the mob chose the slave trader, Sadyk, to lead the
uprising as final confirmation of its true nature. It was not simply Arab
women who were at risk. As Araf himself boasted, "You think, perhaps,
that all the women in our harems are the dark beauties of the East. Oh, no.
We have Italians, we have French, ay, and there are not wanting samples
of your vaunted virtuous English girls among them, duly bought and paid
for" (i.i). In this context it became clear that the British were compelled
to occupation by a love of freedom and the desire to protect female virtue
and not by financial concerns.

Throughout the play the Egyptians presented such profoundly different
values from the British as to suggest not simply cultural difference but an
essential otherness. Araf crassly attempted to use his wealth and influence
to buy Loring's daughter, prompting an incensed Loring to remark: "We
English, when we speak of our children, do not class them with our cattle.
We rear our girls to be the ornaments of our hearth, not as objects of barter
and exchange" (i.i). While the distinction between being "the ornament of

a hearth" and "the ornament of a harem" was lost upon Araf, in the world of the play it was clearly the difference between life as a human being and the life as chattel. Araf himself accounted for his inability to perceive the distinction when he explained in this same scene, "If I speak with passion, remember, the hot blood of the East flows in my veins" (i.i). Araf is not the only character whose temperament was presented as a manifestation of the hot Orient; Sadyk's "veins run fire" (ii.i), and Araf's wife, Suleima, attributed her impetuous actions to the fact of being Arab. Suspecting that Araf is enchanted by another, she lamented, "An Arab woman's love is the full measure of her life, and to lose it is a living death" (i.i). It was hardly surprising, then, when she later stabbed her husband and herself in a fit of passion. Racial difference in women was frequently marked, with Suleima described as a "dusky beauty" and Constance as "pale and pink as the blush rose." Even women defined each other by skin tone. On meeting, Constance and Suleima delivered sequential asides: "She is as beautiful as night" followed by "She is fairer than a morning of spring" (i.i).

The frequent racial marking in the play complicated its assertion that the British occupation was motivated by the desire to protect human freedom wherever it was threatened. The opening scene presented a sharp contrast between the value of English and Egyptian lives when an English tourist, an "elegant girl of twenty," entered, surrounded by a "mob of beggars all shouting together." She flung coppers, for which they "scramble[d]," while she exclaimed "There! you poor lame, lean, blind, miserable, one-legged, one-eyed, filthy, picturesque creatures, take that" (i.i). The scene's (slight) comedy came from the fact that it was the group's abject status that made them "picturesque," but there was obviously no suggestion that their status could or should change. The East's destitution is here part of its attraction, and, significantly, the slave market was a regular amusement in Cook's tours of Egypt.[18] Though a seemingly insignificant moment, *Freedom*'s tourist scene endowed the exotic horde with a limited humanity.

This dehumanization is especially significant if one reads the scene in the context of imperialist melodrama's invariable depiction of a small number of well-armed British soldiers defeating large numbers of crudely armed natives. In *Freedom*, this colonialist *scène à faire* came at the end of the second act when, according to the *Dramatic Notes*, "The Egyptians battering in the gates of the Consulate are opposed and slaughtered in great number by...[a] handful of sailors."[19] The mass of beggars, like the streaming attackers that piled on the stage floor, were indistinguishable from each other but radically different from an elegant tourist or a few valiant sailors. Considering *Freedom*'s frequent references to dark beauties and hot Arab blood, it would seem that the Egyptians – impoverished and "slaughtered in great numbers," as the *Dramatic Notes* blithely stated – were not simply a different race, but a different register of humanity.

According to *Freedom*, the British presence in the East served to elevate the indigenous people (instances of slaughter notwithstanding), bringing technology and morality to a people who were mired in inhuman practices because of their cultural or racial inferiority. Despite these lofty gifts, British motivations were cruelly misinterpreted. When Araf told Loring that "The eyes of every hungry power in Europe gloat upon the fertile valleys of the Nile, and each one thirsts to make our river its pathway to the great East," the banker vehemently denied the charge. Instead, he explained that "we came to your cities as to a market, and with our inventions we bring you progress." Araf was incapable of appreciating the gift of British progress, however, and responded, "with menaces": "Crown the blessing, then, if it be one, by throwing your daughters into our arms. We shall taste the spice of your gift more hotly from their lips and eyes" (I.i). In contrast to Araf's obsession with sexual gratification, Loring recognized the interrelation between free trade and progress, and conceived of geography through these terms. It was not that Araf was incorrect to assert that Europe looked to Egypt as a "pathway to the great East," it was his suggestion that there was something underhanded in this fact that elicited Loring's denial, and it was Araf's insinuation that the desire for open markets was somehow equivalent to his desire for Constance that prompted Loring's anger.

Loring's comparison of cities to markets was a common metaphor of the new geography. The year following the production, in an address to the Manchester Geographical Society, H. M. Stanley would state:

> To him or those who possess [geographical knowledge], the configurations on the world chart appear as clearly defined as though they were the outlines of a man's real estate – the world is only a huge breeding farm, and the various parts round about the shores are like so many stalls at a market-place – and the people therein are only so many vendors and buyers.[20]

Geography was mapped in raw materials and manufactures. It was a logic that had been enshrined at the Great Exhibition and continued to inform Britain's sense of the globe. At the Exhibition, there had been a certain amount of confusion between peoples and products, with attendants classified among the displayed objects. Stanley's exhortation to Britain to develop its geographic knowledge so that it could dominate the global market place similarly combined peoples and products. In his great "breeding farm" it was not clear exactly what or who was being bred. When Araf responded to

Loring's invocation of the moral and economic benefits of free trade with the suggestion that he throw his daughter into the bargain, he was only making explicit a confusion implicit in the geographic imagination. Just as the play made Araf assert that the occupation was motivated by financial interests in order to discredit the idea, the play had him link economic imperialism with human bondage so that the idea could be attributed to a self-serving, lusty, and racially suspect villain.

Britain's commitment to the well-being of the Egyptian population was less evident during the occupation than in melodramas like *Freedom*. To the extent that the British instituted agricultural reforms, it was to make Egypt a more efficient producer of raw materials – chiefly cotton, which largely serviced British manufacturers. These reforms, it has been argued, worsened the condition of the rural poor, creating large landed estates and a destitute landless peasantry. Historians also note that British legal reforms in Egypt largely bypassed shariʿa which continued to govern the relations between men and women. In fact, the Hanafi school of interpretation – which afforded men greatest license in issues of polygamy, divorce, and guardianship – continued to gain precedence.[21] Leila Ahmed notes that Lord Cromer, as consul general during the occupation, created new obstacles to female education in Egypt though he later vociferously attacked female veiling and seclusion, describing them as "the fatal obstacle" to the Egyptian's "attainment of the elevation of thought and character which should accompany the introduction of Western civilization."[22] However, education was apparently unnecessary for women transferring from the harem to the hearth.

KHARTOUM, RACE, AND THE COLONIAL INFRASTRUCTURE

If, for the British theatre, the occupation of Egypt illustrated Britain's commitment to the moral and material improvement of subject peoples, then the war in the Sudan revealed the complex, and ultimately vulnerable, colonial infrastructure required to effect such improvement. From September 1884 to February 1885, British newspapers reported daily on the "Gordon relief expedition." The government contracted the transport of troops to Thomas Cook and Son, already well-known for its Nile tours. Papers detailed the logistical and technological skills marshaled by industry and the military, explaining how the steamers were dragged over the first and second cataracts, how a railway was constructed to convey stores to these points, and accompanying these reports with maps and topographical sketches. In fact, from the time the weekly *Illustrated London News* began reporting on the expedition to the months after the fall of Khartoum, that paper published over 260 illustrations related to the expedition and its battles, some images covering two full pages. The British public was deluged with information on Eastern terrain and how its vast expanses had been mastered by British technology. In addition, the mere fact of the reporting – the remarkable speed by which events transpiring thousands of miles away were not only described but illustrated – served as further proof of the technology, expertise, and daring needed to secure and uplift the East.[23]

Not surprisingly, transportation and communication technology figured prominently in imperial theatre after the fall of Khartoum, and the speed and realism with which reported events were reproduced itself attested to the efficiency of the colonial infrastructure. Harris quickly translated the fall of Khartoum to the stage in a melodrama that opened in September 1885. However, Drury Lane's *Human Nature* was not the first in the field; six months before the production, or roughly one month after papers reported the fall of Khartoum, Sanger's Grand National Amphitheatre (formerly Astley's Amphitheatre) dramatized the war. Drury Lane's *Human Nature* by Henry Pettitt and Augustus Harris, and Sanger's *Khartoum* by William Muskerry and John Jourdain, both recreated the race to save Khartoum, rewriting history in such a way that the desert city remained in British possession. Imperial theatre told a story of irrepressible progress and uplift; colonial imagery was adaptable to every theatrical genre except tragedy.

In highlighting the spectacle of colonial travel, imperialist melodrama departed from a pattern established in earlier exotic plays. The theatrical East, as defined in romantic Eastern plays and the dramatization of oriental romances by poets such as Byron, Moore, and Southey, usually depicted struggles between natives. Similarly, most early Eastern melodramas focused on struggles between pashas, sultans, pharaohs, and sorcerers, as well as Eastern usurpers and rightful heirs, as in *The Spirits of the Moon* and *Zoroaster*. This East was obscure and remote, and often featured supernatural events. When not specifically set in the past, this East demonstrated a timeless quality. Operas and operatic adaptations that featured Europeans in the East were entirely set there; travel to the East was presumed but never depicted. Conversely, characters might be magically transported to the East, as in *Oberon*. Whereas this early East suggested an imaginative landscape removed from a representable geography, the imperialist melodramas of the late-Victorian period defined an East next door in which Europeans vied for mastery. As Heidi Holder has noted, in the imperialist melodramas from the 1880s and 1890s, "the real battles [were] between Europeans, fought *within* a conflict with indigenous people."[24] The East had been transformed into an arena for European expansion – a hinterland in which good and evil (both European) fought, surrounded by a treacherous landscape of arid deserts and warring natives.

Imperialist melodramas perpetuated standard melodramatic devices within this new geography. These plays invariably began in England with familiar misunderstandings and false accusations, which ultimately motivate colonial travel. In *Human Nature* the hero mistakenly suspects his wife of adultery and so joins an expedition to relieve a "desert city" under siege by the "Mahdi." In *Khartoum*, the heroine learns that her husband, who is part of the expedition to relieve Khartoum, has been accused of forgery and so she travels East to inform him of the libel. In both plays, the villain threatens the hero's physical and financial well-being, while menacing the heroine's purity. In *Human Nature* the French villain, Paul de Vigne, has made the English hero, Frank Temple, responsible for a huge financial loss when the Egyptian government backs out of an arms deal the two men had orchestrated at de Vigne's insistence. At the same time, the Frenchman ceaselessly attempts to seduce the hero's unsuspecting wife. In *Khartoum*, the Greek villain, Nicolas Mavrogordato, threatens to have the hero, Captain George Haviland, imprisoned unless his wife Marion submits to Mavrogordato's lust. Both Frenchman and Greek are revealed to be the traitors who betray or attempt to betray the desert city to the Mahdi's siege.

While these plays ultimately erupted into colonial warfare, the battle scenes were no more intrinsic plot elements than the avalanches and floods of Pixérécourt's melodramas. Peter Brooks describes Pixérécourt's third-act cataclysms as the "physical 'acting out' of virtue's liberation from the oppressive efforts of evil." In imperial melodrama as well these sensational scenes of battle, explosion, and natural disaster acted as the last gasp of a pervasive evil before virtue could be read as such and be brought, as Brooks says of Pixérécourt's characters, "into the sphere of public recognition and celebration."[25] The potential dangers of colonial regions constitutes a refocusing of what Eric Bentley calls melodrama's "paranoid" vision[26] onto those peripheral regions where the future of the empire was being decided. Melodrama's traditional concern with the vulnerability of virtue was accompanied with a new concern for the vulnerability of empire. In the process, virtue and empire were conflated. Imperial melodrama's most significant departure from the traditional structure of melodrama was also that feature most significant to defining a new geography: once providence interceded at critical junctures; now the hero relied on telegraphs, steamers, and repeating weapons. Imperial melodrama, like colonial warfare itself, contributed to a popular fascination with new technologies that delivered daily reports and images from the East, enabled troop movement across vast terrain, and (usually) ensured British victories against much larger native forces.[27]

Both *Khartoum* and *Human Nature* gave considerable attention to the spectacle of travel, asking audiences to marvel at the military's ability to move large numbers of troops around the globe at remarkable speeds. Notably, both plays rewrote history; the race was won, the troops arrived in time to save the besieged city or reconquer it. *Khartoum* was produced less than two months after Gordon's death and one day after memorial services for Gordon were conducted at St. Paul's Cathedral and Westminster Abbey, further demonstrating the increased accessibility of the East. *Khartoum* transformed the relief expedition into a lightning race out from England, up the Nile, and across the desert. The play opened at the Portsmouth Dockyard with laborers transporting supplies from the railway lines to a large practicable troopship. Midway through the scene a train appeared carrying additional troops. They disembarked and the train pulled off, revealing "more troops massed behind" along with a crowd to see the soldiers off. The scene culminated with the troops marching onto the troopship, which slowly moved off as crowd and soldiers cheered. Later in the play, audiences witnessed a group of these soldiers at "the Cataract on the Nile" with their "nuggars," broad native boats that the British forces in Egypt towed behind steamers.[28] On stage, the British Grenadiers repeatedly arrived in the nick of time. First they successfully relieved an advance column ambushed at "The Wells" (the only major engagement for the actual relief expedition took place at the Wells of Abu Klea when an advance column of 2,000 British soldiers defeated 10,000 dervishes) and then they pressed on to Khartoum preventing its fall. All the while, Marion Haviland, and her friends, Grace Armytage and Miss Priscilla Prym, accompanied the troops on this Thomas Cook excursion.

In *Human Nature*, British troops similarly relieved a "desert city" under siege by the "Mahdi," an obvious reference to Khartoum.[29] As in *Khartoum*, *Human Nature* depicted a desert camp, a battle, and a scene in which the villain was finally defeated at "The Wells." However, the play's most sensational scene was the soldiers' homecoming. Harris reproduced Trafalgar Square on the Drury Lane stage, and drilled a giant cast representing soldiers and onlookers in what the *Era* described as "the most striking and stirring piece of realism the stage has known."[30] The production concluded with Frank Temple on horseback, leading a procession of soldiers home after their long Eastern tour.

In the spectacle of travel, communication technology could prove as dramatic as any departing steamer or railcar, and the theatre was clearly aware of this fact. While reporting on the relief expedition, newspapers focused attention on the communication system that delivered descriptions of the East, just as they focused attention on the transportation system that opened this once remote region. Telegraph cables not only carried the news, they *were* the news. "Never was a break in telegraphic communication more tantalizing," the *Illustrated London News* announced when reporting that the line to Khartoum was broken and no news was forthcoming on Gordon's planned offensive.[31] Throughout the empire, a growing number of businessmen, diplomats, and soldiers relied on England's network of submarine and overland cables, as well as transit routes. British business, policy, and lives all depended on the free flow of information from the periphery, and when the network was threatened papers made the most of the ensuing drama.

The newest star in the imperial economy, the wartime-press artist or "special," was also dependent on this network of cables and steamers. Specials like Melton Prior of the *Illustrated London News* and Frederick Villiers of the *Graphic* had become celebrities in their own right. It was with some fanfare, as John O. Springhall notes in " 'Up Guards and At Them!' British Imperialism and Popular Art 1880–1914," that the *Illustrated London News* informed its readers on 13 September 1884 that Prior was already on his way to the front.[32] Prior was one of twenty British newsmen reporting on the relief expedition. The competition between papers and the resulting need to differentiate their star reporters from the pack was considerable. In addition to prominently mentioning Prior's name and discussing his sketches in reports on the expedition, the *Illustrated London News* even reported their receipt of Prior's telegraphic messages announcing that sketches were in transit.

The special was aided by new reproduction technology, in addition to steamers and telegraphs. Previously, the artist's sketch served merely as a guide for engravers who then recomposed the subject. However, by 1884 new photo-engraving techniques made it possible to directly reproduce sketches. The *Illustrated London News* published an increasing number of facsimiles during the relief expedition, suggesting that readers demanded the immediate reproduction and the sense of authenticity suggested by the words "photo-engraving." Descriptions that accompanied these facsimiles drew attention to the speed with which they were produced, as when the *Illustrated London News* explained of a Melton Prior image: "This sketch, together with many others, was only received late on Tuesday last and was reproduced by Direct Photo-Engraving Process in ten hours!"[33] Though sketch-artists were initially resistant to using hand cameras (dry-plate, fixed-focus photography had been perfected only recently) at least one soldier brought a camera on the campaign. The *Illustrated London News* thanked an unnamed soldier for sending a photograph of the British camel corps. Sketch-artists would soon take advantage of the technology that would ultimately make them obsolete. When Frederick Villiers returned to the Sudan during the 1898 reconquest, he brought a movie camera and a bicycle, both emblems of modern revolutions in communication and transportation.

Communication technology made a remote and dangerous region safe and accessible. However, as melodrama liked to point out, safety hung on a thin telegraph line. The need to communicate across Eastern deserts, as well as the English public's need for instant reports on the East, is a pressing concern in *Khartoum*. In the play, the dilemma is repeatedly described by Walter Sketchley, a press artist sent by the "General" at Khartoum with vital information for the advancing relief expedition. As Sketchley explained, much more than the city's safety depends on his mission: "Press correspondents now-a-days do not belong to the rose-water brigade – they are quite prepared to share the hardships – aye, and the dangers of any campaign, provided that the British public can have its war news served up every morning at breakfast, fresh and hot, with rolls and coffee!"[34]

As the figure most associated with the modern communication network, Sketchley repeatedly finds ways to convey information when all avenues appear closed. When captured by the Mahdi's troops, he seized an Arab's shield and improvised a "heliograph," flashing a message to the distant troops. Though hardly an example of advanced technology, the bills asserted that the scene depicted "English pluck . . . and modern science." As further proof, the bills included a quote from the *Scientific Review* explaining that the heliograph was a "recent discovery adopted in military tactics" which uses "the rays of a tropical sun" to flash a message to "a distant outpost, even when situated beneath the horizon." Later, when Sketchley reached the advance guard of the relief expedition, he again used "modern science" to facilitate communication. The General's most recent message, "Khartoum all right – can hold out for months," is revealed to mask a dire warning when Sketchley holds the paper to a flame. As Sketchley explains:

read between the lines – the heat brings out the cipher, and in the faint, trembling characters, which every moment grow more distinct, you can trace the agony of the brave hand which penned them, the brave heart's despair, abandoned and alone, – a cry to England's faith and fealty. Listen! (*uncovering, reads through soft music*) "While you are eating, drinking, and resting at your ease – we and those with us – soldiers and servants – are watching by night and by day – treachery is abroad, and our hearts grow weary waiting for the succour which never comes. The end is not far off, when all will be – too late!" (50–51)

The reading of this letter no doubt caused a sensation in the theatre, as it employed much of the actual language of Gordon's last letter to the British Consul General in Egypt.[35] Blockaded in Khartoum and ignored by the Liberal government, Gordon becomes the typical melodramatic victim. In melodrama, cries for help and assertions of innocence go unheard until the final act. The vastness of the empire and the vulnerability of communication systems (not to mention Gladstone's reluctant imperialism) become another of melodrama's silencing devices. In addition to the mute characters, gags, and elaborate misunderstandings common to traditional melodrama, imperial melodrama featured a geography that conspired against speech. Only modern communication technology could breach the perils of the East and reveal the truth obscured by villainy.

Khartoum and *Human Nature*, with their rescue of the city in the last act, were not the only works to adapt events to the melodramatic formula. When the British recaptured the Sudan in 1898, the victory was presented as Gordon's belated rescue. The British victory at Omdurman in that year was commemorated with a medal inscribed "Khartoum." This second Sudan campaign concluded with a memorial service for Gordon. As one journalist wrote of the ceremony, Britain's "long-delayed duty was done...We left Gordon alone again – but alone in majesty under the conquering ensigns of his own people."[36] As Angela Pao writes of French imperial melodrama, "if dramatic authors did indeed rely heavily, even exclusively, on dispatches and commentaries published in the daily papers for their plot outlines and composition of scenes, journalists just as consistently organized their reportage in terms of dramatic scenarios."[37] In tracing out the complex web of relations between the theatre, press, scholarship, and government, it becomes impossible to identify an originating influence.

Both of these plays ascribe a brutality to Eastern people that the plays identified with the harshness of the Eastern climate and topography. In *Human Nature*, the Arabs were simply another of the deadly features of an Eastern landscape which had left the British "choked and blinded by the sand, short of food and water and [without] sleep."[38] In this bleak landscape, the commander of the relief expedition lamented, Arabs descended in "swarming hordes...like mosquitoes – the more you kill the more there seem to be" (iv.i). The full desolation visited by these swarms of Arabs was only evident when a European priest (a member of an apparently substantial group of Europeans at Khartoum) escaped from the fallen city to spur on the relief expedition, describing the horrible events that followed after the villain, Paul deVigne, treacherously opened the city gates to the Mahdi's forces:

The Arabs rushed upon us like a gigantic wave of inhumanity, sweeping all before it, and leaving but horrors in its course. The fiends, mad with triumph, went in gangs, seeking for spoils, wrangling and fighting among themselves for the plunder. Women and children were dragged away to be sold as slaves, while their husbands and fathers were slaughtered before their eyes. Blood flowed in every house, and even in the mosques, until night came on, when, surfeited with slaughter they spared those who were still alive. But we were starved and beaten, until our reason almost left us; and we were beginning to lose all hope, when we heard you were marching to our relief. (iv.i)

The play transformed Khartoum into another Alexandria, creating a European community subject to marauding Arabs and recreating the reported conditions that ostensibly prompted the British invasion of Egypt three years earlier. With the addition of a vicious slave trade (the next scene depicted "European prisoners reduced to slavery" repeating *Freedom*'s depiction of white slavery as a motivation for invasion), *Human Nature* made it clear that the case for the occupation of the Sudan was no less compelling than that of Egypt. The play fulfilled its own logic, and in defiance of actual events the relief mission became an invading force that retook the city.

Khartoum made an even more concerted effort to present the Sudanese as a distinct and primitive race. Bills for the production announced that actual "Soudanese Natives" were featured in the cast.[39] The play asserted the anthropological value of such specimens at the same time as it mocked the desire to study the exotic body. In one scene, Grace Armytage coaxed Priscilla Prym (a comic spinster character) to join her and Sketchley on a stroll along the Nile when the troopship on which they were traveling stopped before a cataract.

GRACE. (*to* Miss Prym) Mr. Sketchley is going to look for some of the Aborigines to put in his sketch book.
MISS P. (*eagerly*) Aborigines? Oh!
GRACE. He says they make beautiful studies, they're such very fine men.
SKETCHLEY. Yes. Magnificent models, and quite *au naturel*. (*aside*) I thought that would fetch her. (31)

An interest in the aborigine's form was revealed as a desire to see "magnificent" naked black bodies, questioning the physiological focus of anthropology as well as the attraction of the production's own extensive cast of "Soudanese Natives."

Even if the Sudanese made "beautiful studies," there was no question of where they sat relative to whites in the racial hierarchy. Elsewhere the Sudanese were sarcastically described as "our dusky friends" and as "wily niggers" (18, 22). Even the few Arab characters who were unaffected by the Mahdi's false teaching recognized the superiority of the British "race." As Ayesha announced to the Mahdi, "The race you war against, though alien to ours, is destined yet to fill this land with faith and freedom that *you* cannot give because you know it not!" (17). Ayesha, ruler of the wild horsemen of Kordofan and known by friend and foe as "The Queen of the Desert," is something of a throwback to a romantic orientalism, in which proud independence and a love of one's native terrain were indications of a pure and primitive nature and had no relation to nationalistic struggle. For Ayesha, there was no question of "submission or resistance" to the British. As she explained: "Our home is in the desert. There our great mother Nature spreads her wide arms to take us to her ample bosom. Let us strike our tents and plunge into the wilderness, at peace with all men!" (17). Conveniently, true Arabs preferred the desert wilds, leaving the cities and coasts for the British. Ayesha's speech patterns also resembled those of exotic characters from the first half of the century. She referred to herself in the third person and occasionally slipped into an antiquated form of English. On separating from the captured English officer whom she secretly loved, Ayesha requested the crucifix he wore as a pledge that "when in happier times, Cross and Crescent are once more at peace, Ayesha shall behold thy face again" (20).

Love affairs between Arabs and Europeans had been a feature of early orientalist works like *Oberon* but were notably absent from imperial melodramas. What had been an element of fantasy in the romantic era was now a troubling possibility. Not surprisingly, then, Ayesha's love did not advance beyond a crush and the audience knew from the outset of the play that the object of her desire was unswervingly committed to Grace (who was only a few miles away on a Nile steamer). The specter of interracial love was made ludicrous in Miss Prym. After she and Grace were taken captive by the Mahdi's forces in one of the play's innumerable plot twists, the spinster proudly stated that she had "made a conquest" of one of the natives. Grace responded, "Not one of these savages?" to which Prym announced that the Mahdi himself had fallen subject to her charms (43). Prym, who was incessantly mocked thoughout the play for her appearance and her excessive attention to men, transformed the threat of miscegenation into a ridiculous impossibility; it was no more possible that a white woman would be attracted to a Sudanese then that an ugly spinster should marry the Mahdi.

In truth, the play asserted, the British did not desire the exotic's body any more than they desired the exotic's land. The prohibition of barbaric practices, the protection of minority communities (especially expatriate Europeans), even the securing of the right of passage did not so much evidence a desire to possess as a desire to cultivate. Britain acted in the name of freedom, of both peoples and commerce. No less an authority than H. M. Stanley had asserted months earlier that England should not "subjugate populous tribes and conquer regions" if for no other reason than that it was unprofitable (though Stanley did recommend holding Khartoum so as to construct a railroad from Suakim to Berber). As Stanley explained, "It has been told to you before, doubtless, and it may be said again, that geographical knowledge clears the path for commercial enterprise, and commercial enterprise has been in most lands the beginning of civilization."[40] In amassing geographical knowledge and in protecting its interests, England was assured of spreading civilization to primitive peoples in inhospitable regions.

THEATRICAL GEOGRAPHERS AND THE STAGING OF COLONIAL SPACE

Theatrical orientalism celebrated geographic knowledge, and this was as evident in the promotional materials and staging of plays as in their plots. The playbill for *Khartoum* included extracts from the *Globe*, *Scientific Review*, and Gordon's last letter. As Heidi Holder points out, these citations did not provide any useful information, but merely reassured audiences that the depicted scenes were documented and truthful.[41] The bills implied that the geography depicted on stage was identical to that depicted in newspapers and journals. This use of tertiary materials to provide productions with geographic authority was especially pronounced at Drury Lane, a theatre regularly criticized for a lack of geographic and historical accuracy. In its review of *Youth*, the *Illustrated London News* complained that "it is somewhat difficult to ascertain with precision where the seat of war in question is situated, and whether it is against Afghans, Boers, or Zulus that [the hero] and his friend exhibit such prodigies of valour."[42] Similarly, *The Times* questioned the historical accuracy of *Freedom* in the sardonic complaint: "It has never been alleged that Arabi endeavored to recruit his harem from the young ladies of the English colony as his representative is here shown to do, or that the contempt of the Arab population for the European residents was excited by the antics of stout old ladies with gingham umbrellas in the bazaars of Cairo."[43] Drury Lane's long history and its unofficial status as England's "National Theatre" necessitated more elevated productions and Harris responded with spring imports such as the Saxe-Meiningen Company and the Comédie Française. Beginning in 1883 the Carl Rosa Opera Company became the regular spring attraction at Drury Lane.

Harris deflected complaints of inaccuracy in the autumn melodramas with quotes from well-known authorities attesting to the truthfulness of the staging, and two exhibitions of artifacts related to the productions: the first accompanying *Human Nature* and the second accompanying *The Armada* (an 1888 production marking as well as reproducing Britain's defeat of the Spanish fleet three centuries earlier). The *Human Nature* exhibition in particular not only highlighted the patriotic nature of the production but also linked it to a vast array of writings on and reproductions of the Sudan. Taken together, *Human Nature* and the exhibition of "Egyptian and Soudanese arms, accoutrements, and relics" provided a thorough illustration of the events and locale of the conflict. The *Era*'s article on the exhibition named the individual officers and press artists who contributed the materials, as well as the battlefields from which they were recovered.[44] As these same battlefields had been frequently represented in sketches and maps in the illustrated papers, the assembled arms, musical instruments, and utensils at the Grand Saloon had the effect of tracing the British advance over hostile Sudanese terrain.

The display of original sketches by Melton Prior and Caton Woodville, artists for the *Illustrated London News*, further clarified the geography evoked by the Exhibition. Presumably, some of these sketches depicted the same battlefields represented by the displayed artifacts. The *Era* described these artifacts as ethnographic, being "illustrative of African life and warfare." However, in the context of the Exhibition's elaborate cross-referencing, the objects become significant for their ability to represent geography as well. Press artists sat at the center of this cross-referencing. Objects and illustrations that were lent by such artist–celebrities as Charles Williams, Melton Prior, and Frederick Villiers shared the stage with the contributions of Admiral Hewett, Lieutenant-General Graham, and General Wolseley. The press not only described the East for the home audience, but also shared in the military's project of collecting, while crossing and claiming territories.

The theme of martyrdom colored Harris's depiction of communication systems within the empire. Even as the Exhibition celebrated the ability to report back a coherent landscape from the periphery of the empire, the repeated subject at the Grand Saloon was the tragic break in communications. Douglas H. Johnson has argued that once it became clear that Khartoum would not be immediately retaken, Gordon was transformed from a soldier into a Christian mystic and martyr – the sacrificial victim of a government that ignored his pleas.[45] The canonization of Gordon was already underway at the Drury Lane Exhibition. Harris amassed an impressive array of

Gordon artifacts: a piece of carpet from Gordon's room in Khartoum, a Sudanese Kourbash he had given as a present, a decoration he struck at Khartoum, and finally a bust of the General. Even *The Times* referred to the collection as the "relics of the martyr of Khartoum."[46]

In this treacherous landscape, communication came at a price. The Exhibition echoed Sketchley's assertion that correspondents were "prepared to share the hardships – aye, and the dangers of any campaign." Among the objects in the glass cases in the center of the room was the revolver worn by John Cameron of the *Standard* when he was shot and killed at Gubat. The death of a correspondent was sharp indication of the vulnerability of communications. All of the correspondents who accompanied the Relief Expedition suffered at least minor wounds, two were killed, and Cameron's death and funeral were the subject of large newspaper illustrations. Audiences at the Exhibition circulated between artifacts and illustrations taken from a region that had dominated the press. "Real" objects combined with past accounts to powerfully evoke both a geography and the systems that delivered this geography. As such, the Drury Lane Exhibition served as a compelling verification of the landscapes produced on the Drury Lane stage.

Harris positioned his illustrations of colonial geography as a service to the nation, bolstering Drury Lane's unofficial status as England's "National Theatre" at a time when some critics were calling for a subsidized theatre precisely because of the fare available at West End theatres like Drury Lane. In Harris's estimation, "the function of [a national theatre] was not so much the reproduction of the plays of the past as a representation of the deeds of the present," as he reportedly explained at the opening of the Soudan Exhibition.[47] Drury Lane was in fact the National Theatre, according to Harris, because it had abandoned Shakespeare and Sheridan for illustrations of colonial conquest. The Soudan Exhibition was further proof of this fact. In these same opening remarks, Harris reportedly explained that "it had been suggested that the Government might have opened an exhibition of that kind; but as Drury Lane is looked upon as the National Theatre, [Harris] thought the same end was attained as if they had done so." In its project of familiarizing the London public with contested colonial regions, Harris presented Drury Lane as an extension of the government.[48] According to Harris, the theatre was even responsible for military recruitment. In the preface to the catalogue of the Soudan Exhibition, Harris reportedly asserted that "the drama may have some share in popularizing the profession of arms amongst the rising generation of Englishmen."[49] The Soudan Exhibition and the press it generated did not simply authenticate *Human Nature* but the entire colonial geography constructed at Drury Lane. When the National Theatre depicted Egypt, the Sudan, South Africa or a host of other regions, audiences could be assured that the stage picture was produced in coordination with and for the benefit of the British military.

At Drury Lane, respectability was in part dependent on the authenticity of the depicted geography, so publicity materials stressed the extensive knowledge of theatre practictioners. A pre-production article published in *The World* depicted *Human Nature* co-author, Henry Pettitt, as a master of geography. The article describes Pettitt as a self-made man, who was first able to obtain a stable position when "his superior knowledge of geography…gained him an usher's desk at the North London Collegiate School." According to the article, Pettitt taught for six years, "taking the boys of North London in imagination all over Europe with the aid of Bradshaw, Cook's Circulars, and Murray's Guides."[50] No specific training or authorities are cited for the development of Pettit's "superior knowledge of geography," and the article would suggest that Pettitt solely employed tourist publications as teaching materials. *Bradshaw's Railway Guide*, promotional circulars for a travel company, and travel guides enabled Pettitt to conjure the world in a classroom. The mention of these popular materials did not diminish Pettitt's authority, but rather celebrated his resourcefulness as a geographer and the new accessibility of geographic information. Routes to the new geographic knowledge abounded, whether one studied guidebooks or the theatre.

Pettitt's sources and his role as a popular geographer underscored the changing status of travel in the colonial period. While a text like *Freedom* clearly ridiculed the young English women now crisscrossing the East, delighting in "lame, lean, and miserable picturesque creatures," the period also looked to the emergence of the tourist industry as opportunity for the elevation of the masses as well as an indication of British prowess in transportation systems. In fact, Gladstone himself would cite modern tourism as one of the great successes of Victorian society when responding to Tennyson's famous attack on the decadence of contemporary culture, *Locksley Hall Sixty Years After* (1886). Gladstone asserted:

Among the humanizing contrivances of the age, I think notice is due to the system founded by Mr. Cook, and now largely in use, under which numbers of persons, and indeed whole classes, have for the first time found easy access to foreign countries, and have acquired some of that familiarity with them, that breeds not contempt but kindness.[51]

When not transporting troops, Cook and Son opened the world to British tourists, disseminating uplifting geographic knowledge.

Pettitt was establishing himself as a popular geographer even before *Human Nature* was produced. At least four of his previous plays depicted Englishmen who made fortunes in exotic lands like India, Bolivia, and Australia, and Pettitt would continue to depict distant regions in his later plays. Many of his plays were partially or entirely set overseas. Pettitt's success was derived from his knowledge of colonial territories, just as his characters' wealth was generated in colonial territories. Pettitt's public image dovetailed with the story he repeatedly told: opportunities awaited the man who would know the exotic. It was a familiar story; Edward Said has gone so far as to assert that all the major English novelists of mid-century accepted a globalized world-view and "could not (in most cases did not) ignore the vast reach of British power." Colonial territories were depicted as realms of possibility that, in turn, supported the domestic order. As Said writes, "Whether it is Sir Thomas Bertram's plantation in Antigua [in *Mansfield Park*] or, a hundred years later, the Wilcox Nigerian rubber estate [in *Howard's End*], novelists aligned the holding of power and privilege abroad with comparable activities at home."[52] The same logic holds true for imperial melodrama. In *Khartoum*, lost honor was regained through colonial warfare, and in *Human Nature*, fidelity was proved after tracking the villain across the Sudanese desert. At both the personal and national level, honor and financial well-being depended on a full knowledge of colonial regions. It is no wonder then that theatre practitioners claimed respectability through the apparent accuracy of the geographies they created.

In defining themselves as geographers, playwrights and managers aped their subject matter; the actual officers and correspondents suggested by *Human Nature* and *Khartoum* were praised for their knowledge of Eastern geography and customs. Descriptions of Gordon often detailed his knowledge of geography. When Gordon was dispatched to the Sudan in January 1884, the *Illustrated London News* began its report by explaining that he had been lately occupied with archeological and topographical studies of Jerusalem.[53] In a review for a published facsimile of Gordon's sketch of his route to Khartoum, the *Athenaeum* announced that "General Gordon lost no opportunity to add to our geographical knowledge."[54] Biographies of Gordon often gave considerable attention to his mapping of the Nile (though he once asserted that he did not care whether the Nile had a source or not). After Gordon's death, his knowledge of Eastern manners and terrain became legendary.

Late-nineteenth-century staging practices, when adapted to orientalist productions, further reinforced audience confidence in the accuracy of the geographies articulated by the theatre. Theatre managers went to great lengths to convince their audiences that the space behind the proscenium provided accurate three-dimensional reproductions of exotic space. The stage lent credibility to the entire geography mapped within the play. If the playwright and manager had fully mastered the contours of this portion of exotic space, it seemed likely that they similarly had mastered the much wider space that connected periphery to metropole, the place of the play with the place of the stage. The stage space, in this sense, acted as synecdoche for the geography created by the play. The stage stood in for the vast terrains through which the protagonist journeyed, and scenic design stood in for a range of geographic practices intended to make distant regions legible and available to the European audience.

Augustus Harris was the undisputed master of these new staging practices. He filled the large Drury Lane stage with built-out settings, a surfeit of realistic detail, carefully choreographed crowd scenes, and armies of supernumeraries – in short, a plethora of unnecessary detail designed to endorse the reality of the scene. Like other managers, Harris wove elements of the "real" into the stage so as to further augment this sense of reality. Animals were of course common on the Victorian stage, and Harris featured many in his melodramas. *Freedom*, for example, opened in a bazaar with "carts drawn by mules" and "camels laden with merchandise." The *Dramatic Notes* stated that this scene represented "with remarkable fidelity the strange figures and contrasts to be seen in the bazaar of an Egyptian city,"[55] and even *The Times* was forced to admit that the Egyptian bazaar was one of a few "admirable examples of art and stage carpentry combined" demonstrating, if nothing else, that "pains [had] been taken to convey an idea of the outward aspect of Egyptian life."[56]

Harris went to great lengths to reassure his audience that they witnessed exact reproductions of the Eastern regions described daily in the press. The extensive display of Sudanese weapons and implements and on-the-spot sketches at Drury Lane's Soudan Exhibition lent credibility to the built-out dunes and Arab city on the Drury Lane stage. Reviewers of *Human Nature* apparently accepted these marks of authenticity and lauded the realism of Harris's Eastern landscapes. The *Truth* asserted that "the accuracy displayed in the scenes illustrative of Egyptian warfare are beyond praise."[57] Unless the paper was staffed with recently returned veterans, one has to assume that the reviewer's opinion was as much the product of the Exhibition and its press as educated scrutiny of the mise-en-scène.

Harris's lavishly detailed reproductions were complemented by fragments of the "real," borrowing state-of-the-art armaments for his imperial melodramas and hiring actual police officers to play the part of officers in the crowd scenes for *Human Nature*. The Soudan Exhibition similarly featured an elaborate mix of the "real" and "represented." In a separate room, adjacent to the Grand Saloon, Harris had recreated the cell of Ahmed Urabi, the Egyptian nationalist whose revolt against the Khedive helped precipitate England's invasion of Egypt in 1882. According to the *Era*, the room was based on a drawing by Frederick Villiers of the *Graphic*, "the carpet, furniture, &c. being those actually used by him during his confinement at Cairo," with other "souvenirs of Arabi" in the room.[58]

Harris was not alone in blurring the boundaries between theatrical artifice and ethnographic display. Readers who learned of the Soudan Exhibition in the *Era* would have also encountered numerous descriptions of the Indian village currently being built in the Albert Palace. The paper explained that snake-charmers, conjurers, Nautch girls, and various native artisans would inhabit reproductions of "gaums" and other native structures.[59] London audiences attended a growing number of such Eastern reproductions. The fragments of the "real" imbedded in these villages and landscapes served as guarantees of authenticity, whether these fragments were objects or people.

As theatres and exhibitions competed for the same public, these different venues increasingly borrowed each other's strategies of reproduction and display. According to the original bill, the production of *Khartoum* at Sanger's Amphitheatre populated its Arab city with actual "Soudanese Natives" and "a large herd of Camels and Dromedaries," much like the ethnic villages featured in the increasingly popular international exhibitions.[60] In case the audience worried that the scenes of warfare lacked such realism, the bill explained that the production had secured "the services of Her Majesty's Household Brigades of Guards, by kind permission of their respective Commanding Officers." Even in domestic scenes, the knowledge that the real was mixed with the theatrical heightened the illusion of reality. However, in the popular mind it was the exhibition that was growing increasingly theatrical in its attempts to recreate exotic landscapes. When the *Illustrated London News* described an Australian aboriginal hut at the Indian and Colonial Exhibition of 1886, the paper attributed the realism of the scene on the Murray River to the fact that "like Mr. Augustus Harris, Sir Samuel Davenport [Executive Commissioner for Australia at the Exhibition] believes in mise-en-scène and goes in for real water."[61] After years of the theatre envying the respectability of the exhibition, the exhibition now seemed intent on adopting the artifice of the theatre.

FANTASTIC LANDSCAPES

The vocabulary of geographic context so dominated British culture that it was present even in theatrical forms that provided relief from the anxieties of empire and offered a return to an earlier romantic sensuality. Pantomime, extravaganza, and ballet rarely made any attempt to reproduce "real" locations. Instead, these forms turned to an exotic romantic iconography which had lost all claims to realism but had retained the transgressive sensuality absent from colonialist depictions of the East. Yet, pantomime, extravaganza, and ballet often employed the same devices that were used by imperial melodramas: lavish built-out sets, the display strategies of museums, and an iconography indebted to the colonial infrastructure. The fantastic landscapes of these non-realistic theatrical forms preserved the tropes of geographic realism even as they promised a departure from blockaded cities and colonial warfare. Both odalisques and telegraph operators resided in these lavish cut-and-paste environments.

Throughout the century, English pantomime inserted references to contemporary events into fantastic story lines and this continued in the late-Victorian period. Similarly, Victorians converted features of the colonial infrastructure into design motifs to be combined with earlier romantic imagery. However, Victorians brought a self-consciousness and energy to these juxtapositions that was distinctly different from the eclecticism commonly associated with the Regency period.[62] In part, this new style of juxtaposition was a product of the heightened sense of period that accompanied the development of the historicist outlook in the nineteenth century. Compounding this was the Victorians' unique conception of their own age as one of transition into a modern future, as Walter Houghton and – more recently – A. Dwight Culler have argued.[63] Victorians looked to the past as if across a giant chasm, carefully delineating the distinct characteristics, the "Spirit," that they believed marked each age. As a consequence, Victorians understood juxtapositions of past and present periods and styles as striking acts of an intense (if not questionable) theatricality. Not surprisingly, then, Victorians reserved these juxtapositions for their most fanciful theatrical forms.

It is first important to note the huge impact that the fall of Khartoum made in popular entertainment venues. For some time after, Gladstone ceased to be known in music halls as the G.O.M. (Grand Old Man) and became instead the M.O.G. (Murderer of Gordon). A number of songs celebrated Colonel Fred Burnaby, the popular officer and explorer who died at Abu Klea. The image of Burnaby bravely resisting native onslaught had become such an ingrained image that eight years later when Harris dramatized the British victories in Burma, the stage directions explained that the hero stood "*in a conspicuous place à la Captain* [sic] *Burnaby, coolly reloading and picking off the enemy.*"[64] Of course, the greatest number of music-hall songs focused on the death of Gordon, the most famous being G. H. MacDermott's "Too late! Too late!"[65] At least one music hall devoted an entire bill to the fall of Khartoum, when the Royal (later known as the Holborn Empire) staged *Shadows of Fate; or, Heroes of the Soudan*, a "Grand Spectacular Entertainment with scenic effects, descriptive war songs, and original music."[66]

Even ballet made reference to the colonial infrastructure, despite the genre's longstanding focus on myth and allegory. It was precisely the ballet's traditional antipathy to modernity that made the oriental romances of Byron and Moore such popular ballet subjects at mid-century. Nonetheless, in the late-Victorian period, English ballet frequently inserted topical references into decidedly ahistorical productions. For example, during the ancient Egypt sequence in the Alhambra spectacle, *Rothmongo* (1879), an Egyptian exclaims in fear at the sight of a hot-air balloon, "It's a judgment!" prompting the character "Surplus" to respond, "Because you've not paid up your Bonded interest regularly, I shouldn't wonder!"[67]

The mixing of romantic and Eastern colonialist imagery grew more common as Europe's direct involvement in the region increased. *Excelsior* (1885), a ballet performed by a Milanese troupe and produced at Her Majesty's Theatre, combined images of fancy with those of Egypt's colonial infrastructure.[68] The *Athenaeum* summarized the represented events:

The progress of Invention is impeded by the genius of Darkness and Superstition. The steamboat of Papin is wrecked by a mob, Volta dreaming of the electric pile, Lesseps plotting the construction of the Suez Canal, and the engineers, French and Italian, boring the Mont Cenis Tunnel, are all impeded by Darkness, who, however, is chased away by Civilization and Light. Opportunities are thus afforded for the presentation of tableaux indicative of the triumphs of steam and electricity, pictures of Egyptian life, and so forth.[69]

The *Era* singled out "the dance of the telegraph messengers" for praise, and then noted "the commendable pains bestowed upon the very difficult representation of the sand storm." The paper also asserted that "the various dances in the Suez Canal scene also deserve to be especially noted" as well as the "judiciously modified treatment of the Indian Nautch."[70] In these allegorical scenes, light and darkness were depicted through the contrast of technology with the harshness of Eastern terrain and behavior. The ever-cynical *Bat* clarified the contrast when it explained that the featured dancer did not appear "until the Spirit of Light had effectively popularized penny steamboats and sixpenny telegrams, had blinded a score of Arabs to show her humanity, and had opened the Suez Canal."[71]

Elements such as the sandstorm and Nautch dance were common to romantic depictions of the East, well before a canal had become the emblem of Egypt. The production's featured dancer also tapped earlier romantic associations. Four months into the run of *Excelsior*, Kate Vaughan was secured for a *pas seul* in the Suez Canal scene. Vaughan is probably known to theatre historians for popularizing the French Quadrille (or Can-Can) at the Gaiety Theatre. However, in Victorian England she was known for her performance of the title role in *Lalla Rookh*, an extravaganza at the Novelty written specially for her. Though Thomas Moore's poem had been adapted to many theatrical forms, Vaughan's performance of the Persian princess had become the standard by the 1880s. The addition of Vaughan in the Suez Canal scene injected the oriental romance – a form with a considerable stage history – into a scene otherwise composed of colonial iconography. This was especially the case as Vaughan appeared in what the *Bat* described as a "Lalla Rookh costume." In *Excelsior*, the colonial infrastructure was imbued with the romantic sensuality that it sorely lacked. At a time when the nation was preoccupied with the vulnerability of communications and transportation in the British Middle East, *Excelsior* combined images of the known East with reassuring images of the desired East.

Pantomime was the non-realistic genre that featured the most extensive references to colonial wars. At least five of the Christmas pantomimes staged in 1882 included scenes inspired by Britain's recent invasion of Egypt. In *Cinderella and the Little Glass Slipper* (Pavilion), not only Cinderella attended the Prince's ball, but the invasion force with commanders Sir Beauchamp Seymour and Sir Garnet Wolseley, and the Khedive himself. Prince Paragon saluted the British heroes with expected words of praise, such as his address to Wolseley:

> You, Sir Garnet, with your gallant force,
> Like a revengeful wave without remorse,
> Swept forth and laid the dusky foeman low.

The Khedive, however, was subject to a certain chastisement for making this "revengeful wave" necessary:

> Khedive, you're welcome too, as our ally,
> To govern better let us hope you'll try;
> The lesson you have learnt, should right direct you,
> And thank your stars you've England to protect you.

Bluff King Hal (Sanger's) apparently made reference to the laying of the Suez–Suakin telegraphic line, which took place during the invasion. According to the *Era*, the pantomime included a scene in which the "submarine communication is formidably guarded by Woolwich infants, dynamite, and gun cotton and telephonic communication is also laid on to Calcutta, Suez, and Cairo."[72] *Robinson Crusoe* (Sadler's Wells) and *Puss in Boots* (Surrey) both included scenes in which children represented the British troops in Egypt. *Puss in Boots* featured "quite an army of little boys, admirably drilled in uniforms according to the Egyptian Expedition, [who] perform military manoeuvres of considerable intricacy to the accompaniment of drum and fife."[73] *Robinson Crusoe* presented "a number of Lilliputian representatives of the Egyptian heroes . . . each in turn being received with much enthusiasm."[74]

Not surprisingly, the pantomime at Drury Lane, *Sinbad the Sailor*, included the most elaborate references to the occupation of Egypt, marking out England's presence in the region.[75] The Egyptian Expedition was first directly mentioned in the episode in which Sinbad disembarked on a small island only to discover that he had climbed onto the back of a whale. In this particular version of the story, however, Sinbad was accompanied by the Khedive of Egypt and together they spied the bombardment of Alexandria, which was revealed in a "Grand Panorama." During the bombardment, Sinbad at first doubted that it was Alexandria they saw because he could not find Cleopatra's Needle, a reference to the Egyptian obelisk that had been transported from Alexandria to London in 1878 and erected by the Thames. England's dominion extended over Eastern cities, monuments, and even fictional characters. According to the pantomime's playbill, when Sinbad is menaced by the Young Egyptian Prince in a later scene, the Diamond Prince warns that Sinbad is a "favourite in London" and that "London is the Capital of England, whose power for the last thousand years he will show." This prompted a procession of the Kings and Queens of England beginning with William the Conqueror and concluding with a "Review of the Troops after their Return from Egypt," making Britain's occupation of Egypt (and its adoption of Sinbad) the culmination of one thousand years of power.

Sinbad contained many of the themes that would surface in *Freedom*, from the contrast between British liberty and oriental tyranny to the uncomfortable acknowledgment of Egypt's stifling debt. However, in *Sinbad* the self-serving nature of these formulations became comically apparent. After the opening transformation scene, the audiences watched as Pasha Kybosh was pursued by an attorney whose "firm to Kybosh money lent / At interest only seventy-five percent." The seizure of the Pasha's "goods and every chattel / Chairs, women, cook, Fat-boy and other cattle" prompted a change of scene to the "Slave Market." Judging from the dialogue in the pantomime scenario, the slave-market scene served as an opportunity to display the chorus as scantily clad exotics, no less a necessity in Harris's imperial pantomimes than the scenes of slaughter were in his imperial melodramas.[76]

Rather than being horrified by the slave trade, the financiers in *Sinbad* are shown to profit from it, as do the male characters that stroll among the wares. Nor is it clear, in *Sinbad*, that Britain's traditional commitment to freedom is antithetical to sexual tyranny. According to the *Illustrated Sporting and Theatrical News*, the procession of British monarchs included notable episodes of their reign "such as the singing of the Great Charter by John and the polygamous tastes of Henry VIII,"[77] suggesting a British corollary to the harem. This somewhat confusing conflation of liberty and sex was followed by a review of British troops. At this point, according to the *Era*, "Sinbad the Sailor, actually, by some magical process [was] transformed into Britannica, who 'never, never, never' will have her subjects slaves, and who sings patriotic songs."[78]

While pantomime delighted in the English occupation of Egypt, there was no reference to the humiliating fall of Khartoum in the pantomimes of 1884 and 1885. Instead, they followed the example set by *Excelsior* and created non-representational landscapes that combined colonial iconography with fantastic imagery. One common device was the allegorical world tour in which a procession of chorus girls represented the armies, industry, and crafts, or history of "all" nations. In effect, the theatre adopted the display strategies of exhibitions that similarly provided microcosms of world geography organized into national pavilions and ethnic villages. In this schema, the great powers displayed their armaments and industry in their own exhibits, while the crafts and natives of lesser powers were displayed in ethnic villages designed by the host country.

The Alhambra ballets also featured these allegorical world tours, and here as well nations were categorized as industrial powers or as objects of ethnography. In December 1885, the Alhambra produced *Le Bivouac*, which included a parade of chorus girls representing the armies of Belgium, Spain, Turkey, Italy, Australia, Russia, Germany, France, and America. The status of the Ottoman Empire was in question, so it is not surprising that five months later the Alhambra preceded *Le Bivouac* with a piece in which "parties of Zulus, North American Indians, and Hindus, Turkish warriors, and New Zealanders succeeded one another in a manner equally bewildering and anachronistic."[79] Apparently it was not clear whether "Turkish warriors" belonged with the great powers or in the ethnic villages with the Zulus. In its review of *Le Bivouac*, the *Bat* took the piece's logic to a natural conclusion:

What with the Indian village at the Albert Palace, the Japaneseries, the promised Indian and Colonial Exhibition next year (will not the Niggeries be a good name for this), and the present Parsee Victoria Company [of Indian acrobats] at the Gaiety Theatre, it seems as if amusement-loving England was only intent on seeing how life is lived far, far away. But why, in our thirst for knowledge of the doings of our fellow men, should it end here, especially with such splendid opportunities for enlarging our knowledge as we at present possess. Why should not Theebaw be engaged to give a representation of a genuine Burmese drunk, while a Soudanese Village would surely solve the Egyptian Question. A few Irishmen that I know of should be perfectly willing to give a joint performance of whiskey and treason, which might tend to the settlement of the Hibernian problem.[80]

The *Bat* contemptuously transformed rebellious regions – Burma, the Sudan, Egypt, and Ireland – into docile displays, revealing how ethnography's purported catholic vision depicts non-Europeans (including the Irish) as timeless objects. English chorus girls and Indian craftsmen were always a pleasure to behold.

Augustus Harris was the undisputed master of these world tours in female bodies. His 1885 Christmas pantomime *Aladdin* (which replaced *Human Nature*) included a "Dream of Fair Women" that featured Theodora, Cleopatra, Semiramis, and Helen of Troy, along with what the *Era* described as "beauties by the dozens, of all nations, of all times."[81] It is worth noting that Harris's Eastern "beauties" were largely derived from the theatre. Sarah Bernhardt had recently appeared in Sardou's *Théodora* at the Gaiety, Cleopatra invariably recalls Shakespeare's tragedy, and Rossini's *Semiramis* continued to be a London favorite – in fact the Drury Lane procession featured music from the opera. After depicting an East in which telegraph lines could be cut and Europeans blockaded by Arab warriors, Harris reproduced an earlier and more benign theatrical East. Harris provided an East of alluring heroines in a geography fashioned from chorus girls. The pantomime also featured Harry Nicholls performing a burlesque version of Kate Vaughan's Suez Canal dance, further highlighting the self-referential qualities of Harris's theatrical landscape.

The following year, at the height of the Indian and Colonial Exhibition and at the start of the Queen's Jubilee celebrations, Harris inserted an even more lavish procession into the Christmas pantomime, *The Forty Thieves*. The procession depicted Great Britain and her colonies. Taking his cue from the Exhibition, Harris included a wealth of detail that audiences could read as ethnographic. A review in the *Era* described the scene: "A troop of Zulus in picturesque native garb follow in the train of Cape Colony, brandishing their assegais and characteristic cowhide shields, their dusky skins showing off to great advantage their gaily beaded devices and fringes, their kilts of divers wild-beast tails, leopard-skin cloaks, uncurled ostrich plumes in their hair, necklets of teeth."[82] Harris not only borrowed the stance of the Exhibition, but its actual displays. India appeared as a chorus girl in a drapery of red and gold brocade that had originally been on display at the Hyderabad court of the Colonial Exhibition. A geography that inspired both pride and anxiety was now controllable, docile, and – quite literally – feminine. The exotic world was delivered via familiar and unthreatening tales; according to the *Bat*, in 1886 there were nine pantomimes based on *Robinson Crusoe*, eight based on *Aladdin*, and four based on *Ali Baba and the Forty Thieves*.[83]

Aladdin, Ali Baba, and Sinbad made regular appearances on the Victorian stage and, in many ways, their popularity encapsulates contradictions inherent in theatrical orientalism. At the same time that British military involvement prompted images of a treacherous and squalid East, Victorian theatre also provided familiar magic lamps and dancing almées. The contradiction was – and is – rarely noted. Edward Lane's promise that the *Nights* provided accurate ethnographic and geographic details was repeated when the explorer, Richard Burton, offered a new translation in 1885–1886. Burton similarly asserted that the tales were more accurate than any travel account and included even longer notes (such that his translation required sixteen volumes). Captain Burton could claim more than scholarly authority; he had served in the East India Company, famously searched for the source of the Nile, and published a popular account of his dangerous pilgrimage to Mecca and Medina disguised as a Muslim. The need for a timeless Orient became only more pressing in the face of nationalist aspirations. The idea that all you needed to know about the East was already contained in the stories you knew from childhood was profoundly appealing to a Britain that had been surprised by Urabi's revolt and the fall of Khartoum.

VICTORIANS TODAY

We, like the Victorians, seek comfort in familiar tales. The year following the Gulf War, Disney released its hugely successful animated feature, *Aladdin*. The film is a harem abduction tale, with an Americanized Aladdin ("call me Al" he explains) rescuing the princess Jasmine from seclusion in

the palace and a forced marriage. As in imperial melodrama, female freedom is paramount – and Jasmine eventually escapes the harem to become
the ornament of Aladdin's hearth. Disney's Orient was no less dangerous
than the one depicted by the news media the year earlier. The dark-skinned
and bearded Jafar effectively controls governmental power but seeks the unprecedented power of the lamp, a power rightfully belonging to Aladdin.
However, if Disney and the media outlets offered similar plots, Disney
offered closure – Eastern villainy was vanquished, a Western-style marriage
restored goodness to the world, and the hero ascended the throne. In contrast, the media went on to depict a post-Gulf War world in which various
Arab villains retain their thrones and stockpile magic lamps at the same
time that the growing strength of political Islam renders an *Aladdin*-like
resolution extremely unlikely.

The harem-abduction trope requires a woman, or a people, desiring and
benefiting from Western liberation. The spread of political Islam has undermined this trope. As Erin Addison argues, Disney's *Aladdin* repressed
the Arab rejection of the West, offering Gulf War America "the mystifica-
tion of power through romantic love, and the packaging of romantic love
as freedom for women."[84] *Aladdin* is an obvious site in which to imagine an
Orient that is more accommodating to Western values given that the tale
was not contained in the original medieval manuscript but was probably
the invention of its first European translator. From its inception, *Aladdin*
was a Western fantasy of a desired Orient. A primary theme of this book has
been that nineteenth-century orientalism was an elaborate project of displacement and self-invention. How striking, then, that in an age in which
global capitalism has undermined local cultures and widened the gulf between the rich and poor (especially poor women), a global corporation like
Disney should rewrite a counterfeit medieval Arabic tale so as to reveal that
Eastern poverty and female oppression will end when romantic love unites
princesses with beggars.

More recently, political leaders have again promised to save brown
women from brown men. In the immediate aftermath of the attack on
the World Trade Center on 11 September 2001, US leaders repeatedly explained that the bombing of Afghanistan was not only the first salvo in
an open-ended war on terrorism, but also a means of freeing Afghani
women from the persecution of the Taliban. Five weeks after the attack on
the World Trade Center, the State Department released a report on "the
Taliban's war against women" on the same day that US First Lady Laura
Bush took over the president's weekly radio address to attack the "brutal oppression of women" in Afghanistan.[85] Such orientalist tropes are selectively

invoked. US leaders did not speak against the mistreatment of women in Saudi Arabia, which had been an important base of operation for the US military. Among Arab nations, the Ba'th regimes of Syria and Iraq have placed some of the strongest restrictions on polygamy and unilateral divorce; however, their more equitable treatment of women had little impact on their status in the West as "rogue nations."

It is not a coincidence that the harem-abduction trope should have reemerged at this time. Its roots, I have shown, date back at least to the start of the twentieth century to a period of radical transformation in which Europeans were suddenly confronted by the greatly expanded scope of known geography, the human timeline, and human diversity. This trope and the others examined in this book helped recreate a sense of "us" and "them," asserting the superiority of the "West" and ultimately facilitating its dominance throughout the world. The history of these tropes and their birth from within the traumas of Western modernity account for their emotional power, and explains why they should reemerge in moments of crisis. These tropes have long informed public opinion in the West, ultimately informing political and military action and transforming the lives of millions of Arabs, often with devastating effects. Now more than ever, the need to examine orientalist imagery and unpack its history is great.

Notes

INTRODUCTION: "REAL SETS," GEOGRAPHY, AND RACE

1. Bill reproduced in William Muskerry and John Jourdain, *Khartoum! Or, The Star of the Desert* (London: Samuel French, [n.d.]), p. 2.
2. Undated clipping, New York Public Library for the Performing Arts, The Billy Rose Theatre Collection, *Human Nature* Clipping File.
3. *Era* 14 November 1885.
4. *Truth*. Undated clipping, New York Public Library for the Performing Arts, The Billy Rose Theatre Collection, *Human Nature* Clipping File.
5. Bert States, *Great Reckonings in Little Rooms: On the Phenomenology of Theatre* (Berkeley, CA: University of California Press, 1985), p. 62.
6. Michel Foucault, "Questions of Geography," *Power/Knowledge: Selected Interviews and Other Writings 1972–1977*, ed. Colin Gordon, trans. Colin Gordon et al. (New York: Random House–Pantheon, 1980), p. 77.
7. Richard Peet, "The Social Origins of Environmental Determinism," *Annals of the Association of American Geographers* 75 (1985), 310.
8. Edward Said, *Orientalism*, 1978 (New York: Vintage–Random House, 1979), p. 55.
9. Johannes Fabian, *Time and the Other: How Anthropology Makes its Object* (New York: Columbia University Press, 1983), p. xiii.
10. An important exception to this tendency is Malek Aloula's examination of orientalist postcards in *The Colonial Harem*, trans. Myrna Godzich and Wald Golzich, Theory and History of Literature, 21 (University of Minneapolis Press, 1986).
11. John MacKenzie, *Orientalism: History, Theory, and the Arts* (Manchester University Press, 1995), p. 14.
12. See Johannes Fabian, *Out of Our Minds: Reason and Madness in the Exploration of Central Africa* (Berkeley, CA: University of California Press, 2000); George W. Stocking, Jr., *Victorian Anthropology* (New York: Free Press–Macmillan, 1987); and Felix Driver, "Geography's Empire: Histories of Geographical Knowledge," *Society and Space* 10 (1992), 23–40.
13. Ann Laura Stoler, *Race and the Education of Desire: Foucault's "History of Sexuality" and the Colonial Order of Things* (Durham, NC: Duke University Press, 1995), p. 205.

14. Michel Foucault, *The History of Sexuality*, 3 vols., trans. Robert Hurley, 1978 (New York: Vintage–Random House, 1990), vol. 1, p. 43.

15. See Timothy Mitchell, *Colonising Egypt*, 1988 (Berkeley, CA: University of California Press, 1991); Edward W. Soja, *Postmodern Geographies: The Reassertion of Space in Critical Social Theory* (London: Verso, 1989); and Tony Bennett, *The Birth of the Museum: History, Theory, Politics*, Culture: Policies and Politics (London: Routledge, 1995).

16. Richard Southern, *Changeable Scenery: Its Origin and Development in the British Theatre* (London: Faber, 1951), p. 356; Sybil Rosenfeld, *A Short History of Scene Design in Great Britain* (Oxford: Blackwell, 1973), p. 137.

17. Alan S. Downer, "Nature to Advantage Dressed: Eighteenth-Century Acting," *PMLA* 58 (1943), 1029; Alan S. Downer, "Players and the Painted Stage: Nineteenth-Century Acting," *PMLA* 61 (1946), 562.

18. Michel Foucault, *The Order of Things: An Archaeology of the Human Sciences*, 1970 (New York: Vintage–Random House, 1973), p. 370.

19. Peet, "Environmental Determinism," 310.

20. Saree Makdisi, *Romantic Imperialism: Universal Empire and the Culture of Modernity* (Cambridge University Press, 1998), p. 6.

21. *Orientalism*, p. 7.

22. Michel de Certeau, *The Writing of History*, trans. Tom Conley (New York: Columbia University Press, 1988), p. 85.

23. Fabian, *Time*, pp. 81, 31.

24. Talal Asad, introduction, *Anthropology and the Colonial Encounter*, ed. Talal Asad (Atlantic Highlands, NJ: Humanities Press, 1973), p. 17.

25. H. R. Mill quoted in Brian Hudson, "The New Geography and the New Imperialism: 1870–1918," *Antipode* 9 (1977), 16.

26. Quoted in Sybil Rosenfeld, *Georgian Scene Painters and Scene Painting* (Cambridge University Press, 1981), p. 18.

27. Rüdiger Joppien, *Philippe Jacques de Loutherbourg, RA 1740–1812* (London: Greater London Council, [1973]), p. 23. Beckford quoted in Richard Daniel Altick, *The Shows of London* (Cambridge, MA: Belknap–Harvard University Press, 1978), p. 122n.

I SPECTACLE AND SURVEILLANCE IN ORIENTALIST PANORAMAS

1. Richard Daniel Altick, *The Shows of London* (Cambridge, MA: Belknap–Harvard University Press, 1978), pp. 460, 463.

2. John Barrell has argued that in the eighteenth century, "The contemplation of landscape was not . . . a passive activity: it involved reconstructing the landscape in the imagination, according to principles of composition that had to be learned." John Barrell, *The Idea of Landscape and the Sense of Place, 1730–1840: An Approach to the Poetry of John Clare* (Cambridge University Press, 1972), p. 6. Analyzing Goethe's *Theory of Colours*, Jonathan Crary has detected "an observer posited by various 'romanticisms' and early modernisms as the active, autonomous producer of his own visual experience." Jonathan Crary,

Techniques of the Observer: On Vision and Modernity in the Nineteenth Century (Cambridge, MA: MIT Press, c.1990), p. 69.

3. Technical features described in Altick, *Shows of London*, pp. 132–133; Ralph Hyde, *Panoramania! The Art and Entertainment of the 'All-Embracing' View* (London: Trefoil Publications, 1988), p. 20; Stephan Oettermann, *The Panorama: History of a Mass Medium*, trans. Deborah Lucas Schneider (New York: Zone Books, 1997), pp. 49–50, and Wolfgang Schivelbusch, *Disenchanted Night: The Industrialisation of Light in the Nineteenth Century*, trans. Angela Davies (Oxford: Berg, 1988), p. 215.

4. Hyde, *Panoramania*, p. 20.

5. Oettermann, *The Panorama*, p. 105.

6. Quoted in Schivelbusch, *Disenchanted Night*, p. 215.

7. *Times* 24 April 1801.

8. Oettermann, *The Panorama*, p. 60.

9. *Description of a View of Constantinople; with its European and Asiatic Suburbs, and a Great Extent of Surrounding Country now Exhibiting at the Panorama Royal, Leicester Square* (London: T. Brettell, 1846), p. 10.

10. Ibid.

11. *A Concise Account of the View of Constantinople with a Map; and an Illustration of the Descriptive Sheets, Which are Given to Each Person Who Goes to Those Paintings at the Panorama, Leicester Square* (London: Panorama and Messrs. Richardsons, 1801), p. 6.

12. *Description of a View of Constantinople*, p. 6.

13. *A Concise Account of the View of Constantinople*, p. 6.

14. *Description of a View of Constantinople*, p. 3.

15. Saree Makdisi, *Romantic Imperialism: Universal Empire and the Culture of Modernity* (Cambridge University Press, 1998), p. 125.

16. Stephen Bann, *The Inventions of History: Essays on the Representation of the Past* (Manchester University Press, 1990), p. 116.

17. Quoted in Bann, *Inventions of History*, p. 117.

18. Bann, *Inventions of History*, p. 117.

19. Quoted in Patrick Conner, ed., *Inspiration of Egypt: Its Influence on British Artists, Travelers and Designers, 1700–1900* (Brighton Museum, 1983), p. 29.

20. Pieter van der Merwe, comp., *The Spectacular Career of Clarkson Stanfield, 1793–1867* (Tyne and Wear County Council Museums, 1979), p. 89.

21. Charles Dibdin, Jr., *History and Illustrations of the London Theatres* (London: Printed for the Proprietors of the "Illustrations of London Buildings," 1826), p. 82.

22. John Britton, *The Autobiography of John Britton* (London, 1850), p. 101n.

23. Handbill quoted in Altick, *Shows of London*, p. 199.

24. Wolfgang von Hagen, *Frederick Catherwood, Archt.*, introd. Aldous Huxley (New York: Oxford University Press, 1950), pp. 41–42.

25. Ibid., p. 42.

26. Friedrich Nietzsche, *The Use and Abuse of History*, trans. Adrian Collins (New York: Library of Liberal Arts–Macmillan, 1957), p. 18.

27. 21 August 1841, 643.

28. Quoted in Altick, *Shows of London*, p. 136. Altick states that the exchange was between Robert Barker and Nelson, though Oetterman's assertion that the exchange was between Henry Aston Barker and Nelson is more likely.

29. *Memoirs of Thomas Frognall Dibdin*, quoted in Altick, *Shows of London*, p. 135.

30. *The Siege of Acre; or, Descriptive Collections Relative to the Late Scene of Conquest in Syria Between the British and Turkish Force, Under the Orders of Sir W. Sidney Smith, and the Republican French, Commanded by General Buonaparte* (London: W. Glendinning, 1801).

31. *The Slaves in Barbary; or, British Vengeance* (Royal Circus 1818). *Doctor Faustus and the Black Demon; or, Harlequin and the Seven Fairies of the Grotto* (Adelphi 1823) discussed in David Mayer III, *Harlequin in His Element: The English Pantomime, 1806–1836* (Cambridge, MA: Harvard University Press, 1969), p. 299. *Peristrephic Panorama of the City of Algiers* (Hull Athenaeum Society, 1818) discussed in van der Merwe, *Spectacular Career*, p. 84. *The Bombardment of Algiers by Lord Exmouth* discussed in Katharine Sim, *David Roberts R.A., 1796–1864: A Biography* (London: Quartet Books, 1984), p. 44, and van der Merwe, *Spectacular Career*, p. 81.

32. *Harlequin and Number Nip* (Covent Garden 1827) reviewed in *The Times* 27 December 1827 and discussed by Sim, *David Roberts*, p. 46. *Harlequin and the Astrologer of Stepney; or, the Enchanted Fish and the Fated Ring* (Surrey 1827) discussed in Mayer, *Harlequin*, p. 300. *Harlequin and Cock Robin* (Drury Lane 1827) discussed in Altick, *Shows of London*, p. 202.

33. Quoted in Mayer, *Harlequin*, p. 301.

34. Pieter van der Merwe, "Roberts and the Theatre," *David Roberts*, comp. Hellen Guiterman and Briony Llewellyn (Oxford: Phaidon Press and Barbican Art Gallery, 1986), p. 41.

35. Altick, *Shows of London*, p. 176.

36. Quoted in Altick, *Shows of London*, p. 176.

37. *Description of a View of the Bombardment of St. Jean D'Acre with the City and Surrounding Country* (London: George Nichols, 1841), p. 5.

38. *Athenaeum* 6 February 1841, 115.

39. Quoted in Altick, *Shows of London*, p. 177.

40. Leaflet, Panorama file, Theatre Museum, London.

41. *Times* 27 December 1861.

42. *Description of A View of the City of Cairo and the Surrounding Country* (London: T. Brettell, [1847]), p. 3.

43. *Illustrated London News* 20 March 1847.

44. *Description of A View of the City of Cairo*, pp. 6, 7.

45. Jonathan Culler, "Semiotics of Tourism," *American Journal of Semiotics* 1. 1–2 (1981), 132.

46. David Roberts RA, *The Holy Land* (Israel: Terra Sancta Arts, 1982), p. 13. This book contains images taken from the first edition, with the original introduction, and selections from Roberts's Middle Eastern diary.

47. Sim, *David Roberts*, p. 152.
48. *Illustrated London News* 20 March 1847.
49. *Description of A View of the City of Cairo*, p. 4.
50. The nineteenth-century history of English travel in the Middle East is comprehensively discussed in Sarah Searight's *The British in the Middle East* (New York: Atheneum, 1970), from which the above discussion is derived.
51. *Illustrated London News* 8 November 1845.
52. William Makepeace Thackeray, *Notes of a Journey from Cornhill to Grand Cairo*, 1845, introd. Sarah Searight (Heathfield: Cockbird, 1991), p. 132.
53. *Illustrated London News* 30 March 1850.
54. *Athenaeum* 29 March 1851, 219.
55. Quoted in Hyde, *Panoramania*, p. 143.
56. Altick, *Shows of London*, p. 208.
57. Stocqueler would later write *The Battle of Alma* for Astley's Amphitheatre. According to Richard Altick, Stocqueler continued to lecture at panoramas throughout the 1850s, *Shows of London*, pp. 208, 480.
58. Michel Foucault, *Discipline and Punish: The Birth of the Prison*, trans. Alan Sheridan, 1978 (Vintage–Random House, 1979), p. 217.
59. *Description of Constantinople* (London: W. J. Golbourn, 1854) [n.p.].
60. *Athenaeum* 18 February 1853, 214.
61. Foucault, *Discipline and Punish*, p. 207.
62. Michel Foucault, "Questions on Geography," Colin Gordon, trans., *Power/Knowledge: Selected Interviews and Other Writings, 1972–1977* (New York: Pantheon Books, 1980), pp. 71, 76.
63. Quoted in Timothy Mitchell, *Colonising Egypt* (Berkeley: University of California Press, 1991), p. 95.
64. Brian Hudson, "The New Geography and the New Imperialism: 1870–1918," *Antipode* 9 (1977), 12.
65. Mitchell, *Colonising Egypt*, p. 35.
66. Quoted in Mitchell, *Colonising Egypt*, p. 29.
67. *Illustrated London News* 29 November 1851, supplement.
68. Quoted in Kenneth Paul Bendiner, "The Portrayal of the Middle East in British Painting, 1835–1860," PhD dissertation, Columbia University (1978), p. 6.
69. *Illustrated London News* 1 June 1850.
70. Quotations are taken from a handbill in the Theatre Museum, London.
71. Quoted in Raymund Fitzsimons, *The Baron of Piccadilly: The Travels and Entertainments of Albert Smith, 1816–1860* (London: Bles, 1967), p. 77.
72. *Illustrated London News* 8 June 1850.
73. Fitzsimons, *Baron*, p. 83.
74. Quotation taken from a handbill in the Theatre Museum, London.
75. *Athenaeum* 27 July 1850, 793.
76. *Mirror* quoted in Altick, *Shows of London*, p. 231.
77. Thackeray, *Notes of a Journey*, p. 63.

2 FANTASIES OF MISCEGENATION ON THE ROMANTIC STAGE

1. F. W. Hawkins, *The Life of Edmund Kean* (London: 1869; New York: Benjamin Bloom, 1969), p. 221.
2. Nicholas Hudson, "From Nation to Race," *Eighteenth-Century Studies* 29.3 (1996), 247; Nancy Stepan, *The Idea of Race in Science, 1800–1960* (London: Macmillan, 1982), pp. ix–xvii; George W. Stocking, Jr., *Race, Culture, and Evolution: Essays in the History of Anthropology* (New York: Free Press, [1968]), see especially "French Anthropology in 1800," pp. 13–41.
3. Ivan Hannaford, *Race: The History of an Idea in the West* (Washington, DC: Woodrow Wilson Center Press, 1996), p. 229.
4. Charles Lamb, "On the Tragedies of Shakespeare, Considered with Reference to Their Fitness for Stage Representation," *Essays of Charles Lamb*, ed. George Armstrong Wauchope (Boston: Ginn, 1904), pp. 252–253.
5. Jonathan Bate, ed. *Romantics on Shakespeare* (London: Penguin Books, 1992), p. 483. Mythili Kaul notes that questions concerning Othello's race – whether Shakespeare intended him to be black or even if blacks could behave nobly – "were repeatedly raised in the nineteenth century, the era of expanding colonization and imperialist consolidation when arguments for and against slavery were at their height." Mythili Kaul, "Background: Black or Tawny? Stage Representations of Othello from 1604 to the Present," *Othello: New Essays by Black Writers*, ed. Mythili Kaul (Washington, DC: Howard University Press, 1997), p. 5. Such concerns informed theatrical reviews as early as the late-eighteenth century. Kaul cites a 1787 review of Kemble's Othello that raised the issue of the character's race: "We must approve his [Kemble's] dressing Othello in Moorish habit ... but is it necessary the Moor should be as *black* as a native of Guiney?" p. 6. Virginia Mason Vaughan thoroughly examines the question of Othello's race in the Jacobean and later periods in *Othello: A Contextual History* (Cambridge University Press, 1994). See especially pp. 13–34, 51–70, 158–162.
6. Stepan, *Race*, p. 10.
7. William Hazlitt, *A View of the English Stage: or, A Series of Dramatic Criticism* (London: Robert Stodart, Anderson and Chase, 1818), pp. 109–110.
8. W. B. Proctor, *The Life of Edmund Kean* (1835; New York: Benjamin Bloom, 1969), p. 31; New York Public Library for the Performing Arts, Billy Rose Theatre Collection, Edmund Kean Clipping File.
9. Thomas Colley Grattan, "My Acquaintance with the Late Edmund Kean," *New Monthly Magazine* 39 (1833), 7–16. Few reviewers remarked on Kean's substitution of brown pigment for burnt cork when performing Othello, though in 1816 (two years after Kean's debut in that role) Hazlitt complained while reviewing Kean: "[Othello] was black: but that is nothing." William Hazlitt, *Hazlitt on Theatre*, ed. William Archer and Robert Lowe (1895, reprint, New York: Hill and Wang, 1957), p. 69. See also Ruth Cowhig, "Actors, Black and Tawny, in the Role of Othello – and their Critics," *Theatre Research International* 4 (1979), 133–146. Nonetheless, it is generally accepted by theatre historians that

Kean ushered in the "bronze-age" of Othellos, to borrow Mythili Kaul's phrase (p. 8).

10. New York Public Library for the Performing Arts, Billy Rose Theatre Collection, Edmund Kean Iconography.

11. William St. Clair, "The Impact of Byron's Writings: an Evaluative Approach," *Byron: Augustan and Romantic*, ed. Andrew Rutherford (New York: St. Martin's Press, 1990), p. 21.

12. Quoted in Harold Newcomb Hillebrand's *Edmund Kean* (New York: Columbia University Press, 1933), p. 159.

13. Much more damning accounts circulated, such as published insinuations of homosexual acts and the rumor that Byron had demanded anal sex from Lady Byron. Incest only became widely associated with Byron after the publication of Harriet Beecher Stowe's *Lady Byron Vindicated* in 1870. See Louis Crompton, *Byron and Greek Love: Homophobia in Nineteenth-Century England* (Berkeley, CA: University of California Press, 1985), especially pp. 225–235, 261–262.

14. Playbill at Theatre Museum, London.

15. Quoted in Marjorie Garber, *Vested Interests: Cross-dressing and Cultural Anxiety* (New York: Routledge, 1992), p. 317.

16. Byron makes the comment in his author's notes for *The Giaour*.

17. Daniel W. Wilson, "Turks on the Eighteenth-Century Operatic Stage and European Political, Military, and Cultural History," *Eighteenth-Century Life* 2 (1985), 79–92.

18. William Dimond, *The Bride of Abydos: A Romantic Drama, in Three Acts* (London: T. H. Lacey, [n.d.]), p. 21.

19. Dimond, *Bride*, p. 5.

20. 12 February 1818, 125.

21. St. Clair, "Impact of Byron," p. 17.

22. Samuel Claggett Chew, *Byron in England, His Fame and After Fame* (New York: C. Scribner's Sons, 1924), p. 41.

23. John Baldwin Buckstone, *Don Juan. A Romantic Drama* (London: J. Dicks [1828]), p. 10.

24. Malcolm Kelsall, *Byron's Politics* (Brighton, Sussex: Harvester Press, 1987), p. 159.

25. *The Seraglio* I.i. Manuscript in the Lord Chamberlain's collection.

26. *Illustrated London News* 5 October 1844.

27. Ibid., 12 October 1844.

28. Ibid., 21 December 1844.

29. John Sweetman, *The Oriental Obsession: Islamic Inspiration in British and American Art and Architecture, 1500–1920*, Cambridge Studies in the History of Art (Cambridge University Press, 1988), p. 105.

30. Ibid., p. 107.

31. *Times* 20 April 1824.

32. Stanley Mayes, *The Great Belzoni* (London: Putnam 1959), pp. 258, 261.

33. *Times* 30 April 1821.

34. Clipping, Theatre Museum, London.

35. *Times* 20 April 1824.
36. Quoted in J. R. Planché, *Recollections and Reflections: A Professional Autobiography*, 2 vols. (New York: Da Capo Press, 1978), vol. i, p. 37.
37. Playbill, Theatre Museum, London.
38. *Drama* April 1824, 89–90.
39. Pieter van der Merwe, "The Life and Theatrical Career of Clarkson Stanfield 1793–1867," PhD thesis, University of Bristol (1979), p. 115.
40. *Drama* April 1824, 86.
41. *Illustrated London News* 10 April 1847.
42. *Theatrical Inquisitor and Monthly Mirror* 10 June 1817, 447.
43. Guildhall clippings c26.53 t.
44. *Elphi Bey; or, the Arab's Faith* (iii.iii). Quotations taken from the manuscript in the Lord Chamberlain's collection.
45. *Theatrical Inquisitor and Monthly Mirror* 10 June 1817, 446–447.
46. Ibid., January 1814, 30.
47. Ibid., April 1817, 304–305.
48. Ibid., June 1817, 448.
49. Muhsin Jassim Musawi, *Scheherazade in England: A Study of Nineteenth-Century English Criticism of the Arabian Nights* (Washington, DC: Three Continents Press, 1981), p. 15.
50. See Werner William Beyer, *The Enchanted Forest* (New York: Barnes and Noble, 1963).
51. *Times* 23 June 1800.
52. J. R. Planché, *Oberon: A Romantic and Fairy Opera* (London: Hunt & Clarke, 1826), p. 2.
53. Quoted in Sybil Rosenfeld, "The Grieve Family," *Anatomy of an Illusion: Studies in Nineteenth-Century Scenic Design* (Amsterdam: Scheltema and Holkema, 1969), p. 41.
54. Unidentified review, clipping, Theatre Museum, London.
55. A. L. Campbell, *The Demon of the Desert; or, The Well of the Palms* (London: J. Duncombe and Company, [n.d.]), i.i; ii.vi.

3   THE BUILT-OUT EAST OF POPULAR ETHNOGRAPHY

1. Richard Daniel Altick, *The Shows of London* (Cambridge, MA: Belknap–Harvard University Press, 1978), pp. 45–49.
2. Tony Bennett, *The Birth of the Museum: History, Theory, Politics*, Culture: Politics and Policies (London: Routledge, 1995), p. 39.
3. Barbara Kirshenblatt-Gimblett, "Objects of Ethnography," *Exhibiting Cultures: The Poetics and Politics of Museum Display*, ed. Ivan Karp and Steven D. Lavine (Washington: Smithsonian Institution Press, 1991), p. 392.
4. Sybil Rosenfeld, *Georgian Scene Painters and Scene Painting* (Cambridge University Press, 1981), p. 35. Rosenfeld cites the memoir of the pantomime's librettist, John O'Keeffe, though elsewhere she suggests that there are inaccuracies in this text.

5. John Whale, "Indian Jugglers: Hazlitt, Romantic Orientalism and the Difference of View," *Romanticism and Colonialism: Writing and Empire, 1780–1830*, ed. Tim Fulford and Peter J. Kitson (Cambridge University Press, 1998), p. 208.

6. British Museum, Department of Prints and Drawings, *A Collection of cuttings from newspapers, etc., relating to the Olympic Theatre, from 1805 to 1841*, MS Notes. 2 vols. (1805–1841), Theatre Cuttings 47 and 48. Cited in Whale, "Indian Jugglers," p. 209.

7. William Hazlitt, *The Complete Works of William Hazlitt*, ed. P. P. Howe, 21 vols. (New York: AMS Press, 1967), vol. VIII, pp. 82–83.

8. David Bromwich, *Hazlitt, The Mind of a Critic* (1983; New Haven, CT: Yale University Press, 1999), p. 354.

9. Nigel Leask, *British Romantic Writers and the East: Anxieties of Empire* (Cambridge University Press, 1993), p. 22.

10. Whale, "Indian Jugglers," p. 213.

11. William Hazlitt, *Works*, p. 81.

12. *Illustrated London News* 24 June 1843.

13. Ibid. 15 June 1850.

14. Ibid. 12 August 1854.

15. *Athenaeum* 22 June 1845, 863.

16. Richard M. Dorson, *The British Folklorists, A History* (University of Chicago Press, 1968), p. 84.

17. Arthur Keith, "Presidential Address. How Can the Institute Best Serve the Needs of Anthropology?" *Journal of the Royal Anthropological Institute of Great Britain and Ireland* 47 (1917), 14, 15.

18. George W. Stocking, Jr., *Victorian Anthropology* (New York: Free Press–Macmillan, 1987), p. 245.

19. William Ryan Chapman, "Arranging Ethnology: A. H. L. F. Pitt Rivers and the Typological Tradition," *Objects and Others: Essays on Museums and Material Culture*, ed. George W. Stocking, Jr., History of Anthropology, 3 (Madison, WI: University of Wisconsin Press, 1985), p. 22.

20. Paul Greenhalgh, *Ephemeral Vistas: The "Expositions Universelles," Great Exhibitions and World's Fairs, 1851–1939*, Studies in Imperialism (Manchester University Press, 1988), p. 85.

21. *Times* 30 April 1851.

22. Quoted in Jeffrey A. Auerbach, *The Great Exhibition of 1851: A Nation on Display* (New Haven, CT: Yale University Press, 1999), p. 180.

23. John Allwood, *The Great Exhibitions* (London: Studio Vista, 1997), p. 22.

24. *Times* 2 May 1851.

25. John Tallis, *Tallis' History and Description of the Crystal Palace, and the Exhibition of the World's Industry in 1851*, 3 vols. (London: Tallis, 1851), vol. I, p. 15.

26. Ibid., vol. I, p. 19.

27. The report is in *The Crystal Palace and its Contents*, which appears to be a compilation of earlier published reports on the Exhibition ([London]:

W. M. Clark, 1851), p. 7. In the rush to produce books on the Exhibition, publishers borrowed extensively from papers.

28. Henry Mayhew and George Cruikshank, *1851 or, The Adventures of Mr. and Mrs. Sandboys and Family: Who Came Up to London to Enjoy Themselves and to See the Great Exhibition* (London: David Bogue, [1851]), p. 2.
29. British Museum, Department of Prints and Drawings, British Roy PV11.
30. Auerbach, *Great Exhibition*, p. 159.
31. *Illustrated London News* 31 May 1851.
32. Tallis, *Crystal Palace*, vol. 11, pp. 134–135.
33. *Illustrated London News* 31 May 1851.
34. *The Crystal Palace and its Contents*, pp. 43–44.
35. *Times* 15 May 1851.
36. *Illustrated London News* 31 May 1851.
37. John MacKenzie, *Propaganda and Empire: The Manipulation of British Public Opinion, 1880–1960* (Manchester University Press, 1984), p. 114. See also Greenhalgh, *Ephemeral Vistas*, p. 85, and Allwood, *Great Exhibitions*, p. 45.
38. Thomas Richards, *The Commodity Culture of Victorian England: Advertising and Spectacle, 1851–1914* (Stanford University Press, 1990), p. 25.
39. Tallis, *Crystal Palace*, vol. 11, p. 92.
40. *Times* 1 May 1851.
41. Stocking, *Victorian Anthropology*, p. 5.
42. *The Crystal Palace and its Contents*, p. 43.
43. *Illustrated London News* 12 July 1853.
44. Altick, *Shows of London*, p. 209.
45. *Athenaeum* 30 August 1851, 932.
46. As exhibitions increasingly felt the need to provide contextual information, displays were augmented by written and spoken commentary. Barbara Kirshenblatt-Gimblett distinguishes between the people and implements displayed at such exhibits, "ethnographic objects," and the accompanying spoken and written commentary, "ethnographic documents." She discusses an earlier instance at the Egyptian Hall in which a Mexican Indian who was installed in an in situ display described the surrounding reproductions. The native, in her words, did "double duty as ethnographic specimen and museum document." "Objects of Ethnography," p. 404.
47. Edward Said, *Orientalism*, 1978 (New York: Vintage–Random House, 1979), pp. 176–177.
48. Tallis, *Crystal Palace*, vol. 1, p. 33.
49. Ibid., vol. 1, p. 37.
50. *Illustrated London News* 31 May 1851.
51. Stocking, *Victorian Anthropology*, pp. 111–117.
52. Stocking, *Victorian Anthropology*, p. 5.
53. Tallis, *Crystal Palace*, vol. 1, p. 23.
54. Michael Darby, *The Islamic Perspective: An Aspect of British Architecture and Design in the Nineteenth Century* (London: World of Islam Festival Trust, 1983), p. 105.

55. Quoted in Tallis, *Crystal Palace*, vol. 1, p. 19.

56. Quoted in Richards, *Commodity Culture*, p. 28.

57. Richard Southern, *Changeable Scenery, Its Origin and Development in the British Theatre* (London: Faber and Faber, 1952), p. 324.

58. Altick, *Shows of London*, p. 155.

59. *Illustrated London News* 3 May 1845.

60. Quoted in Darby, *Islamic Perspective*, p. 126.

61. Darby, *Islamic Perspective*, p. 128.

62. Altick, *Shows of London*, p. 491; Darby, *Islamic Perspective*, p. 127.

63. Information on reconstruction and redecoration taken from Raymond Mander and Joe Mitchenson, *The Lost Theatres of London* (New York: Taplinger, 1968), pp. 42–46; Victor Glasstone, *Victorian and Edwardian Theatres: An Architectural and Social Survey* (London: Thames and Hudson, 1975), pp. 50–51.

64. See in particular his Elephant and Castle, London; remodeling of the Tivoli, London; Hackney Empire, London; Richmond, London; Empire, Edinburgh; Olympic Theatre, Liverpool; and Grand Opera House, Belfast. Brian Mercer Walker, ed., *Frank Matcham: Theatre Architect* (Belfast: Blackstaff Press, 1980).

65. Quoted in Altick, *Shows of London*, p. 293. Information on Chinese Collection taken from Altick, *Shows of London*, pp. 292–294.

66. According to *The Times*, between the Chinese and Turkish exhibits, the pagoda "was occupied simultaneously or successively by a panorama or two, a collection of South African skins, enlivened by a Bosjesman [Bushman] and a family of Zulu Caffres" (9 August 1854). The inclusion of terms that are now derogatory does not lessen the possibility that the pagoda developed a reputation for ethnographic display at this time.

67. *Illustrated London News* 19 August 1854; *Illustrated London News* 30 September 1854; *Times* 9 August 1854.

68. *Illustrated London News* 19 August 1854.

69. *Illustrated London News* 30 September 1854.

70. Edward P. Alexander, "Artistic and Historical Period Rooms," *Curator* 7 (1964), 263–281.

71. Quoted in Auerbach, *Great Exhibition*, p. 116.

72. Michel de Certeau, *The Writing of History*, trans. Tom Conley (New York: Columbia University Press, 1988), pp. 209–210. Lévi Straus quoted in de Certeau, *Writing of History*, p. 210.

73. Ira Jacknis, "Franz Boas and Exhibits: On the Limitations of the Museum Method of Anthropology," *Objects and Others: Essays on Museums and Material Culture*, ed. George W. Stocking, Jr. (Madison, WI: University of Wisconsin Press, 1985), p. 82.

74. Said, *Orientalism*, p. 162.

75. *Times* 9 August 1854.

76. Patrick Beaver, *The Crystal Palace, 1851–1936: A Portrait of Victorian Enterprise* (London: Hugh Evelyn, 1970), pp. 83–84.

77. Auerbach, *Great Exhibition*, p. 201.

78. *Illustrated London News* 21 August 1851.
79. R. G. Latham, *The Natural History Department of the Crystal Palace Described* (London: Crystal Palace Library, 1854), p. 6.
80. In 1853, Reimer's Anatomical and Ethnological Museum occupied a portion of Savile House; however the inclusion of "Aztec Lilliputians" in the waxwork "Gallery of All Nations" throws the display's scientific rigor into doubt. See Altick, *Shows of London*, pp. 341–342.
81. Alfred Russel Wallace, *My Life: A Record of Events and Opinions*, 2 vols. (London: Chapman and Hall, 1905), vol. 1, p. 322. Wallace explains that Latham employed Italian modelers who had been trained in schools of classical sculpture. "The result," he explains, "was very curious, and often even ludicrous, a brown Indian man or girl being given the attitudes and expressions of an Apollo or a Hercules, a Venus or a Minerva."
82. *Illustrated London News* 21 August 1852.
83. "Our Museums, Their Desiderata and Arrangement," *Athenaeum* 29 November 1851, 1253–1254.
84. Owen Jones, *The Alhambra Court in the Crystal Palace* (London: Crystal Palace Library, 1854), pp. 14–15.
85. Quoted in John MacKenzie, *Orientalism: History, Theory, and the Arts* (Manchester University Press, 1995), p. 122. While Jones never explicitly rejected industrialism, it is possible to read his interest in Islamic architecture in relation to the medievalism of the later Arts and Crafts movement. For Jones, as for later designers, the desire to revive a lost craftsmanship was part of a larger concern over the splintering effects of modernity.
86. *Guide to the Palace and Park* (London: Charles Dickens and Evans, [1886]), p. 7.
87. Jones, *Alhambra*, p. 39.
88. *Guide to the Palace and Park*, p. 8; *The Royal Album of Crystal Palace Views* [n.p., n.d.].
89. Peter J. Bowler, *The Invention of Progress: The Victorians and the Past* (Cambridge, MA: Basil Blackwell, 1989), p. 39.
90. Latham, *Natural History*, pp. 31, 34.

4   THE BIBLICAL EAST IN THEATRES AND EXHIBITIONS

1. Kenneth Paul Bendiner, "The Portrayal of the Middle East in British Painting, 1835–1860," PhD dissertation, Columbia University (1978), p. 7.
2. Richard Daniel Altick, *The Shows of London* (Cambridge MA: Belknap–Harvard University Press, 1978), p. 394.
3. John Russell Stephens, *The Censorship of English Drama, 1824–1901* (Cambridge University Press, 1980), pp. 97–98.
4. Stephens, *Censorship*, p. 97.
5. Playbills, London Theatre Museum.
6. Martin Meisel, *Realizations: Narrative, Pictorial, and Theatrical Arts in Nineteenth-Century England* (Princeton University Press, 1983), p. 171.

7. Quoted in Meisel, *Realizations*, p. 173.
8. *Athenaeum* 12 September 1840, 716–717.
9. Neil Asher Silberman, *Digging for God and Country: Exploration, Archeology, and the Secret Struggle for the Holy Land, 1799–1917* (New York: Knopf, 1982), pp. 37–47.
10. Quoted in Altick, *Shows of London*, p. 394.
11. *Illustrated London News* 23 January 1847.
12. Quoted in Altick, *Shows of London*, p. 394.
13. *Illustrated London News* 16 March 1846.
14. Quoted in Stephens, *Censorship*, p. 105.
15. Stephens, *Censorship*, pp. 102–103.
16. Theatre Museum, London.
17. *Observer* 13 April 1834.
18. William Charles Macready, *The Diaries of William Charles Macready, 1793–1873*, 2 vols., ed. William Toynbee (New York: G. P. Putnam, 1912), vol. I, p. 116.
19. Seton Lloyd, *Foundations in the Dust: A Story of Mesopotamian Exploration* (London: Oxford University Press, 1947), p. 77.
20. In its review of the 1839 *Artaxerxes* the *Athenaeum* wrote that "the effect of the semi-barbarous costumes, the ponderous and richly decorated architecture, and the colossal figures of bulls and hippogriffs of grotesque sculpture, is strikingly characteristic" (19 October 1839, 797). Another reviewer remarked: "We are transported back to the real ancient Persians, the times of winged horses, peaked beards, and Babylonish bricks." Quoted in Sybil Rosenfeld, "The Grieve Family," *Anatomy of an Illusion: Studies in Nineteenth-Century Scene Design* (Amsterdam: IFTR, 1969), p. 41.
21. Quoted in Meisel, *Realizations*, p. 174.
22. Meisel, *Realizations*, p. 170.
23. *Illustrated London News* 26 March 1853.
24. Lloyd, *Mesopotamian Exploration*, p. 137.
25. Edmund S. Carpenter writes that degenerationist theory was supported by the views of historians of and travelers in exotic lands, who "persuasively pointed out that in distant lands were to be found semi-barbarian natives living amid the ruins of 'lost' civilizations, unable to reproduce the works of their forefathers ... Moral and intellectual refinements, so readily assigned to these earlier civilizations, were found wanting in the rude tribes encountered by Europeans in the region, and their absence was taken by many as an indication of degenerationism." According to Carpenter, this view persisted until destroyed by E. B. Tylor's comparative method gained prominence in the second half of the nineteenth century. "The Role of Archeology in the Nineteenth-Century Controversy between Developmentalism and Degeneration," *Pennsylvania Archeologist* 20 (1950), 7–8.
26. George W. Stocking, Jr., *Victorian Anthropology* (New York: Free Press–Macmillan, 1987), p. 71.
27. Peter J. Bowler discusses the attempts of British geologists to "retain a link between the new geology and traditional accounts of the creation and deluge" in *The Invention of Progress: The Victorians and the Past* (Oxford: Basil Blackwell,

1989), pp. 162–163. In "From Chronology to Ethnology: James Cowles Prichard and British Anthropology, 1800–1850," George W. Stocking, Jr., argues that the English belief that the Mosaic records served as the base and sustenance of European civilization was the natural response of thinkers who grew to maturity at a time when this civilization seemed threatened by the atheistic barbarism of the French Revolution. Introductory essay, *Researches into the Physical History of Man*, by James Cowles Prichard (University of Chicago Press, 1973), p. xlvi.

28. *Athenaeum* 22 February 1851, 225–226.

29. Ibid. *Illustrated London News* 22 February 1851. *Era* 23 February 1851. The published text for *Azaël* featured a lengthy description of the costumes. This description often employed vague language that suggested accuracy without actually giving details, in phrases such as "cap of the Egyptian fashion" and "turban after the oriental fashion." Edward Fitzball, *Azaël, The Prodigal* (London: John Duncombe, [n.d.]).

30. The maquettes that I cite for this production are housed at the Blythe House Annex of the Theatre Museum, London.

31. Giovanni Battista Belzoni, *Plates Illustrative of the Researches and Operations of G. Belzoni in Egypt and Nubia* (London: J. Murray, 1820).

32. *Illustrated London News* 22 February 1851.

33. *Athenaeum* 22 February 1851, 225–226.

34. Austen Henry Layard, *The Monuments of Nineveh, from Drawings Made on the Spot* (London: J. Murray, 1849).

35. *Illustrated London News* 22 February 1851.

36. Familiar theatrical imagery often appeared in supposedly scholarly reproductions of the ancient East. For example, even as formulaic a piece as *The Bride of the Nile, or the Lily of Memphis and the Oracle of Latona* (Royal Amphitheatre 1845) could be praised by the *Illustrated London News* for "introducing us to several new facts connected with the manners, customs and idiosyncrasies of the ancient Egyptians." *Illustrated London News* 6 September 1845.

37. *Illustrated London News* 22 February 1851.

38. *Athenaeum* 22 February 1851.

39. Richard Schoch, *Shakespeare's Victorian Stage: Performing History in the Theatre of Charles Kean* (Cambridge University Press, 1998), p. 83.

40. Barbara Kirshenblatt-Gimblett, *Destination Culture: Tourism, Museums, and Heritage* (Berkeley, CA: University of California Press, 1998), p. 23.

41. Hayden V. White, "Foucault Decoded: Notes from the Underground," *History and Theory* 12 (1973), 47.

42. Stephen Bann, *The Clothing of Clio: A Study of the Representation of History in Nineteenth-Century Britain and France* (Cambridge University Press, 1984), p. 85.

43. Eilean Hooper-Greenhill, *Museums and the Shaping of Knowledge* (London: Routledge, 1992), p. 17.

44. Tony Bennett, *The Birth of the Museum: History, Theory, Politics*, Culture: Policies and Politics (London: Routledge, 1995), p. 39.

45. Kirshenblatt-Gimblett, *Destination Culture*, p. 19.

46. John Elsner, "The House and Museum of Sir John Soane," *The Cultures of Collecting*, ed. John Elsner and Roger Cardinal (Cambridge, MA: Harvard University Press, 1994), pp. 170–171.

47. *Times* 30 April 1821.

48. Stanley Mayes, *The Great Belzoni* (London: Putnam, 1959), pp. 258, 261.

49. The redesign of this room is discussed in Patrick Conner, ed., *The Inspiration of Egypt: Its Influence on British Artists, Travellers and Designers, 1700–1900* (Brighton Borough Council, 1983), pp. 67–68. An outline etching of the room appears in Richard D. Altick's *Shows of London*, p. 245.

50. *Times* 30 April 1821.

51. Richard Altick provides thorough descriptions of some of Bullock's exhibits, *Shows of London*, pp. 235–252.

52. George Brown Goode, "The Museums of the Future," *The Origins of Natural Sciences in America: The Essays of George Brown Goode*, ed. Sally Gregory Kohlstedt (Washington, DC: Smithsonian Institution Press, 1991), p. 322.

53. Mayes, *Belzoni*, pp. 42–51, 254. According to Mayes, Belzoni played such roles as the Black Chief in *Philip Quarll*, an imitation of Robinson Crusoe, and performed a strong-man routine at Bartholomew's Fair in, what a contemporary described as, "oriental dress." Even before he departed for the East, the exotic figured in Belzoni's performances.

54. Richard Foulkes explains that Phelps omitted most of the play's references to the incestuous affair between Antiochus and his daughter when he cut Gower's speeches from the production. "Samuel Phelps's *Pericles* and Layard's Discoveries at Nineveh," *Nineteenth-Century Theatre Research* 5 (Autumn 1977), 85–92. However, audience members who were familiar with the play or who understood the riddle posed to Pericles would certainly associate Antiochus with the perceived moral degeneracy of Nineveh. The Nineveh artifacts were featured in the production's many Eastern Mediterranean locations and were used, according to a contemporary playgoer, to emphasize "the instability of fortune" (quoted in Foulkes, "Phelps's", p. 87). The many reversals of fortune depicted in the play were accentuated by the implication that, like Nineveh, these cities too would fall with breathtaking speed.

55. Playbill note reproduced in Charles Kean (adapter), *Sardanapalus, King of Assyria: a tragedy, in five acts by Lord Byron* (London: T. H. Lacey, [1853]).

56. *Illustrated London News* 18 June 1853.

57. *Era* 19 June 1853, 10.

58. Martin Meisel discusses the scene painting for *Sardanapalus* and its reliance on the artifacts at the British Museum in his analysis of the nineteenth-century theatre's use of spectacular effect as evidence of what Charles Lamb disparagingly called "the material sublime." *Realizations: Narrative, Pictorial, and Theatrical Arts in Nineteenth-Century England* (Princeton University Press, 1983), pp. 181–183.

59. *Synopsis of the Contents of the British Museum*. Quoted in William Ryan Chapman, "Arranging Ethnology: A. H. L. F. Pitt Rivers and the Typological Tradition," *Objects and Others: Essays on Museums and Material Culture*, ed.

George W. Stocking, Jr. (Madison, WI: University of Wisconsin Press, 1985), p. 23.

60. Edward Miller, *That Noble Cabinet: A History of the British Museum* (Athens, OH: Ohio University Press, 1974), p. 196. Speaking before the Brooklyn Institute in 1889, George Brown Goode described the British Museum's Assyrian and Egyptian galleries as "museums of themselves." Goode, "Museums of the Future," p. 345.

61. *Illustrated London News* 21 August 1852.

62. Kean (adapter), *Sardanapalus*.

63. *Athenaeum* 18 June 1853, 745. *Illustrated London News* 18 June 1853.

64. Tracy C. Davis, *Actresses as Working Women: Their Social Identity in Victorian Culture*, Gender and Performance (London: Routledge, 1991), pp. 100–101.

65. Kean (adapter), *Sardanapalus*, pp. 55, 56, 2, 21.

66. *Illustrated London News* 18 June 1853.

67. James Prichard, "Anniversary Address to the Ethnological Society of London on the Recent Progress of Ethnology," Ethnological Society of London, *Journal* 2 [1850], 128–129.

68. *Era* 10 June 1853, 10.

69. [J. F. Murray], "The World of London," *Blackwood's Magazine* 51 (1842) quoted in Altick, "Shows of London," p. 442.

70. Goode, "Museums of the Future," p. 322.

71. John William Cole, *The Life and Theatrical Times of Charles Kean, F.S.A. Including a Summary of the English Stage for the Last Fifty Years, and a Detailed Account of the Management of the Princess's Theatre from 1850 to 1859*, 2 vols. (London: Richard Bentley, 1879), vol. II, pp. 65–66.

72. Kean (adapter), *Sardanapalus*, p. 55.

73. Owen Jones, *Description of the Egyptian Court Erected in the Crystal Palace by Owen Jones . . . and Joseph Bonomi* (London: Crystal Palace Library, 1854), p. 3.

74. *Illustrated London News* 9 October 1852.

75. Jones, *Egyptian Court*, p. 25.

76. *Illustrated London News* 2 April 1853. See also, R. A. Hayward, *Cleopatra's Needle* (London: Moorland, 1978), pp. 25, 75.

77. Austen Henry Layard, *The Nineveh Court in the Crystal Palace* (London: Crystal Palace Library, 1854), pp. v, vi, 52, 55, 57, 62, 64, 66.

78. Jones, *Egyptian Court*, p. 3.

79. Ibid., pp. 14–15. Each word in the translation appeared beneath the corresponding hieroglyph.

80. *Illustrated London News* 17 June 1854.

5 THE GEOGRAPHY OF IMPERIAL THEATRE

1. J. N. L. Baker, "Mary Somerville and Geography in England," *Geographical Journal* 3 (1948), 216.

2. Brian Hudson, "The New Geography and the New Imperialism: 1870–1918," *Antipode* 9 (1977), 12.

3. Richard Peet, "The Social Origins of Environmental Determinism," *Annals of the Association of American Geographers* 75 (1985), 310.

4. H. R. Mill quoted in Hudson, "Geography," 16. The influence of neo-Lamarckian racism on geography is discussed in Peet, "Environmental Determinism."

5. See George Stocking, Jr., *Victorian Anthropology* (New York: Free Press–Macmillan, 1987), pp. 239–273.

6. Ibid., p. 262.

7. George Stocking, Jr., *Race, Culture, and Evolution: Essays in the History of Anthropology* (New York: Free Press–Macmillan, 1968), p. 119.

8. *Illustrated London News* 14 February 1885.

9. For discussions of these melodramas, see James Stottlar, " 'A House Choked with Gunpowder and Wild with Excitement': Augustus Harris and Drury Lane's Spectacular Melodrama," *When They Weren't Doing Shakespeare*, ed. Judith L. Fisher and Stephen Watt (Athens, GA: University of Georgia Press, 1989), pp. 212–229, and Michael Booth "Soldiers of the Queen: Drury Lane Imperialism," *Melodrama: The Cultural Emergence of a Genre*, ed. Michael Hays and Anastasia Nikolopoulu (New York: St. Martin's Press, 1996), pp. 3–20. Booth discusses the production styles of Drury Lane's autumn melodramas in *Victorian Spectacular Theatre, 1850–1910*, Theatre Production Studies (Routledge: London, 1981). See especially pp. 69–74.

10. *Times* 14 September 1885.

11. Lord Chamberlain's Collection.

12. Booth, "Soldiers," p. 8.

13. *Era* 27 June 1883.

14. II.ii. All quotes from *Freedom* are taken from an unpublished printed script in the Theatre Collection at Princeton University.

15. D. C. M. Platt, *Finance, Trade, and Politics in British Foreign Policy, 1815–1914* (Oxford University Press, 1968), p. 158.

16. Clement M. Henry, *The Mediterranean Debt Crescent: Money and Power in Algeria, Egypt, Morocco, Tunisia, and Turkey* (Gainesville, FL: University Press of Florida, 1996), p. 215.

17. The Earl of Cromer, *Modern Egypt*, 2 vols. (New York: Macmillan, 1908), vol. 1, p. 41.

18. For a description of tourist outings to Egyptian slave markets see Edmund Swinglehurst, *The Romantic Journey: The Story of Thomas Cook and Victorian Travel* (New York: Harper, 1974), p. 82.

19. *Dramatic Notes* August 1883, 34.

20. H. M. Stanley, "Central Africa and the Congo Basin; or, The Importance of the Scientific Study of Geography," *The Journal of the Manchester Geographical Society* 1 (1885), 8.

21. Amira El-Azhary Sonbol, *The New Mamluks: Egyptian Society and Modern Feudalism* (Syracuse, NY: Syracuse University Press, 2000), pp. 71–79, 93–96; Leila Ahmed, *Women and Gender in Islam: Historical Roots of a Modern Debate* (New Haven, CT: Yale University Press, 1992), pp. 145–146.

22. Quoted in Ahmed, *Women and Gender in Islam*, p. 153.

23. The British first applied the telegraph to military purposes during the Crimean War. J. S. Bratton discusses how theatre managers used telegraphic dispatches to dramatize events of this war in "Theatre of War: the Crimean on the London Stage, 1854–5," *Performance and Politics in Popular Drama: Aspects of Popular Entertainment in Theatre, Film and Television, 1800–1976*, ed. David Bradby, Louis James, and Bernard Sharratt (Cambridge University Press, 1980), pp. 119–137. Angela C. Pao explains that from the time of the Crimean conflict onward, French imperial theatre used the acceleration in communication made possible by the telegraph to dramatize victories before the battles had even been fought. *The Orient of the Boulevards: Exoticism, Empire, and Nineteenth-Century French Theatre*, New Cultural Studies (Philadelphia, University of Pennsylvania Press, 1998), p. 135.

24. Heidi Holder, "Melodrama, Realism, and Empire on the British Stage," *Acts of Supremacy: The British Empire on Stage, 1790–1930*, ed. J. S. Bratton et al. (Manchester University Press, 1991), p. 142.

25. Peter Brooks, *The Melodramatic Imagination: Balzac, Henry James, Melodrama, and the Mode of Excess* (1976; New York: Columbia University Press, 1985), p. 32.

26. Eric Bentley, *The Life of the Drama* (New York: Applause, 1964), p. 202.

27. Daniel R. Headrick convincingly argues that technological innovations shaped the development of nineteenth-century imperialism in *The Tools of Empire: Technology and European Imperialism in the Nineteenth Century* (Oxford University Press, 1985).

28. In point of fact the commander of the relief expedition, General Garnet Wolseley, refused to use native boats and instead ordered eight hundred boats specially constructed in London to navigate the cataracts at low water. These ships proved too light and fragile to navigate the Nile rapids. Later in the scene, an explanation is provided for the often reported capsizing of Wolseley's low boats; an Arab "fellaheen" cuts the nuggar free and it is "borne by current… strikes rock and founders."

29. In fact, both the review in *The Times* (14 September 1885) and in the *Athenaeum* (19 September 1885) assume the play depicts the recent war in the Sudan.

30. *Era* 19 September 1885, 14.

31. *Illustrated London News* 29 March 1885.

32. John Springhall, "'Up Guards and At Them!' British Imperialism and Popular Art 1880–1914," *Imperialism and Popular Culture*, ed. John M. MacKenzie (Manchester University Press, 1992), pp. 49–72.

33. *Illustrated London News* 23 February 1884.

34. William Muskerry and John Jourdain, *Khartoum!; or, The Star of the Desert* (London: Samuel French, n.d.), p. 29.

35. The double letter also served to explain the apparent contradiction between Gordon's last desperate letter and earlier dispatches that asserted the city could "hold out for years."

36. Quoted in Douglas H. Johnson, "The Death of Gordon: a Victorian Myth," *Journal of Imperial and Commonwealth History* 10 (1982), 304.

37. Pao, *Orient*, p. 123.

38. (IV.i). Quotations from *Human Nature* are taken from the printed edition in the Harvard Theatre Collection.
39. Bill reproduced in William Muskerry and John Jourdain, *Khartoum! Or, The Star of the Desert* (London: Samuel French, [n.d.]), p. 2.
40. Stanley, "Africa," 10.
41. Holder, "Melodrama," p. 140.
42. Quoted in Holder, "Melodrama," p. 142.
43. *Times* 6 August 1883.
44. *Era* 14 November 1885, 7.
45. As Johnson explains, the increased emphasis on Gordon's religious character is evidenced in a number of pamphlets and sermons published after his death. In them, Gordon is referred to as a "Christian Hero," "The Youngest of the Saints," a "Hero and a Saint," "England's Hero and Christian Soldier," "The Forsaken Hero," and "The Hero Sacrificed." Johnson, "Gordon," 302.
46. *Times* 1 December 1885.
47. *Era* 14 November 1885, 7.
48. The *Bat*, a journal that was critical of Victorian spectacular theatre, linked its criticism of Harris's management to its criticism of the war:

> We ratepayers were charged about thirty millions sterling for the Soudan war. All we got for the money, a few swords, some Mahdi's uniforms, a shield or two, a coat of mail, and some wooden saddles have been handed over to Augustus Harris. And certainly we must be poor patriots indeed if we grudge that paltry sum to decorate the walls of the grand saloon of the National Theatre.
>
> To those whose disgust that the course taken by England both with regard to Egypt and the Soudan does not destroy any interest in the relics, the show must be instructive and entertaining. And it is satisfactory to notice that the collection is much better shown and catalogued at Drury Lane than it would have been had it been exhibited by public authorities at a national museum. 17 November 1885, p. 499.

49. *Era* 14 November 1885, 7.
50. Reprinted in the *Era* 19 September 1885, 16.
51. Quoted in Richard Shannon, *The Crisis of Imperialism, 1865–1915* (London: Hart-Davis, 1974), p. 201.
52. Edward Said, *Culture and Imperialism*, 1993 (New York: Knopf, 1994), p. 76.
53. *Illustrated London News* 26 January 1884.
54. *Athenaeum* 28 February 1885, 283.
55. *Dramatic Notes* August 1883, 33.
56. *Times* 6 August 1883.
57. Undated clipping, New York Public Library for the Performing Arts, The Billy Rose Theatre Collection, *Human Nature* Clipping File.
58. *Era* 14 November 1885, 7.
59. *Era* 17 October 1885, 7.
60. The conflation of "natives" with "dromedaries" at both the theatre and the exhibition demonstrates an ongoing confusion as to whether authenticity was a feature of cultural practice or an indwelling quality. It also displays a limited sensitivity to the humanity of displayed peoples. For an analysis of human

display at exhibitions see Paul Greenhalgh, *Ephemeral Vistas: The "Expositions Universelles," Great Exhibitions and World's Fairs, 1851–1939* (Manchester University Press, 1988), especially pp. 82–111.

61. *Illustrated London News* 29 May 1886.
62. On exoticism in Regency eclecticism, see John Steegman's *The Rule of Taste: From George I to George IV* (New York: Russell and Russell, 1968), pp. 154–175.
63. Walter Houghton, *The Victorian Frame of Mind, 1830–1870* (New Haven: Yale University Press, 1957). A. Dwight Culler, *The Victorian Mirror of History* (New Haven, CT: Yale University Press, 1985).
64. Booth, "Soldiers," p. 13.
65. For analysis of this and other music-hall songs lauding the British military, see David Russell, " 'We Carved Our Way to Glory': the British Soldier in Music Hall and Song and Sketch, *c.* 1880–1914," *Popular Imperialism and the Military*, ed. John M. MacKenzie (Manchester University Press, c.1992), p. 66.
66. Advertised in the *Bat* 14 April 1885, 1.
67. Information taken from Lord Chamberlain's Collection manuscript and bill from the Theatre Museum, London.
68. The ballet was first performed at La Scala, Milan, on 11 January 1881. See Ivor Guest, *Ballet in Leicester Square: The Alhambra and the Empire, 1860–1915* (London: Dance Books, 1992), p. 37.
69. *Athenaeum* 30 May 1885, 705.
70. *Era* 17 October 1885, 8.
71. *Bat* 20 October 1885, 428.
72. *Era* 30 December 1882, 4.
73. *Illustrated Sporting Theatrical News* 30 December 1882, 391.
74. *Era* 30 December 1882, 4.
75. Information on *Sinbad* is taken from the pantomime scenario in the Lord Chamberlain's Collection, British Museum, and from a playbill at the Theatre Museum, London.
76. Exotic undress in the Drury Lane pantomime, *Robinson Crusoe*, is discussed in Tracy Davis, *Actresses as Working Women: Their Social Identity in Victorian Culture* (London: Routledge, 1991), pp. 120–121.
77. *Illustrated Sporting and Theatrical News* 30 December 1882, 382.
78. *Era* 30 December 1882, 4.
79. Ibid. 29 May 1886, 10.
80. *Bat* 22 December 1885, 587.
81. *Era* 21 November 1885, 15.
82. *Era* review reprinted in its entirety in Booth, *Victorian Spectacular Theatre*, pp. 165–171.
83. *Bat* 28 December 1886, 883.
84. Erin Addison, "Saving Other Women from Other Men: Disney's *Aladdin*," *Camera Obscura: A Journal of Feminism and Film Theory* 31 (1993), 19.
85. David Stout, "Mrs. Bush Cites Women's Plight Under Taliban," *New York Times* 18 March 2001, late edn.: B1.

Select bibliography

ARCHIVAL COLLECTIONS

British Library, Department of Manuscripts, Lord Chamberlain's Plays
British Museum, Department of Prints and Drawings
Harvard Theatre Collection
New York Public Library, Humanities and Social Sciences, Asian and Middle Eastern Division
New York Public Library, Humanities and Social Sciences, Rare Books Division
New York Public Library for the Performing Arts, The Billy Rose Theatre Collection
New York University, Fales Library Collection
Theatre Museum, London
University of London, Special Collections
Victoria and Albert Museum, Prints and Drawings
Yale University, Beinecke Rare Books and Manuscript Library
Yale University, Center for British Art, Department of Rare Books and Manuscripts

NEWSPAPERS AND PERIODICALS

Athenaeum
The Builder
Era
Illustrated London News
Illustrated Sporting Theatrical News
Sketch
The Times

PERIODICALS REPRODUCED IN BRITAIN'S LITERARY HERITAGE: NINETEENTH-CENTURY THEATRE PERIODICALS

Actors by Daylight, and Pencilings in the Pit (part III, reel 4)
The Bat (part II, reels 2–4)
The Call-Boy (part III, reel 4)

The Cicerone (part III, reel 4)
The Drama; or, Theatrical Pocket Magazine (part I, reel 8)
Dramatic Notes (part III, reels 8–10)
The Dramatic Review, a Weekly Journal of Literature, Art, Music and the Drama
(part III, reel 6)
The Mask (part III, reel 6)
Oxberry's Weekly Budget of Plays and Magazine of Romance, Whim, and Interest
(part III, reel 4)
The Players (part III, reels 5–6)
The Programme and Playbill (part II, reel 22)
The Stage Directory (part II, reel 1)
Tallis's Dramatic Magazine and General Theatrical and Musical Review (part III,
reel 5)
The Theatre (part I, reels 9–18)
The Theatrical Inquisitor (part I, reels 2–6)
The Theatrical Mirror and Playgoers' Companion (part I, reel 9)
The Theatrical Programme and Entre'acte (part I, reel 9)
The Theatrical Times (part II, reel 1)
Theatricals (part II, reel 22)
The Weekly Theatrical Reporter and Music Hall Review (part III, reel 6)

CONTEMPORARY BOOKS, ARTICLES, AND PUBLISHED PLAYS

Belzoni, Giovanni Battista, *Plates Illustrative of the Researches and Operations of
G. Belzoni in Egypt and Nubia*, London: J. Murray, 1820.
Britton, John, *The Autobiography of John Britton*, London: published by author,
1850.
Buckstone, John Baldwin, *Don Juan. A Romantic Drama*, London: J. Dicks
[1828].
Campbell, A. L., *The Demon of the Desert; or, The Well of the Palms*, London:
J. Duncombe and Co., [n.d.].
Cole, John William, *The Life and Theatrical Times of Charles Kean, F.S.A. Including
a Summary of the English Stage for the Last Fifty Years, and a Detailed Account
of the Management of the Princess's Theatre from 1850 to 1859*, 2 vols., London:
Richard Bentley, 1879.
*A Concise Account of the View of Constantinople with a Map; and an Illustration
of the Descriptive Sheets, Which Are Given to Each Person Who Goes to Those
Paintings at the Panorama, Leicester Square*, London: Panorama and Messrs.
Richardsons, 1801.
Cromer, Earl of, *Modern Egypt*, 2 vols., New York: Macmillan, 1908, vol. 1.
The Crystal Palace and its Contents, [London]: W. M. Clark, 1851.
Denon, Vivant, *Voyage dans la Basse et la Haute Egypte*, 2 vols. and atlas, Paris:
H. Gaugain, 1829, atlas.
Description of Constantinople, London: W. J. Golbourn, 1854.

Description of a View of Constantinople; with its European and Asiatic Suburbs, and a Great Extent of Surrounding Country Now Exhibiting at the Panorama Royal, Leicester Square, London: T. Brettell, 1846.

Description of a View of the Bombardment of St. Jean D'Acre with the City and Surrounding Country, London: George Nichols, 1841.

Description of A View of the City of Cairo and the Surrounding Country, London: T. Brettell, [1847].

Description of A View of the City of Damascus and the Surrounding Country now exhibited at the Panorama, Leicester Square. Painted by the Proprietor Robert Burford. London: T. Brettell, Rupert Street, Haymarket, 1841.

Dibdin, Jr., Charles, *History and Illustrations of the London Theatres*, London: Printed for the Proprietors of the "Illustrations of London Buildings," 1826.

   Professional and Literary Memoirs of Charles Dibdin the Younger, Dramatist and Upward of Thirty Years Manager of Minor Theatres, ed. Georges Speaight, London: Society for Theatre Research, 1956.

Dimond, William, *The Aethiop: or, The Child of the the Desert*, New York: Samuel French, [n.d.].

   The Bride of Abydos, London: T. H. Lacey, [1818].

Fitzball, Edward, *Azaël, The Prodigal*, London: John Duncombe, [n.d.].

   The Earthquake; or, The Spectre of the Nile, London: John Cumberland, [1829].

   Thalaba, the Destroyer, London: John Lowndes, 1826.

Goode, George Brown, "The Museums of the Future," *The Origins of Natural Sciences in America: The Essays of George Brown Goode*, ed. Sally Gregory Kohlstedt, Washington, DC: Smithsonian Institution Press, 1991, 321–348.

Grattan, Thomas Colley, "My Acquaintance with the late Edmund Kean," *New Monthly Magazine* 39 (1833), 7–16, 143–151.

Guide to the Palace and Park, London: Charles Dickens and Evans, [1886].

Hawkins, F. W., *The Life of Edmund Kean*, London: 1869; New York: Benjamin Bloom, 1969.

Hazlitt, William, *The Complete Works of William Hazlitt*, ed. P. P. Howe, 21 vols., New York: AMS Press, 1967, vol. VIII.

   Hazlitt on Theatre. ed. William Archer and Robert Lowe. 1895. Reprint, New York: Hill and Wang, 1957.

   A View of the English Stage: or, A Series of Dramatic Criticism, London: Robert Stodart, Anderson and Chase, 1818.

Hopkins, Albert A., *Magic: Stage Illusions and Scenic Diversions, Including Trick Photography*, 1898. Reprint, as *Magic: Stage Illusions, Special Effects and Trick Photography*, New York: Dover, 1976.

Jones, Owen, *The Alhambra Court in the Crystal Palace*, London: Crystal Palace Library, 1854.

   Description of the Egyptian Court Erected in the Crystal Palace by Owen Jones . . . and Joseph Bonomi, London: Crystal Palace Library, 1854.

Kean, Charles (adapter), *Sardanapalus, King of Assyria: a tragedy, in five acts by Lord Byron*, London: T. H. Lacey, [1853].

Lamb, Charles, "On the Tragedies of Shakespeare, Considered with Reference to Their Fitness for Stage Representation," *Essays of Charles Lamb*, ed. George Armstrong Wauchope, Boston: Ginn, 1904, pp. 237–258.

Latham, R. G., *The Natural History Department of the Crystal Palace Described*, London: Crystal Palace Library, 1854.

Layard, Austen Henry, *The Monuments of Nineveh, From Drawings Made on the Spot*, London: J. Murray, 1849.

The Nineveh Court in the Crystal Palace, London: Crystal Palace Library, 1854.

Lloyd, Seton, *Foundations in the Dust: A Story of Mesopotamian Exploration*, London: Oxford University Press, 1947.

Macready, William Charles, *The Diaries of William Charles Macready, 1793–1873*, 2 vols., ed. William Toynbee, New York: G. P. Putnam, 1912.

Mayhew, Henry and George Cruikshank, *1851, or, The Adventures of Mr. and Mrs. Sandboys and Family: Who Came Up to London to Enjoy Themselves and to See the Great Exhibition*, London: David Bogue, [1851].

Muskerry, William and Jourdain, John, *Khartoum! Or, The Star of the Desert*, London: Samuel French, [n.d.].

Nietzsche, Friedrich, *The Use and Abuse of History*, trans. Adrian Collins, New York: Library of Liberal Arts–Macmillan, 1957.

O'Keeffe, John, *A Short Account of the New Pantomime called Omai; or, A Trip Round the World*, London: T. Cadell, 1785.

Planché, J. R., *Oberon: A Romantic and Fairy Opera*, London: Hunt & Clarke, 1826.

Recollections and Reflections: A Professional Autobiography, 2 vols., New York: Da Capo Press, 1978.

Prichard, James, "Anniversary Address to the Ethnological Society of London on the Recent Progress of Ethnology," Ethnology Society of London, *Journal* 2 [1850], 119–149.

Proctor, W. B., *The Life of Edmund Kean*, 1835; New York: Benjamin Bloom, 1969.

The Royal Album of Crystal Palace Views [n.p., n.d.].

The Siege of Acre; or, Descriptive Collections relative to the late scene of conquest in Syria between the British and Turkish Force, Under the Orders of Sir W. Sidney Smith, and the Republican French, Commanded by General Buonaparte, London: W. Glendinning, 1801.

Stanley, H. M., "Central Africa and the Congo Basin; or, The Importance of the Scientific Study of Geography," *The Journal of the Manchester Geographical Society* 1 (1885), 6–25.

Tallis, John, *Tallis's History and Description of the Crystal Palace, and the Exhibition of the World's Industry in 1851*, 3 vols., London: Tallis, 1851.

Thackeray, William Makepeace, *Notes of a Journey from Cornhill to Grand Cairo*, 1845, introd. Sarah Searight, Heathfield: Cockbird, 1991.

Wallace, Alfred Russel, *My Life: A Record of Events and Opinions*, 2 vols., London: Chapman and Hall, 1905, vol. 1.

SECONDARY MATERIALS

Addison, Erin, "Saving Other Women from Other Men: Disney's *Aladdin*," *Camera Obscura: A Journal of Feminism and Film Theory* 31 (1993), 5–26.

Ahmed, Leila, *Women and Gender in Islam: Historical Roots of a Modern Debate*, New Haven, CT: Yale University Press, 1992.

Alexander, Edward P., "Artistic and Historical Period Rooms," *Curator* 7 (1964), 263–279.

Allwood, John, *The Great Exhibitions*, London: Studio Vista, 1997.

Aloula, Malek, *The Colonial Harem*, trans. Myrna Godzich and Wald Golzich, Theory and History of Literature, 21, University of Minneapolis Press, 1986.

Altick, Richard Daniel, *The Shows of London*, Cambridge MA: Belknap–Harvard University Press, 1978.

The English Common Reader: A Social History of the Mass Reading Public, 1800–1900, University of Chicago Press, 1957.

Arundel, Dennis Drew, *The Story of Sadler's Wells, 1683–1977*, Newton Abbot: David and Charles, 1978.

Asad, Talal, introduction, *Anthropology and the Colonial Encounter*, ed. Talal Asad, Atlantic Highlands, NJ: Humanities Press, 1973.

Auerbach, Jeffrey A., *The Great Exhibition of 1851: A Nation on Display*, New Haven, CT: Yale University Press, 1999.

Bachelard, Gaston, *The Poetics of Space*, trans Maria Jolas, new edition, foreword John R. Stilgoe, Boston, MA: Beacon Press, 1994.

Baker, J. N. L., "Mary Somerville and Geography in England," *Geographical Journal* 3 (1948), 207–222.

Bann, Stephen, *The Clothing of Clio: A Study of the Representation of History in Nineteenth-Century Britain and France*, Cambridge University Press, 1984.

Bann, Stephen, *The Inventions of History: Essays on the Representation of the Past*, Manchester University Press, 1990.

Romanticism and the Rise of History, New York: Twayne, 1995.

"The Sense of the Past: Image, Text, and Object in the Formation of Historical Consciousness in Nineteenth-Century Britain," *The New Historicism*, ed. Aram Veeser. New York: Routledge, 1989, pp. 102–115.

Barrell, John, *The Idea of Landscape and the Sense of Place, 1730–1840: An Approach to the Poetry of John Clare*, Cambridge University Press, 1972.

Bate, Jonathan (ed.), *Romantics on Shakespeare*, London: Penguin Books, 1992.

Beaver, Patrick, *The Crystal Palace, 1851–1936: A Portrait of Victorian Enterprise*, London: Hugh Evelyn, 1970.

Bendiner, Kenneth Paul, "The Portrayal of the Middle East in British Painting, 1835–1860," PhD dissertation, Columbia University (1978).

Bennett, Tony, *The Birth of the Museum: History, Theory, Politics*, Culture: Policies and Politics, London: Routledge, 1995.

Bentley, Eric, *The Life of the Drama*, New York: Applause, 1964.

Beyer, Werner William, *The Enchanted Forest*, New York: Barnes and Noble, 1963.

Booth, Michael, *English Melodrama*, London: Herbert Jenkins, 1965.

"Soldiers of the Queen: Drury Lane Imperialism," *Melodrama: The Cultural Emergence of a Genre*, ed. Michael Hays and Anastasia Nikolopoulu, New York: St. Martin's Press, 1996, pp. 3–20.

Theatre in the Victorian Age, Cambridge University Press, 1991.

Victorian Spectacular Theatre, 1850–1910, Theatre Production Studies, Routledge and Kegan Paul: London, 1981.

Bowler, Peter J., *The Invention of Progress: The Victorians and the Past*, Cambridge, MA: Basil Blackwell, 1989.

Bratton, J. S., "Theatre of War: the Crimean on the London Stage, 1854–5," *Performance and Politics in Popular Drama: Aspects of Popular Entertainment in Theatre, Film and Television, 1800–1976*, ed. David Bradby, Louis James, and Bernard Sharratt, Cambridge University Press, 1980, pp. 119–137.

Bromwich, David, *Hazlitt, The Mind of a Critic*, 1983, New Haven, CT: Yale University Press, 1999.

Brooks, Peter, *The Melodramatic Imagination: Balzac, Henry James, Melodrama, and the Mode of Excess*, 1976, New York: Columbia University Press, 1985.

Butler, Marilyn, "Byron and the Empire in the East," *Byron: Augustan and Romantic*, ed. Andrew Rutherford, New York: St. Martin's Press, 1990, pp. 63–81.

Campbell, Michael J., *John Martin, Visionary Printmaker*, New York: Campbell Fine Art and New York Art Gallery, 1992.

Carpenter, Edmund S., "The Role of Archeology in the Nineteenth-Century Controversy between Developmentalism and Degeneration," *Pennsylvania Archeologist* 20 (1950), 5–18.

Çelik, Zeynep, *Displaying the Orient: Architecture of Islam at Nineteenth-Century World's Fairs*, Berkeley, CA: University of California Press, 1992.

Certeau, Michel de, *The Writing of History*, trans. Tom Conley, New York: Columbia University Press, 1988.

Chew, Samuel Claggett, *Byron in England, His Fame and After Fame*, New York: C. Scribner's Sons, 1924.

Chapman, William Ryan, "Arranging Ethnology: A. H. L. F. Pitt Rivers and the Typological Tradition," *Objects and Others: Essays on Museums and Material Culture*, ed. George W. Stocking, Jr., History of Anthropology, 3, Madison, WI: University of Wisconsin Press, 1985, pp. 15–48.

Conner, Patrick (ed.), *Inspiration of Egypt: Its Influence on British Artists, Travellers and Designers, 1700–1900*. Brighton Museum, 1983.

Conner, Patrick, *Oriental Architecture in the West*, London: Thames and Hudson, 1979.

Cowhig, Ruth, "Actors, Black and Tawny, in the Role of Othello – and Their Critics," *Theatre Research International* 4 (1979), 133–146.

Crary, Jonathan, *Techniques of the Observer: On Vision and Modernity in the Nineteenth Century*, Cambridge, MA: MIT Press, c.1990.

Crompton, Louis, *Byron and Greek Love: Homophobia in Nineteenth-Century England*, Berkeley, CA: University of California Press, 1985.

Culler, A. Dwight, *The Victorian Mirror of History*, New Haven, CT: Yale University Press, 1985.

Culler, Jonathan, "Semiotics of Tourism," *American Journal of Semiotics* 1. 1–2 (1981), 127–140.

Darby, Michael, *The Islamic Perspective: An Aspect of British Architecture and Design in the Nineteenth Century*, London: World of Islam Festival Trust, 1983.

Davis, Tracy C., *Actresses as Working Women: Their Social Identity in Victorian Culture*, Gender and Performance, London: Routledge, 1991.

Dawson, Warren R. and Uphill, Eric P., *Who Was Who in Egyptology*, London: Egypt Exploration Society, 1972.

Dorson, Richard M., *The British Folklorists, A History*, University of Chicago Press, 1968.

Downer, Alan S., "Nature to Advantage Dressed: Eighteenth-Century Acting," *PMLA* 58 (1943), 1002–1037.

"Players and the Painted Stage: Nineteenth-Century Acting," *PMLA* 61 (1946), 522–576.

Driver, Felix, *Geography Militant: Cultures of Exploration and Empire*, Oxford: Blackwell, 2001.

"Geography's Empire: Histories of Geographical Knowledge," *Society and Space* 10 (1992), 23–40.

"Power, Space, and the Body: a critical Assessment of Foucault's Discipline and Punish," *Society and Space* 3 (1985), 425–446.

Elfenbein, Andrew, *Byron and the Victorians*, Cambridge Studies in Nineteenth-Century Literature and Culture, 4, Cambridge University Press, 1995.

Elsner, John, "The House and Museum of Sir John Soane," *The Cultures of Collecting*, ed. John Elsner and Roger Cardinal, Cambridge, MA: Harvard University Press, 1994, pp. 155–176.

Fabian, Johannes, *Out of Our Minds: Reason and Madness in the Exploration of Central Africa*, Berkeley, CA: University of California Press, 2000.

Fabian, Johannes, *Time and the Other: How Anthropology Makes its Object*, New York: Columbia University Press, 1983.

Fisher, Sydney Nettleton, *The Middle East, A History*, 3rd edn., New York: Alfred A. Knopf, 1979.

Fitzsimons, Raymund, *The Baron of Piccadilly: The Travels and Entertainments of Albert Smith, 1816–1860*, London: Bles, 1967.

Edmund Kean: Fire from Heaven, New York: Dial Press, 1976.

Foucault, Michel, *Discipline and Punish: The Birth of the Prison*, trans. Alan Sheridan, 1978, New York: Vintage–Random House, 1979.

The History of Sexuality, 3 vols., trans. Robert Hurley, 1978, New York: Vintage–Random House, 1990, vol. 1.

The Order of Things: An Archaeology of the Human Sciences, 1970, New York: Vintage–Random House, 1973.

"Questions of Geography," *Power/Knowledge: Selected Interviews and Other Writings 1972–1977*, ed. Colin Gordon, trans. Colin Gordon et al., New York: Random House–Pantheon, 1980, pp. 63–77.

Foulkes, Richard, "Samuel Phelps's *Pericles* and Layard's Discoveries at Nineveh," *Nineteenth-Century Theatre Research* 5 (Autumn 1977), 85–92.

Fried, Michael, *Absorption and Theatricality: Painting and Beholder in the Age of Diderot*, University of Chicago Press, 1980.

Garber, Marjorie, *Vested Interests: Cross-dressing and Cultural Anxiety*, New York: Routledge, 1992.

Glasstone, Victor, *Victorian and Edwardian Theatres: An Architectural and Social Survey*, London: Thames and Hudson, 1975.

Greenhalgh, Paul, *Ephemeral Vistas: The "Expositions Universelles," Great Exhibitions and World's Fairs, 1851–1939*, Studies in Imperialism, Manchester University Press, 1988.

Guest, Ivor, *Ballet in Leicester Square: The Alhambra and the Empire, 1860–1915*, London: Dance Books, 1992.

Guiterman, Helen and Briony Llewellyn (comps.), *David Roberts*, Oxford: Phaidon Press and Barbican Art Gallery, 1986.

Haddawy, Husain, introduction, *The Arabian Nights*, trans. Husain Haddawy, New York: W. W. Norton, 1990.

Hagen, Wolfgang von, *Frederick Catherwood, Archt.*, introduction Aldous Huxley, New York: Oxford University Press, 1950.

Hannaford, Ivan, *Race: The History of an Idea in the West*, Washington, DC: Woodrow Wilson Center Press, 1996.

Hayward, R. A., *Cleopatra's Needle*, London: Moorland, 1978.

Hazelton, Nancy, "The Grieve Family: Patterning in Nineteenth-Century Scene Design," *Theatre Survey* 32.1 (1991), 31–42.

Headrick, Daniel R., *The Tools of Empire: Technology and European Imperialism in the Nineteenth Century*, Oxford University Press, 1985.

Henry, Clement M., *The Mediterranean Debt Crescent: Money and Power in Algeria, Egypt, Morocco, Tunisia, and Turkey*, Gainesville, FL: University Press of Florida, 1996.

Hillebrand, Harold Newcomb, *Edmund Kean*, New York: AMS Press, 1966.

Hobsbawm, E. J., *The Age of Empire, 1875–1914*, New York: Pantheon Books, 1987.

Holder, Heidi, "Melodrama, Realism, and Empire on the British Stage," *Acts of Supremacy: The British Empire on Stage, 1790–1930*, ed. J. S. Bratton et al., Studies in Imperialism, Manchester University Press, 1991, pp. 129–149.

Hooper-Greenhill, Eilean, *Museums and the Shaping of Knowledge*, The Heritage: Care-Preservation-Management, London: Routledge, 1992.

Houghton, Walter, *The Victorian Frame of Mind, 1830–1870*, New Haven, CT: Yale University Press, 1957.

Howell, Margaret J., *Byron Tonight: A Poet's Plays on the Nineteenth-Century Stage*, Surrey: Springwood Books, 1982.

Hudson, Brian, "The New Geography and the New Imperialism: 1870–1918," *Antipode* 9 (1977), 13–19.

Hudson, Nicholas, "From Nation to Race," *Eighteenth-Century Studies* 29.3 (1996), 12–19.

Hyde, Ralph, *Panoramania! The Art and Entertainment of the 'All-Embracing' View*, London: Trefoil Publications, 1988.

Jacknis, Ira, "Franz Boas and Exhibits: On the Limitations of the Museum Method of Anthropology," *Objects and Others: Essays on Museums and Material Culture*, ed. George W. Stocking, Jr., History of Anthropology, 3, Madison, WI: University of Wisconsin Press, 1985, pp. 75–111.

Johnson, Douglas H., "The Death of Gordon: a Victorian Myth," *Journal of Imperial and Commonwealth History* 10 (1982), 285–310.

Joppien, Rüdiger, *Philippe Jacques de Loutherbourg, RA 1740–1812*, London: Greater London Council, [1973].

Jullian, Philippe, *The Orientalists: European Painters of Eastern Scenes*, Oxford: Phaidon, 1977.

Kaul, Mythali, "Background: Black or Tawny? Stage Representations of Othello from 1604 to the Present," *Othello: New Essays by Black Writers*, Washington, DC: Howard University Press, 1996, pp. 1–22.

Keith, Arthur, "Presidential Address. How Can the Institute Best Serve the Needs of Anthropology?" *Journal of the Royal Anthropological Institute of Great Britain and Ireland* 47 (1917), 12–30.

Kirshenblatt-Gimblett, Barbara, *Destination Culture: Tourism, Museums, and Heritage*, Berkeley, CA: University of California Press, 1998.

"Objects of Ethnography," *Exhibiting Cultures: The Poetics and Politics of Museum Display*, ed. Ivan Karp and Steven D. Lavine, Washington, DC: Smithsonian Institution Press, 1991, pp. 386–443.

Leask, Nigel, *British Romantic Writers and the East: Anxieties of Empire*, Cambridge Studies in Romanticism, 2, Cambridge University Press, 1993.

" 'Wandering through Eblis'; Absorption and Containment in Romantic Exoticism," *Romanticism and Colonialism: Writing and Empire, 1780–1830*, ed. Tim Fulford and Peter J. Kitson, Cambridge University Press, 1998, pp. 165–188.

Malcolm Kelsall, *Byron's Politics*, Brighton, Sussex: Harvester Press, 1987.

McClintock, Anne, *Imperial Leather: Race, Gender and Sexuality in the Colonial Contest*, New York: Routledge, 1995.

MacKenzie, John, *Orientalism: History, Theory, and the Arts*, Manchester University Press, 1995.

Propaganda and Empire: The Manipulation of British Public Opinion, 1880–1960, Manchester University Press, 1984.

Makdisi, Saree, *Romantic Imperialism: Universal Empire and the Culture of Modernity*, Cambridge Studies in Romanticism, 27, Cambridge University Press, 1998.

Mander, Raymond and Mitchenson, Joe, *The Lost Theatres of London*, New York: Taplinger, 1968.

Mayer III, David, *Harlequin in His Element: The English Pantomime, 1806–1836*, Cambridge, MA: Harvard University Press, 1969.

Mayes, Stanley, *The Great Belzoni*, London: Putnam 1959.

Meisel, Martin, *Realizations: Narrative, Pictorial, and Theatrical Arts in Nineteenth-Century England*, Princeton University Press, 1983.

Miller, Edward, *That Noble Cabinet: A History of the British Museum*, Athens, OH: Ohio University Press, 1974.

Mitchell, Timothy, *Colonising Egypt*, 1988, Berkeley, CA: University of California Press, 1991.

Musawi, Muhsin Jassim, *Scheherazade in England: A Study of Nineteenth-Century English Criticism of the Arabian Nights*, Washington, DC: Three Continents Press, 1981.

Norris, Hilary, "A Directory of Victorian Scene Painters," *Theatrephile* 1.2 (1984), 38–52.

Oettermann, Stephan, *The Panorama: History of a Mass Medium*, trans. Deborah Lucas Schneider, New York: Zone Books, 1997.

Pao, Angela C., *The Orient of the Boulevards: Exoticism, Empire, and Nineteenth-Century French Theatre*, New Cultural Studies, Philadelphia, University of Pennsylvania Press, 1998.

Peet, Richard, "The Social Origins of Environmental Determinism," *Annals of the Association of American Geographers* 75 (1985), 309–333.

Platt, D. C. M., *Finance, Trade, and Politics in British Foreign Policy, 1815–1914*, Oxford University Press, 1968.

Playfair, Giles, *Kean*, New York: Dutton, 1939.

Pratt, Mary Louise, *Imperial Eyes: Travel Writing and Transculturation*, London: Routledge, 1992.

Richards, Thomas, *The Commodity Culture of Victorian England: Advertising and Spectacle, 1851–1914*, Stanford University Press, 1990.

Roberts, David, *The Holy Land*, Israel: Terra Sancta Arts, 1982.

Rosenfeld, Sybil, "The Grieve Family," *Anatomy of an Illusion; Studies in Nineteenth-Century Scenic Design*, Amsterdam: Scheltema and Holkema, 1969.

Georgian Scene Painters and Scene Painting, Cambridge University Press, 1981.

A Short History of Scene Design in Great Britain, Drama and Theatre Studies, Oxford: Blackwell, 1973.

Russell, David, " 'We Carved Our Way to Glory': the British Soldier in Music Hall and Song and Sketch, *c.* 1880–1914," *Popular Imperialism and the Military*, ed. John M. Mackenzie, Studies in Imperialism, c.1992, Manchester University Press, pp. 50–79.

Said, Edward, *Culture and Imperialism*, 1993, New York: Knopf, 1994.

Orientalism, New York: 1978, Vintage–Random House, 1979.

Saxon, A. H., *Enter Foot and Horse: A History of Hippodrama in England and France*, New Haven, CT: Yale University Press, 1968.

Schivelbusch, Wolfgang, *Disenchanted Night: The Industrialisation of Light in the Nineteenth Century*, trans. Angela Davies, Oxford: Berg, 1988.

Schoch, Richard, *Shakespeare's Victorian Stage: Performing History in the Theatre of Charles Kean*, Cambridge University Press, 1998.

Searight, Sarah, *The British in the Middle East: A Social History of the British Overseas*, New York: Atheneum, 1970.

Shannon, Richard, *The Crisis of Imperialism, 1865–1915*, The Paladin History of England, London: Hart-Davis, 1974.

Silberman, Neil Asher, *Digging for God and Country: Exploration, Archeology, and the Secret Struggle for the Holy Land, 1799–1917*, New York: Knopf, 1982.

Sim, Katharine, *David Roberts R.A., 1796–1864: A Biography*, London: Quartet Books, 1984.

Soja, Edward W., *Postmodern Geographies: The Reassertion of Space in Critical Social Theory*, Haymarket, London: Verso, 1989.

Sonbol, Amira el-Azhary, *The New Mamluks: Egyptian Society and Modern Feudalism*, Syracuse, NY: Syracuse University Press.

Southern, Richard, *Changeable Scenery: Its Origin and Development in the British Theatre*, London: Faber, 1951.

Springhall, John, "'Up Guards and At Them!' British Imperialism and Popular Art 1880–1914," *Imperialism and Popular Culture*, ed. John M. Mackenzie, Manchester University Press, 1992, pp. 49–72.

St. Clair, William, "The Impact of Byron's Writings: An Evaluative Approach," *Byron: Augustan and Romantic*, ed. Andrew Rutherford, New York: St. Martin's Press, 1990, pp. 1–25.

States, Bert, *Great Reckonings in Little Rooms: On the Phenomenology of Theatre*, Berkeley, CA: University of California Press, 1985.

Steegman, John, *The Rule of Taste: From George I to George IV*, New York: Russell and Russell, 1968.

Stepan, Nancy, *The Idea of Race in Science: Great Britian, 1800–1960*, London: Macmillan, 1982.

Stephens, John Russell, *The Censorship of English Drama, 1824–1901*, Cambridge University Press, 1980.

Stocking, Jr., George W., *Race, Culture, and Evolution: Essays in the History of Anthropology*, New York: Free Press–Macmillan, 1968.

  "From Chronology to Ethnology: James Cowles Prichard and British Anthropology, 1800–1850," introduction to James Cowles Prichard, *Researches into the Physical History of Man*, Classics in Anthropology, University of Chicago Press, 1973, pp. ix–cx.

  Victorian Anthropology, New York: Free Press–Macmillan, 1987.

Stoler, Ann Laura, *Race and the Education of Desire: Foucault's History of Sexuality and the Colonial Order of Things*, Durham, NC: Duke University Press, 1995.

Stottlar, James, "'A House Choked with Gunpowder and Wild with Excitement': Augustus Harris and Drury Lane's Spectacular Melodrama," *When They Weren't Doing Shakespeare*, ed. Judith L. Fisher and Stephen Watt, Athens, GA: University of Georgia Press, 1989, pp. 212–229.

Sweetman, John, *The Oriental Obsession: Islamic Inspiration in British and American Art and Architecture, 1500–1920*, Cambridge Studies in the History of Art, Cambridge University Press, 1988.

Swinglehurst, Edmund, *The Romantic Journey: The Story of Thomas Cook and Victorian Travel*, New York: Harper, 1974.

Thomas, Nicholas, *Colonialism's Culture: Anthropology, Travel and Government*, Princeton University Press, 1994.

Thomas, Nicholas, "Licensed Curiosity: Cook's Pacific Voyages," *The Culture of Collecting*, ed. John Elsner and Roger Cardinal, Cambridge, MA: Harvard University Press, 1994, pp. 116–136.

Thornton, Lynne, *The Orientalists: Painters–Travelers, 1828–1908*, Paris: ACR Edition, 1983.

Van der Merwe, Pieter, "The Life and Theatrical Career of Clarkson Stanfield 1793–1867," PhD thesis, University of Bristol, 1979.

"Roberts and the Theatre," *David Roberts*, comp. Hellen Guiterman and Briony Llewellyn, Oxford: Phaidon Press and Barbican Art Gallery, 1986, pp. 27–46.

Van der Merwe, Pieter (comp.), *The Spectacular Career of Clarkson Stanfield, 1793–1867*, Tyne and Wear County Council Museums, 1979.

Vaughan, Virginia Mason, *Othello: A Contextual History*, Cambridge University Press, 1994.

Watkins, Daniel P., *Social Relations in Byron's Eastern Tales*, London: Associated Universities Press, 1984.

Whale, John, "Indian Jugglers: Hazlitt Romantic Orientalism and the Difference of View," *Romanticism and Colonialism: Writing and Empire, 1780–1830*, ed. Tim Fulford and Peter J. Kitson, Cambridge University Press, 1998, pp. 206–220.

Walker, Brian Mercer (ed.), *Frank Matcham: Theatre Architect*, Belfast: Blackstaff Press, 1980.

White, Hayden V. "Foucault Decoded: Notes from the Underground," *History and Theory* 12 (1973), 23–54.

Wilson, Daniel W., "Turks on the Eighteenth-Century Operatic Stage and European Political, Military, and Cultural History," *Eighteenth-Century Life* 2 (1985), 79–92.

Wilson, Frances (ed.), *Byromania: Portraits of the Artist in Nineteenth- and Twentieth-Century Culture*, London: Macmillan, 1999.

Index